BASEBALL GOES TO WAR

WILLIAM B. MEAD

Farragut
Publishing
Company

Copyright © 1985 by William B. Mead.

First published in 1978 by Contemporary Books, Inc., under the title
Even the Browns. Copyright © 1978 by William B. Mead.

Expanded edition published in 1982 by Van Nostrand Reinhold Company
Inc., under the title *The Ten Worst Years of Baseball*. Copyright © 1978,
1982 by William B. Mead and Harold Rosenthal.

ISBN: 0-918535-02-6
Library of Congress Catalog Card Number 85-45528

All Rights Reserved
Printed in the United States of America

To my wife and daughter,
who are not baseball fans,
and our two sons, who are.

CONTENTS

Preface

It took a world war to win the St. Louis Browns a pennant, and to me it seemed a small enough price to pay. Like any normal boy growing up in St. Louis during the early 1940s, I had an abiding love affair with the glamorous Cardinals, who, as best I can recall, never lost a game. It seemed that the Browns never won a game until that wonderful war brought them the 1944 pennant, and in so doing bestowed upon me another love, one that could be indulged while the Cardinals were out of town.

It didn't cost much. Every spring I would pick up my Knothole passes—one for the Browns, one for the Cardinals—at the public library. Thus enrolled as a member of the Knothole Gang, I could get in free to any day game, doubleheaders excepted.

Once or twice or three times a week, my brother Alden and I would leave our big white house in Webster Groves, a respectable suburb, walk down Gray Avenue past Bristol School to Lockwood Avenue, and catch a Manchester Line streetcar headed downtown. The older streetcars were yellow, and had hard cane seats. Sometimes we were lucky enough to get on one of the newer models, which were painted red and had some padding to sit on.

I knew it was about time to get off when the smell of the stock-yards—a stench for which I have nothing but the fondest memories—rolled through the open windows. A short ride on the Grand Avenue streetcar brought us to Grand and Dodier, where sat Sportsman's Park, the most beautiful edifice ever built.

Unlike the sterile stadiums of today, Sportsman's Park satisfied the senses. The neighborhood was strikingly shabby. The heat bore down much more intensely on the city sidewalks than in the green suburb we had left behind, where the temperature might have been only, say, ninety degrees. As we walked into the Knothole section in left field, the unswept grime crunched underfoot, and the park reeked of beer and other drippings. As one of the more egalitarian institutions in town, the Knothole Gang smelled pretty bad, too. I once attended with a friend who picked up a case of what was initially diagnosed as chiggers, a country bug, the louse being a city beast foreign to our experience.

Sportsman's Park was no namby-pamby garden museum for people who liked to watch ivy grow or admired blank green walls. The outfield walls and the scoreboard gave you something interesting to read.

"Falstaff Beer, Choicest Product of the Brewer's Art."

"Avoid 5 o'clock shadow; GEM razors and blades."

"Here's How! Get Hyde Park Beer."

"Drink Stag Beer."

Even the scoreboard clock: "Official Time: LONGINES."

"Griesedieck Bros. Light Lager Beer."

"Drink Alpen Brau."

"First Choice of Men Who Work and Fight. LIFEBUOY. Stops B.O."

(The Lifebuoy sign had the current National and American league standings printed on either side of the advertising message, thus earning more than its share of attention.)

For a nickel, we would buy an official scorecard, having knowingly passed up the unofficial scorecards hawked outside the park. At today's ball parks, you pay a dollar for a slick-paper booklet so full of ads that you can hardly find the lineups, which invariably include two or three players benched a week before with injuries and two or three others who were traded or farmed out during the last road trip. In contrast, those nickel scorecards, using some miracle of printing now apparently lost to mankind, were printed just before the game, and always had the correct lineups.

Those scorecards had good ads, too. In addition to the five local beers that also bought space in the outfield, they included ads for the hotels at which the Browns and Cardinals stayed while traveling.

"The Sherry-Netherland, Cincinnati."

"The New Yorker, Home of Ultra-Violet Ray Bathrooms."

Although those hotel ads obviously were coerced by the St. Louis ballclubs in exchange for their patronage, they were not ineffective. When I first traveled to New York on my own, at the age of 21, I stayed at the New Yorker, and indeed would not have considered any other hotel.

The Knothole Gang was chaperoned by a mean old man with only one arm, named Wingy. Far from promoting the noble Knothole concept, which was to woo today's youngsters so they would be tomorrow's paying customers, Wingy cursed the children and angrily spun his empty sweat-shirt sleeve like a propeller. Bolder Knotholers would goad Wingy by rolling empty bottles down the steps, comparing skills to see how far one could roll before it smashed. A partially melted snow cone would occasionally fly overhead, dripping sugared lime or orange. Wingy did not take such insults sitting down. At the end of his rope one day in 1944, he tried to clear the Knothole section during the ninth inning of a Brownie game. The Browns were behind but these were not the losing Browns of past years, and we Knotholers refused to budge. As Wingy screamed and whirled his empty sleeve in angry frustration, the Browns vindicated us, rallying to win the game.

When I mention the Browns or their pennant year, most people quickly mention Pete Gray, the one-armed outfielder, or Eddie Gaedel, the midget. A mention of wartime baseball always evokes the name of Gray, and no one else. It is as if some diabolical historian-in-the-sky has decided that those two names are all that is to be remembered of the St. Louis Browns, and of four wartime baseball seasons. If that's all you want, turn to those chapters and be done with it. But neither man was around when the Browns won their pennant, and to a true Brownie fan, neither Gray nor Gaedel stood out all that much anyway. Counting Wingy, Gray was the third one-armed Brownie. The second was a batting-practice pitcher named Orville Paul, who wore no glove and, after pitching a ball, would pick up another from a tray beside him. Gaedel, who stood 3 feet 6 inches tall, could be described as a short, weak, right-handed hitter who was afraid to swing at the ball. I do not have room to list every Brownie player who fit that description.

Two tides of history came together to bring the Browns their pennant in 1944. One was the story of the Browns themselves, and the other was the devastating effect of World War II on the teams that had humiliated the Browns for so many years. That is what this book is about. I read hundreds of old newspapers, principally the *Sporting News*, and talked to about three dozen players, managers, and others who participated in the events described. So the book is not written from childhood memories.

But I was there. When you read of the second-to-last day of the 1944 season, when Denny Galehouse of the Browns shut out the Yankees 2 to 0, and brought the pennant race to its dramatic climax the next day, let your mind glance toward the left-field corner of Sportsman's Park, lower deck. That 11-year-old kid wearing glasses is my brother, Alden. The chubby 10-year-old beside him is me.

CHAPTER 1

The National Pastime Joins Up

Baseball has long been recognized as a reflection of American values. There is somehow more to it than the playing of a game for the entertainment of spectators. Many fans, myself included, were brought up with a feeling for baseball bordering on the religious. Sportswriters and baseball officials quite naturally do all they can to nourish this attitude, because it enhances their business and magnifies the importance of their work.

This unique role in American life was hard to maintain during World War II, but baseball managed it. Patriotic jingoism was the language of the day. No institution voiced it more loudly, nor identified itself with the war effort more closely, than did organized baseball. Trotting out capital letters in plenty, The Game gloried in its role as The National Pastime, one of the Institutions American Boys were Fighting to Preserve.

This stance contained an element of self-interest bordering on desperation. Baseball officials feared for their business. Frivolous activities were frowned upon during the war, and athletes not in military service were sometimes criticized as draft dodgers, though they were not. So baseball adopted a stern wartime visage, did its best to improve morale and inspire the populace, raised vast amounts of money in War Bond sales and war charity contributions, and made sure that the game got at least as much credit as it deserved. "Duty and Service and Baseball always have been synonymous," baseball's weekly newspaper, the *Sporting News*, proclaimed in a typically gushy wartime editorial.

On the home front, baseball's contributions began immediately after Pearl Harbor. Players and officials took 10 percent of their pay in War Bonds. Servicemen in uniform were allowed to attend games free in most cities. Fans actually threw foul balls back onto the field so they could be given to military posts for recreational use. In 1942, the St. Louis Browns admitted 39,000 servicemen without charge, and donated 912 baseballs that fans had returned.

More important were dozens of benefit games staged by major and minor league teams to raise money for War Bonds, the USO, the Red Cross, and the Army and Navy relief agencies. There were all kinds of wartime collection drives. Kitchen grease was collected and recycled—really to make soap, although the government, fearing that the truth would cause a run on soap supplies, maintained that grease was needed for explosives. The Louisville Colonels of the American Association collected 2,587 pounds of grease at a "Waste Fat Night." The Cincinnati Reds collected cigarettes instead of tickets at a "Smokes for Service Men" benefit game that included twenty vaudeville acts. At Shreveport, Louisiana, Mrs. George Roby contributed some scrap aluminum to gain admission to an "Aluminum Night" game and found, upon returning to her car, that other fans had contributed her aluminum hubcaps.

For three straight seasons, 1942 through 1944, each of the sixteen major league teams promoted one home game a year as a benefit for the Army and Navy relief funds, which aided the families of servicemen. The first one was held in early May of 1942 at Ebbets Field in Brooklyn. Even the players, umpires, and sportswriters paid their way in; 42,822 tickets were sold, netting the Navy Relief Society more than $60,000. A military parade preceded the game, in which the Dodgers beat the Giants, 7 to 6, on a home run by Dolf Camilli.

At Yankee Stadium, $80,000 was raised at the Yankees' 1942

war charity game. To help attract fans, Walter Johnson, 54, threw seventeen pitches to Babe Ruth, 47, who hit two of them into the stands. In Detroit, the charity game raised $68,000, even though the opposition was the Browns. Altogether, the sixteen games netted $506,000 for war charities in 1942, $326,500 in 1943, and $328,500 in 1944.

A second All-Star game was staged in 1942 to benefit war charities. On July 6 at the Polo Grounds in New York, the American League, without a single Brownie in the lineup, beat the National League 3 to 1 in the regular All-Star game and earned the right to play the Service All-Stars the following night in Cleveland. The American League won that game 5 to 0, knocking out Bob Feller of the Navy in the second inning. Feller recalls a trickler by Tommy Henrich of the Yankees as the key hit. The two games raised $100,000 to buy baseball equipment for military recreation, $60,000 for the Army and Navy relief funds, and $60,000 in War Bonds and War Stamps. The *Sporting News* called the Cleveland game "a spectacle such as one sees only once in a lifetime."

"Rumbling tanks, jumping jeeps, drilling Marines, music from the famous Great Lakes Naval Station's band, parading the colors of the Army, Navy and Coast Guard, and 65,000 awed persons filling one of the nation's great stadia made an unforgettable spectacle," the story continued. "As though it were a contagion, one could feel the patriotic fervor of the entire 65,000; it sent needles shooting down one's spine, started honest tears trickling down the cheeks, and made one murmur to one's self: 'Thank God, I am an American!'"

During the All-Star break, there was talk of putting the 1942 World Series on tour so more money could be raised. The notion was dropped, but $363,000 from Series receipts was given to wartime charities. Together with money from the benefit games in each major league city, the two All-Star games, $259,000 from minor league benefit games, and receipts from various smaller affairs, organized baseball contributed $1,295,000 to war charities in 1942 alone. "Definitely," said the *Sporting News*, "the detractors of the game are in wild retreat."

In 1943, the charity games were upstaged by a spectacle conceived and promoted by Shirley Povich, who covered the Washington Senators for the Washington *Post*. Povich:

The war effort was total. Everybody was in a passion to win this war. Our heroes, so called, were in the armed services. What do we do on the home front? Well, hurray, everything we can. So we got the bright idea of having a game to sell War Bonds. We pegged it to the idea that if we could fill the park, we could buy a United States cruiser. That was the target—so many million dollars to buy a cruiser for the Navy.

I put in motion the idea that we could have a game between the Senators and the Navy All-Stars, most of whom were operating out of Norfolk and Newport News. Bob Feller pitched at Norfolk; Padgett was down there catching; Phil Rizzuto, Benny McCoy—they had all the big leaguers.

The Navy agreed to the game. Every admission would be a War Bond. If you bought a fifty-dollar bond, I think, you got a general admission seat. If you bought a thousand-dollar bond you got one box seat. I got a call from a man who said to me that he would like to have a box seat at the game. I said, "Well, good." He said, "How many seats in a box?" I said, "Well, some have eight seats, some ten, some twelve." He said, "Can I have twelve seats?" I said, "Yes, if you'll buy $12,000 worth of bonds." He said, "Tell me where I can get them." I said, "I'll have them delivered to you at the Mayflower Hotel." He said, "Fine, I'll be here and write a check." That was Del Webb. He later owned the Yankees, but then he was just a baseball fan who had come in from Phoenix, Arizona. Might have been the highest price ever paid to see a ball game.

I got Bing Crosby to come down and sing behind second base, and Kate Smith to come down and sing "God Bless America." Did I pay them? Absolutely not; not even expenses. It was no trouble getting them. Everybody responded to these things during the war; all you had to do was ask.

I got Al Schacht, the famous baseball clown, simulating a home run in slow motion. Al was the pitcher, and he went through a slow-motion act of pitching to nobody in particular at the plate, and then in slow motion, my God, it's been hit over the fence. Al turns around toward right field to watch this ball go over the fence. In pantomime, you see; he was a great actor. We didn't need anybody at the plate, Al put on such a show.

But at that moment, just as the ball seems to be sailing over the right field fence, Babe Ruth himself, unadvertised, appeared out of the dugout and circled the bases. The Babe himself. In uniform. A little showmanship, eh? I didn't know I was such a showman.

Povich's showmanship raised $2,125,375, the second largest athletic gate in history; only the Dempsey-Tunney fight had earned more. The date was May 24, 1943; Crosby sang "Dinah," "As Time Goes By," and "White Christmas." The Babe took the microphone and urged the fans to buy even more War Bonds. Sir Archibald Wavell, a British war hero, gave an inspiring speech. "I always thought the first World Series I played in was the most thrilling event I would ever take part in or see," said Rizzuto, the Yankee shortstop then playing for the Navy, "but the show in Washington outdid that." He singled home two runs and survived a rundown between third and home as the Navy edged the Senators, 4 to 3. The Navy pitcher was Broadway Charley Wagner, who had beaten the Senators five times the previous year for the Boston Red Sox.

Povich's innovation was embellished in New York. On June 8, 1943, at a luncheon in the Waldorf-Astoria ballroom sponsored by the New York and Brooklyn chapters of the Baseball Writers Association of America, former mayor Jimmy Walker auctioned off players from the three New York teams for a total of $123,850,000 in War Bond pledges. Dixie Walker of the Dodgers drew an $11,250,000 bid from the Brooklyn Club, a social organization. The Esso Marketeers bought Carl Hubbell of the Giants for $3,000,000, and the National Bronx Bank paid $3,500,000 for Joe Gordon of the Yankees. In addition to fulfilling the pledges, a sponsor had to buy bonds in line with his player's achievements during the remainder of the season. The amounts were $2,500 for each single, $5,000 for a double, $7,500 for a triple and $10,000 for a home run. Pitchers earned the allied cause $35,000 for each victory, $50,000 for a shutout.

On August 26, 1943, twenty-six players from the three New York teams played as the War Bond All-Stars against a team of Army baseball stars including Hank Greenberg of the Tigers, Enos Slaughter of the Cardinals, and Sid Hudson of the Senators. The game drew 38,000 fans to the Polo Grounds and sold a staggering $800,000,000 in War Bond pledges. The War Bond All-Stars won, 5 to 2. By September of 1943, the three New York baseball teams had participated in the sale of enough War Bonds to fill nearly a quarter of New York City's War Bond goal.

Baseball's contributions won allies where they were needed. In

November of 1943, Senator Scott Lucas, Democrat of Illinois, rose to praise the game for its financial contributions to the war effort. Lucas said that since Pearl Harbor, organized baseball had turned in $3,128,698 to war charities, $2,289,702 in admission taxes, and, from the National League alone, a bit over $1 billion in War Bond sales. "My sincere hope is that nothing will be done by any agency of the government which will in any way disturb the continuation of this great American institution during the emergency," Lucas told his colleagues.

Altogether, the major leagues contributed $2,900,000 to war charities during World War II. Beyond Lucas's figures, no tabulation was kept of War Bond sales or of contributions from the minor leagues. The final benefit games were played in July of 1945. No All-Star game was played that summer because of travel restrictions; seven interleague war charity games were played instead. In Boston, Chicago, New York, Philadelphia, and St. Louis, the local National and American league teams played each other. In Cleveland, the Indians played the Cincinnati Reds; in Washington, the Senators played the Brooklyn Dodgers. Bert Shepard, who had lost one leg in the war, pitched for Washington, and won. The games raised $245,000 for war relief funds.

In addition to the special events, War Bonds and War Stamps were sold at booths in baseball parks, and players addressed War Bond rallies. Brooklyn players hawked bonds through the stands one Easter; what Dodger fan could deny a personal request from Dixie Walker or Billy Herman? In April of 1943, Branch Rickey, general manager of the Dodgers and a steadfast churchman, agreed for once to attend a Sunday game. The occasion that prompted Rickey to violate the Sabbath was a U.S. Treasury Department ceremony honoring the Dodger Spring Offensive War Bond Campaign, which helped bring Brooklyn War Bond sales to $180,000,000, nearly double the borough's springtime quota.

Shortly after the 1942 World Series, won by the Cardinals, St. Louis sportscasters France Laux and Bob Lyle auctioned the glove of Terry Moore, Cardinal center fielder, for a $5,000 War Bond. The gloves of second baseman Jimmy Brown and pitcher Ernie

White went for $1,000 War Bonds; baseballs autographed by the Cardinals raised as much as $550 each. A week later, Laux outdid himself at a street rally in Centralia, Illinois, hammering down various Cardinal artifacts for a total of $102,150 in bonds. An autographed baseball went for $7,699 and team pictures for $9,500; even a turkey, which by no means resembled a cardinal, drew $1,000.

At the Philadelphia Sports Writers Dinner in early 1943, Connie Mack's portrait was auctioned for $16,000 in Bonds. The crowd was whipped up by Jimmy Gorman, 18, a wounded Marine who described the manner in which he and his comrades had killed Japanese soldiers on Guadalcanal. "When Jimmy hauled out a trophy of his Pacific adventure—a Japanese flag—the diners were stumped," Stan Baumgartner of the Philadelphia *Inquirer* wrote in the *Sporting News.* "They wanted to cheer Jimmy, but they wanted to hiss the Japanese flag and they did so with a venom that singed the decorations of the hall."

In September of 1943, the major leagues offered to send two teams on tour to entertain troops in the South Pacific. Players were to donate their time, and many volunteered; the squads were of all-star quality with players such as Bucky Walters and Johnny Vander Meer of the Cincinnati Reds, Bob Elliott of the Pittsburgh Pirates, Stan Musial of the St. Louis Cardinals, Bill Dickey and Charlie Keller of the New York Yankees, Tex Hughson and Bobby Doerr of the Boston Red Sox, Luke Appling of the Chicago White Sox, and Rudy York of the Detroit Tigers. The players were lectured by the *Sporting News* to put behind them any notion of a "vacation or a merry-making junket," and by Branch Rickey to make the games "blood and thunder affairs." After all preparations had been made, the War Department reversed itself and canceled the trip, pleading a shortage of ships and airplanes. A tour by boxers Joe Louis and Billy Conn also was canceled. Drew Pearson's "Washington Merry-Go-Round" column reported that the tours had been scrubbed by Secretary of War Henry L. Stimson, who "felt that the troops would resent the sight of apparently healthy ballplayers not in service uniform; would not realize that each ballplayer of military age had been exempted from the draft because of some physical infirmity."

However, a number of players, managers, umpires, and sportswriters did entertain U.S. troops on tours sponsored by the USO. Following the 1944 World Series, twenty-nine baseball notables were divided into five groups, each of which toured a separate war zone; the trips lasted several months. Sportswriters served as masters of ceremonies for the players, managers, and umpires, who showed baseball movies, told anecdotes, and answered questions.

One soldier's enthusiasm led the *Sporting News* to overplay its hand. In late 1943, U.S. troops in the Aleutian Islands were visited by Stan Musial and Danny Litwhiler of the Cardinals, Dixie Walker of the Dodgers, Hank Borowy of the Yankees, and Frankie Frisch, manager of the Pirates. Pfc. Howard T. Kosbau, sports editor of the *Sourdough Sentinel,* a service newspaper serving that area, wrote that "the soldiers here would rather talk with big league ballplayers than with Betty Grable." Apparently confident that Kosbau's view was prevalent, the *Sporting News* offered $50 for the best letter from a serviceman answering this question:

"Which would you prefer—an earful of big leaguers' gab or an eyeful of Betty Grable's gams?"

The advertisement pictured Miss Grable on a blanket, wearing a bathing suit and high-heeled shoes. Swallowing its pride, the *Sporting News* announced six months later that the winner, Major Alfred C. Brown, stationed in North Africa, had polled the men in his unit; 90 percent of them voted for Miss Grable's legs. "Put yourself in our place!" wrote the major. "For over a year we've had nothing feminine to observe but Arab women, their bodies completely covered with dirty white robes, their heads and faces covered, with possibly just one eye peeping out. Compare this constant view to that of one squint of Betty's gams. Brother, let's exchange places!"

Essential industries at home needed help, too. With labor short on the apple farms of Virginia's Shenandoah Valley, seven members of the Washington Senators, including Manager Ossie Bluege and star pitcher Dutch Leonard, spent a 1943 open date picking apples. Paul Florence, president of the Birmingham Barons of the Southern Association, set aside an acre of land and told his players to plant a victory garden.

Although many of these deeds were impressive, it would have been hard for any civilian institution to live up to the words that were written to describe baseball's wartime role and to exhort even greater effort.

Like a chameleon, baseball changed color to match the hue of public feeling toward the war. As the 1941 season opened with America still at peace, the *Sporting News* published cartoons contrasting the United States and Europe. The former showed a boy in the stands cheering as a runner slid into base. The latter pictured a lad beside a heap of rubble, grieving for his dead grandmother. "Europe's national pastime seems to be war; America's is baseball," the caption declared. By May of 1943, a cartoon in the same publication was urging fans to "run a Hun, bap a Jap, bop a Wop."

With relish, stories were told of baseball's connections with the battlefronts. General Douglas MacArthur, hero of the Pacific, was proudly identified as the left fielder for Army against Navy in a game between the two service academies in 1901. MacArthur was hitless that day but got on base somehow, stole a base, and scored a run. Brigadier General Frank A. Armstrong, who commanded the first attack in Europe by U.S. heavy bombers, was written up as the military's highest ranking former professional baseball player. Armstrong had played a season with Kinston (North Carolina) in the Virginia League.

Three Germans posing as U.S. soldiers were exposed by their ignorance of the game and were shot. In England, U.S. airmen complained that the Luftwaffe was bombing their baseball diamonds. On the South Pacific island of New Britain, Japanese soldiers shouted, "To hell with Babe Ruth!" as they charged a Marine emplacement. "Thirty Japanese struck out for good," reported the *Sporting News* with satisfaction. Solicited for a comment, Ruth said, "I hope every Jap that mentions my name gets shot, and to hell with all Japs anyway."

On another Pacific island, a dead Japanese soldier named Hikichi Kazuo was identified by newspaper clippings in his pocket as a star third baseman for Osaka of Japan's major league. A German soldier astounded his American captors by yielding up a copy of the *Sporting News;* he explained that he once lived in Washington Heights, New York, and was a Dodger fan. The war gave one minor league player the hope of settling an old score. Upon enlisting in the Navy, Fred Collins of Kansas City in the American Association said he wanted to find an individual whom he had encountered while pitching years before against a touring Japanese team. "I would have had a shutout but for this little yellow guy," Collins said. "He hit me for two home runs. I just want to get my hands on him."

Baseball's most ardent wartime evangelist was Daniel M. Daniel of the New York *World-Telegram,* who moonlighted extensively for the *Sporting News.* In his enthusiasm, Daniel sometimes seemed to confuse the major leagues with the Army or the Marine Corps. "Baseball marches on," Daniel wrote in February of 1942. "It marches on in martial tread, cognizant of its duties and its responsibilities, and the hazards which confront it on land, sea and in the air." (As things turned out, no baseball team encountered hostile land forces, none took to the sea or air, and none was attacked by enemy ships or airplanes.) A year later, Daniel borrowed from the hymnbook. "Onward baseball soldiers, marching to the fray," he wrote of players entering military service, adding this rhyme:

The best players of all,
Heed Uncle Sam's call.

Those who did not were also supported. "The *Sporting News* extends to every ballplayer who is in a position to go on with his profession in 1943, the hand of support," an editorial said. "It tells every such player that in going on, he is not entering upon a year of nefarious activity."

Daniel was keen on ceremony. He saw baseball and America as indivisible, and believed that the opening day of each season should be a fulsome display of this coupling. Rhapsodizing about President Franklin D. Roosevelt's appearance at the 1941 opener, Daniel called the President's opening toss "the most amazing thing in the world," in sharp contrast with the attitude of Axis leaders.

"'Frivolous,' snorts Hitler. 'Ridiculous,' gutturals Mussolini. 'Marvelous,' says the American, as he sees behind the curtain—as he grasps the things connoted by Mr. Roosevelt's throwing out the ball and remaining to watch the fight to its decision. . . .'"

In the future, wrote Daniel, the opening ceremony should include a parade to the center field flagpole of the baseball commissioner, the presidents of all the major and minor leagues, the presidents of all sixteen major league clubs, the thirty-two most outstanding players in baseball, and, lest anyone be left out, "every man of any position in all baseball.

"Arouse yourselves, you men in high office and you men of baseball position!" the editorial continued. "Let this annual opening in Washington become a tremendous pageant dedicating anew, every April, the great game of baseball to the great people of America."

Americans have long used sporting vernacular to describe conflicts of every kind; World War II may have set a record for idiomatic home runs and strikeouts. After the St. Louis Cardinals overcame Brooklyn's large lead to win the 1942 pennant, the brewer of Alpen Brau, a St. Louis beer that did not survive postwar competition, was moved to liken the home team to the Allies, and, by inference, the Dodgers to the Axis powers. The large newspaper advertisement pictured a frightened Hitler listening to the chirping of a cardinal perched on a baseball bat, and said:

"Listen to the little Red Bird, Adolf . . . it's telling you
            YOUR LEAD ISN'T BIG ENOUGH EITHER!

"Sure, Adolf, you got off to a flying start! That foul-play combination, Hitler to Hirohito to Benito, worked like a charm in the early innings.

"You banged the ball all over the map . . . because you started playing *your* game before anyone else had a fair chance to warm up and put a team on the field.

"That's just what you counted on! But what you didn't count on, Adolf, was the fact that *a fighting spirit can overcome any lead.*

"You're starting to realize that now. The United Nations are hitting their stride. They have started smashing your pitchers all over the lot . . . putting men on bases everywhere. Soon they'll be scoring on your home plate!

"There's only one flag that you and your teammates are ever going to run up in the game *you* started. It's the white flag of surrender.

"In the World Series that lies ahead, we trust it's in the Cards to *win*, as surely as we know it's in the cards for Hitler, Hirohito and Benito to *lose*.

"Alpen Brau Beer

"Columbia Brewing Company, St. Louis, Missouri"

The choicest words were reserved for the threat that baseball perceived to its existence during the war. Sportswriters and baseball officials repeatedly cited the game's contribution to military and civilian morale. People who believed that professional sports should be suspended during wartime, or that athletes should automatically be drafted, were portrayed as misguided fools or, by implication, traitors. In a February, 1943, editorial, the *Sporting News* conceded that the Allies could win the war without baseball. "But the path to triumph would be longer, and for those on the home front, certainly much more onerous," the editorial warned. "It would be bad for our nation if we were forced to become a nation of sobbers and kill-joys. We must have the movies, we must have baseball. No rational analysis possibly can reach any other conclusion."

Actually, few did. In April, 1942, the Gallup Poll reported that 64 percent of those polled believed that professional sports should continue during the war; 24 percent said they should not. By a 9 to 2 margin, respondents to a poll conducted by the Athletic Round Table of Spokane, Washington, favored the continuation of professional baseball; the margin was 8 to 1 in a similar poll conducted by the Pittsburgh *Post-Gazette*.

Somewhat less scientific polls conducted by the *Sporting News* produced results even more top-heavy in favor of continuing professional baseball. In one, the publication posed the question to servicemen via radio broadcasts, asking for replies by mail. "There came back a thunderous 'yes,' uttered by hundreds of militant voices, with no uncertain emphasis in favor of playing ball," the *Sporting News* reported. Pfc. Wayne L. Ashworth, a clerk at Fort Benning, Georgia, won ten dollars for the best reply.

"Baseball discontinued?" Ashworth wrote. "Would you like to discontinue the use of salt and pepper on your eggs, dressing on your salad, icings on your cakes and catsup or mustard on your hotdogs? ... Discontinue baseball and you remove something from our morale—something that only baseball can fill."

On February 7, 1943, at the annual dinner of the New York Chapter of the Baseball Writers Association of America, baseball was given ringing endorsements by a succession of notables.

"When there is no more reason for self-reliance in this country, then and then alone will there be no more reason for baseball," said Captain Eddie Rickenbacker, the World War I aviation hero.

"Hitler has killed a great many things in the past few years," said Quentin Reynolds, a well-known foreign correspondent. "Do not let him kill baseball!"

Wendell Willkie, the 1940 Republican presidential candidate, said that he had met thirty American servicemen on a Libyan battlefield and every one of them asked for a report on the pennant races. "Let us all here tonight make a resolution to preserve not alone baseball, but all of precious America," Willkie said.

"No matter how feeble are the nine men we'll put on the field, I think they'll be strong enough, without the help of any lobby in Washington, to survive," said Judge Kenesaw Mountain Landis, the commissioner of baseball.

Turning serious after watching a parody of himself by actor Lou Costello, New York Mayor Fiorello H. LaGuardia said, "Our people don't mind being rationed on sugar and shoes, but those men in Washington will have to leave our baseball alone!" The crowd of 1,300 rose in applause.

One of baseball's most outspoken supporters during the war was Senator Albert B. (Happy) Chandler, Democrat of Kentucky. "I'm for winning the war, and for keeping baseball," Chandler said in an interview at the Kentucky Derby in 1942. "We can, and must, do both."

That had the proper ring. So did a letter in early 1944 from Bob

Feller, then on the battleship U.S.S. *Alabama*, to Ed McAuley, a Cleveland sportswriter. "The most obvious and biggest peeve among servicemen is directed at those who are attempting to scuttle competitive athletics," Feller wrote. Ty Cobb, 58, expressed similar sentiments from the home front. "I hope that league baseball, even if it is played by old men, will receive some official recognition that it is essential to morale," Cobb said. "If worse came to worst, I'd get back into harness myself to help preserve it."

Baseball players were exhorted to work for the national good in many ways. At a winter meeting, the club presidents voted to require players to carry their own luggage; wardrobe trunks were forbidden. At various stages of the war, players were urged editorially to improve the physical fitness of the populace, work in war factories during the winter, vote full World Series shares to players in military service, avoid being photographed while pantomiming a soldier, avoid being photographed in pleasurable pursuits like hunting or swimming, and avoid being photographed in such miserable conditions as a rainstorm, unless they could strike an uncomplaining pose.

The latter three admonitions were intended to prevent any public feeling that athletes were ridiculing soldiers, lolling in the sun or complaining of the rain, while so many other young men were being killed in battle. The *Sporting News* suggested particular caution in hunting, lest an accident contrast the conditions under which athletes and soldiers fired their guns. "All praise to the player whose career ends from a wound on the battlefield," the publication said. "But small sympathy to the player who . . . insists on risking the end of his career to bring down a jack rabbit."

Like other industries, baseball found many ways to mix patriotism with profits. The *Sporting News* itself offered subscriptions to servicemen for $3.75 a year; the regular rate was $7. As an example to others, the publication reprinted a letter from Warren C. Giles, vice president and general manager of the Cincinnati Reds, ordering subscriptions for all Reds and Red farmhands in service. "CINCINNATI REDS REMEMBER THEIR MEN IN THE SERVICE!" the headline said. For a while, the weekly newspaper carried an "Honor Roll" of teams that gave *Sporting News* subscriptions to players in service. When Hank Greenberg of the Tigers wrote from his Army base for a subscription, the *Sporting News* reprinted his letter, headlined "Soldier Calls for his Bible."

Baseball payrolls declined during the war as established players entered military service and were replaced by athletes whose skills could not command large salaries. Nevertheless, club owners did not hesitate to cite the conflict as a reason for restraining the greed of their players. This posture, of course, served the greed of the owners. When Dutch Leonard asked for a raise in 1942 after winning eighteen games for the seventh-place Washington Senators the season before, Clark Griffith turned him down. "In these war times, with conditions as they are, anybody ought to welcome the same salary as he received last year," Griffith said.

The Detroit Tigers were even more patriotic; they offered salaries of $11,000 to pitcher Buck Newsom and first baseman Rudy York, who had earned $32,500 and $20,000, respectively, in 1941. Newsom took issue, and was traded to Washington.

In a February 1942 editorial, the *Sporting News* cautioned players that holding out for higher salaries in wartime would appear unseemly to the fans. Besides, club owners faced "huge hazards," the editorial said, including air raids. "They have calculated just what they can afford to pay the players—and they have not given the club treasuries all the best of it," the editorial said, concluding: "LET'S HAVE NO MORE OF THIS NONSENSE!" Pitcher Wayne Osborne of the Hollywood Stars in the Pacific Coast League, no doubt a serious reader of the *Sporting News*, offered to take a pay cut, but was assured by the owner of his club that he would be doing his bit if he merely sought no raise.

When the government imposed controls on salaries and prices later in 1942 to restrain inflation, the major leagues asked whether they were free to cut a player's pay. The government replied that a player could not be paid less than the lowest-paid member of his team received in 1942, or more than his highest-paid teammate of 1942. Within that range, a team was free to raise or lower salaries.

The rule helped the New York Giants acquire Ernie Lombardi, the 1942 National League Batting champion, from the Boston Braves, whose highest salary in 1942 was the $12,500 paid to shortstop Eddie Miller. Lombardi wanted $15,000 for 1943; the Braves were willing to pay it but could not. They swapped Lombardi to the Giants, whose salary ceiling was the $17,500 paid to shortstop Billy Jurges. In exchange, the Braves got catcher Hugh Poland and second baseman Connie Ryan, neither of whom threatened the salary barrier.

As more and more players were conscripted and salary controls were eased, the shoe shifted to the other foot. The scarcity of players gave those remaining a strong bargaining position. In 1944 and 1945, major league clubs were bedeviled by holdouts. After winning twenty-two games in 1942 and twenty-one in 1943, pitcher Mort Cooper of the Cardinals had the effrontery to return a contract offering him $12,000 for 1944; he said he wanted $17,500. Sam Breadon, the Cardinal owner, invoked patriotism to shame Cooper. "Certainly, at a time like this, it is unwise for players who have been excused from military service for some reason or another to publicize their dissatisfaction with the contracts which have been sent them," Breadon said. "I do not think it makes very good reading for persons who have their boys on the fighting fronts."

Cooper signed, but the next spring he held out again. So did shortstop Marty Marion, who recalled that 1945 salary disagreement with humor:

I was the Most Valuable Player in the league in 1944, and Mr. Breadon sent me a contract the next year for $13,000. I sent it back to him and told him I would not play for $13,000. I wanted $15,000, which was pretty small money. But at that particular time we had two boys on the ballclub named the Cooper boys [Mort's younger brother, Walker, was the Cardinal catcher], and Mr. Breadon had promised the Cooper boys that they would be the highest-paid players on the club. So he told me, "I can't pay you what you want because I promised the Coopers they would get the highest salaries, and they're not getting that much." I said, "I don't give a damn what Cooper makes; I won't play for $13,000." So he gave me the $15,000 to play that year, and he called the Cooper boys in and gave them the same thing. He didn't even have to tell them what he paid me, but he was fair. Mort bought me a new hat for getting him a raise.

CHAPTER 2

The Browns Break Water

Public service and posturing aside, baseball's greatest contribution to the war effort was its manpower. The United States raised an armed force of nearly sixteen million men during World War II, and those drafted first were hale, hearty men in their 20s and 30s. That naturally drained away most of the best professional baseball players, hurting better teams the most and drying up their usual source of replacements, the minor league farm systems.

Many of the best players enlisted, including baseball's three preeminent stars, Joe DiMaggio, Bob Feller, and Ted Williams. These men were patriotic; besides, they felt public pressure to enter military service as an example to others. Most of the men left behind to play baseball were physical culls and athletes of extraordinary youth or old age.

Gradually, this state of affairs made a contender of the St. Louis Browns. Nothing short of a world war could have done so. Among the sixteen major league teams, only the Browns had never won a pennant. They had last come close in 1922, when the great George Sisler lifted the Browns to second place, one game behind the Yankees. Since then, the Browns had finished in the first division only five times, never as high as second.

Moreover, this woebegone team seemed to be going from bad to worse. The Browns entered the 1940s bereft of talent, money, fans, and hope. Their play was dreadful, and their players so accustomed to thrashings that they sometimes seemed to cringe around the field like whipped hounds. Fans, so few and silent, could hear the Brownie infielders take turns fulfilling their ritual obligation to encourage the pitcher, following the script and monotone that all baseball players learn, just as they learn to chew tobacco.

First, the Brownie first baseman: "Humm Babe humm Babe chuck Babe." Then, after a pitch or two, the first baseman would fall silent, and the second baseman would pick up the chant. And so around the otherwise lifeless Brownie infield. (In this unchanging baseball script, nearly all pitchers are named "Babe." A more imaginative fielder will sometimes christen a pitcher with some other name, such as "Shooter," as in "Cumm Shooter Cumm Shooter Cumm Shooter." Or, in a more personal vein, "Left-hander" or "Right-hander," a chant that ends with an exclamation, as in "Ho [meaning go] you left-handuhh!")

The Brownies had little to chant about. In 1939, they lost 111 games, winning only forty-three. Years later, players of similar futility, the early New York Mets, were embraced by hometown fans like ragged teddy bears. The Browns, in contrast, were spurned like lepers. One day in 1933, only thirty-four fans showed up to watch them play. The major league attendance record for a single game is 84,587; the Browns failed to draw that many for their entire season of home games in 1935, and by 1939 had increased their home attendance to only 109,000. St. Louis, proud of its shoe factories and breweries, had a sardonic slogan that put the Browns in civic perspective: "First in shoes, first in booze, and last in the American League."

Sportsman's Park, the baseball stadium where the Browns and the Cardinals played, was so abused by continuous play during the hot St. Louis summers that the infield usually lost most of its grass by midseason. Some local high schools had greener diamonds. The players dressed in a drab clubhouse with bare concrete floors, and washed in showers that sometimes were simply curved pipes, with no shower heads. Nothing was air-conditioned, not even the cramped and airless cubicle where the umpires dressed alongside the water heater.

This tawdry background somehow helped to lend the Cardinals a rakish and exciting air. They were the brigands of baseball, the "Gashouse Gang." They won, and the fans loved them. The same setting made the Browns look their miserable worst.

Unnoticed at first, the Browns began to thrive in the austere atmosphere of World War II. While utterly lacking the kind of young hero whose enlistment might be recorded by newsreel cameras, the Browns were rich with aged and ailing journeymen who failed to qualify for military service. Moreover, they were skilled at acquiring and managing more players of the same variety, including drunks and rogues cast off as troublemakers by other teams and, in one case, by the Army itself. These worn and frayed strands of playing talent became the yarn of major league baseball during World War II. The Browns had been knitting their teams from such scraps since well before Hitler's first blitzkrieg; the war placed a premium on that kind of knitting.

Better teams, such as the New York Yankees, Boston Red Sox, and Brooklyn Dodgers, found wartime conditions difficult and somehow degrading. Indeed, Yankee President Edward G. Barrow spent much of the war publicly curling his lip at wartime promotions such as night baseball, and wartime expedients such as the part-time use of men whose main jobs were in war factories. Other teams hired these players with reluctance. William O. DeWitt, the Brownie general manager, invented the practice.

As the war wore on, the rest of the American League was sucked dry of talent by the military draft. But the Browns improved. Finally, in 1944, they surfaced, like an ugly stump in a draining lake.

This process took time, and was not without interruption. The military draft started slowly, and was capricious, taking some players for three or four years while others, equally young and healthy, served one year or less. Teams wafted up and down from season to season, blown by military currents largely beyond their control.

CHAPTER 3

Hammerin' Hank and Losing Pitcher: Baseball's Peacetime Soldiers

Although the fact is largely forgotten, the United States began drafting its World War II Army in late 1940, more than a year before the U.S. was drawn into the war by Japan's attack on the Naval base at Pearl Harbor. On October 16, 1940, a date carefully selected to avoid conflict with the state fairs that abound during autumn, every American male between the ages of 21 and 36 was required to register for the draft. Since President Franklin D. Roosevelt and most members of Congress were still promising that they would try to keep the United States out of the war, the draft supposedly was for training only; each man would be released after serving one year. With millions registering and only thousands then needed, selection was to be by lottery. The lower a man's lottery number, the more likely he would be drafted.

The *Sporting News* covered draft registration day with photographs of four prominent players registering—Joe DiMaggio of the Yankees and his brother Dominic of the Red Sox, in San Francisco; Bob Feller, of the Indians, in Cleveland; and Bucky Walters, of the World Champion Cincinnati Reds, in Philadelphia. The occasion provided an opportunity for the long-winded hyperbole that was common in sportswriting of that era, and the *Sporting News* did not let the chance slip by.

"Uncertain as to what 1941 held for them, but nevertheless walking up to the registration desk and taking pen in hand as unperturbed and as courageously as they have walked up to the plate, swinging a bat, the nation's army of ballplayers heeded the first call of Uncle Sam and was prepared to answer the second fully aware that on them and their generation rests the strength of the defensive arm of their nation," wrote Edgar G. Brands, the weekly's editor. Setting the tone for its coverage throughout the war, the *Sporting News* tempered that patriotic drumbeat with the suggestion that baseball players might warrant special favor. Brands wrote: "Whether they will be excused for the one-year training period because of their indispensability to baseball, whether they will be permitted to serve in off-season hitches, whether a team loses none, only one player, several, a star or only an ordinary performer—all these 'ifs' rest in the laps of the gods, the final policy adopted and the drawing of numbers, which will designate those who most don the uniform, beginning November 18." Brands speculated, correctly as it turned out, that many players might spend their service time entertaining the troops. Wishfully, he added: "Assurances have been given in high official quarters that all athletes in camp will be given an opportunity to keep on competitive edge while there." As for the major leagues, he wrote prophetically, "It looks like the start of an era of very young men and the aged veterans in baseball for the next four years, the length of time in which conscription is to be enforced."

Among the players registering that day were Hank Greenberg, 29, left fielder of the Detroit Tigers, and Hugh Mulcahy, 27, right-handed pitcher for the Philadelphia Phillies. Among regular performers, two players of more widely differing fortunes could hardly have been found in the major leagues. Greenberg was baseball's leading home run slugger. In 1938 he hit fifty-eight homers, only two short of Babe Ruth's record. In 1940 he batted .340 and led the American League in home runs with forty-one, doubles with fifty, runs batted in with 150, and slugging average with .670. The Tigers won the 1940 American League pennant and Greenberg was voted the league's Most Valuable Player. He was known throughout baseball as "Hammerin' Hank."

Mulcahy was a pitcher good enough to start every fourth game for the Phillies and to finish most of them. But even a good pitcher cannot win with a bad team, and the Phillies were dreadful. In 1938, 1939, and 1940, seasons of 154 games each, the Phils lost 105 games, 106, and 103, respectively, finishing last each year. Mulcahy shouldered his share of the load, losing twenty games in 1938, sixteen in 1939, and twenty-two in 1940. In both 1938 and 1940, he was the National League's only twenty-game loser. In fact, Mulcahy lost so many games that it became part of his name. He is listed in the record books to this day as Hugh (Losing Pitcher) Mulcahy.

When the first dr..ft lottery was held on November 18, 1940, the low numbers held by Greenberg and Mulcahy exposed them to early induction. The sporting pages were full of military talk, much of it speculative. Billy Southworth, Jr., a star outfielder with Toronto of the International League and the son of the St. Louis Cardinals' manager, joined the Army Air Corps and became the first professional baseball player to enlist. Another minor leaguer, outfielder Bill Embick of the Harrisburg, Pennsylvania, Senators, was the first player drafted. Johnny Gorsica, a Detroit pitcher whose real name was Gorsykowski, was rumored to have joined the Polish Air Squadron, an arm of Britain's Royal Air Force, but the report proved to be false. On February 2, 1941, at the eighteenth annual dinner of the New York Chapter of the Baseball Writers Association of America, writers spoofed the forthcoming military careers of ballplayers with skits staged at "Fort Dicks." Rud Rennie of the New York *Herald-Tribune* sang a composition entitled "If Greenberg Fights Like He Can Slug."

But in fact, no major leaguers were drafted immediately and none enlisted. Toward the end of 1940, the owners of several major league teams talked of forming a committee to discuss the draft status of ballplayers with government officials. But Judge Landis, the tyrannical and puritanical commissioner of baseball, killed the idea and forbade any lobbying by baseball men.

The commissioner's order was consistent with the patriotic

stance adopted by baseball during World War I, which drew 247 major league players into service. In June of 1918, the government had ordered all civilian men of military age either to join the armed forces or to take a job in an industry considered essential to the war effort. Actors and opera singers, among others, sought and got exemptions from this "work or fight" order. Baseball did not apply, asking only for permission to complete an abbreviated 1918 season. Secretary of War Newton D. Baker allowed the season to run through Labor Day. He also permitted a World Series, in which Babe Ruth pitched two victories as the Boston Red Sox beat the Chicago Cubs, four games to two. Only the Armistice saved baseball from skipping the 1919 season.

Fearing that World War II might lead to another such curtailment, other baseball officials echoed Landis's message of self-sacrifice only to a point. "Baseball is ready, yes eager, to do its duty in national defense," said Ford Frick, president of the National League. "Baseball wants no favors in this respect. It expects no exemptions, except," Frick added, "such as the authorities may decide to favor it with."

With the United States still at peace, some Selective Service officials saw no harm in deferring men who had important business to attend to. Jimmy Stewart was deferred for six months by his Hollywood draft board, which reasoned that the nation could not readily spare his acting talents. "The baseball folks are not going to ask that this ruling be regarded as precedent, but they are watching things closely," reported the *Sporting News.*

Unknown to Judge Landis, Clark C. Griffith, a turn-of-the-century pitching star who had owned the Washington Senators for more than two decades, was watching things at first hand. Griffith, nicknamed "The Old Fox," knew the pathways of power in Washington, and truly believed that baseball's most appropriate contribution would be not the mobilization of players but the building of morale, resulting from soldiers and war workers watching games and playing ball themselves. During World War I, Griffith contributed enthusiastically to a drive in which the major leagues donated a vast amount of balls, bats, and other equipment for use by our doughboys in France. A freighter carried off this precious cargo with great fanfare, only to be torpedoed and sunk by a German submarine.

In 1941, Griffith undertook a discreet role as baseball's resident lobbyist. One who remembered Griffith's work was General Lewis B. Hershey, who ran the Selective Service System through World War II, the Korean War, and most of the Vietnam conflict. Hershey:

Old Man Landis was hell for high water that they weren't going to go messing around. But I used to have lunch maybe once a month with Griff and sometimes the president of the National League, Ford Frick, who happened to have been a Hoosier who came from not too far from where I did. Old Fox always said, "Now, don't let Landis know I'm seeing you." Landis was the fellow that Griff looked toward and shivered.

Griffith was trying to keep a ball team on the field. One of our problems was to get through people's heads the fact that we couldn't possibly take all these people, even in two to three years. I think our first call was about 10,000, and they were all volunteers; one of them was the president of the New York Stock Exchange. Everyone gets frightened when there's a thunderstorm but not many houses get hit. The fact that we were going to draft a few people the first year or so wouldn't have hurt the baseball business to amount to anything.

We talked a lot of times about whether there was any possibility of a deferment. Of course, you can't have right without somebody saying what right is, and you can't have wrong without somebody saying what's wrong. But I don't think it seemed to a lot of us that you could start out deferring people from service to play ball. As the war went on, it got to the place where there wasn't any reason for Griff to talk to me. About the only thing I could have advised him on was, "Why the hell don't you try to get some of these cripples?"

On April 24, 1941, the *Sporting News* led off with a wildly optimistic story by Daniel M. Daniel of the New York *World-Telegram*. Daniel quoted Griffith as predicting that the government would soon announce a plan to limit the induction of major league players.

"Just what the plan will be, I cannot say," Griffith said. "There may be an order which would prevent the drafting of more than one player of any major league club until the 1941 season is over. Perhaps the limit will be fixed at two players. Then again, the Adjutant General's office may allow all our draft eligibles to remain in the major leagues until October, and in the meantime order military drill for all players in baseball. This, you will recollect, was done in 1917 and 1918." (Indeed it was. At the request of Ban Johnson, then president of the American League, all American League teams were given Army instructors in 1917 and competed for a $500 prize in pregame drills. The Browns won the drilling award and perhaps spent themselves; they finished seventh in the league standings.)

No such consideration was forthcoming from the government. "He'd seen the wrong people, probably," said General Hershey. In fact, Griffith may have been drawing wishful conclusions from an isolated favor done for him by none other than Hershey.

Besides Greenberg and Mulcahy, the only major league players of any note who faced induction that spring of 1941 were the two batting stars of Griffith's Washington Senators, Cecil Travis and Buddy Lewis. In 1940, Travis batted .322 and Lewis hit .317. WhenTravis's draft board in Georgia and Lewis's in North Carolina announced in early April that the two ballplayers would be inducted within a month, Shirley Povich of the Washington *Post* wrote in the *Sporting News* that the result would be "virtual devastation of the Washington infield.

"The United States may be gathering its greatest peace-time Army, but Manager Bucky Harris of the Senators is of the mind that Uncle Sam has already declared war—on the Washington club," Povich wrote. As it turned out, both players were deferred until after the 1941 season. Lewis, now an automobile dealer in Lowell, North Carolina, recalled the circumstances. Lewis:

I was in the first draft here in Gadsden County, in early 1941. What was my attitude? Well, I didn't particularly like it. At that time, there was no war and no real vision of war. Hell, you kind of hated to just leave. I had already signed my professional baseball contract for that year, and I was supporting my two parents; I was the only support they had. So it didn't seem right, and I felt like I should have had a complete deferment. My draft board never did give me a deferment. Clark Griffith got it through General Hershey. Griffith being a friend of his, he gave me a deferment until the end of the baseball season.

General Hershey:

Who? They played where? We postponed a lot of people for a lot of reasons. I grew up on a farm, and I had no problem in my mind with a guy in July or August being deferred to get his crop in. A crop's a crop; I have no quarrel with baseball players, no prejudice against them. Another thing, when you're inducting 10 or 15 thousand, well, you had so many more that were just as obligated to go, and if a fellow was going anyway, you didn't have to worry too much about public opinion if the guy goes eventually.

(Hershey was consistent. In a similar situation years later, he recalled, "We got in quite a tangle with this hips boy in entertainment. The fellow with the swivel hips. Yeah, Presley. Well, you know that boy registered, and it happened that the war wasn't on and we weren't taking anybody much. He used to come to his local board every time he was back in Memphis and say, 'When it's time for me, let me know.' So he finally got a contract singing somewhere and was about two-thirds through the damned thing, and the local board said, 'Come on in here.' He appealed, and it came in here, and I said to that local board, 'You would let him bring in his wheat, wouldn't you?' But I doubt if they deferred him; their backs were up.")

So, apparently, were the backs of Mulcahy's draft board in Massachusetts and Greenberg's in Michigan. Mulcahy was inducted into the Army on March 8, 1941. Greenberg followed on May 7, after playing the season's first nineteen games. "I am 100 percent in favor of military training and will do my best," Mulcahy told a *Sporting News* correspondent. "If there is any last message to be given to the public," said Greenberg, "let it be that I'm going to be a good soldier." The *Sporting News* bade Greenberg farewell with a drawing of him in military uniform against a background of the American flag. Above hovered the ghostly form of Hammerin' Hank in his Detroit flannels. "As exemplified by Greenberg, baseball is asking no special concessions and expects no favors that are not granted others," said a *Sporting News* editorial. "But diamond performers inducted into the service are entitled to the same consideration given those skilled in other lines and should be permitted to utilize their talents by being assigned to work they know better than others." With obvious disapproval, the editorial reported that Mulcahy was pitching only occasionally at Camp Devens, Massachusetts, and expressed hope that Greenberg would not be similarly misused. "We look not only for Hank to be slugging the ball for some camp team, but for him to be directing the physical activities of large groups, for which he is especially fitted, and giving more material aid to the upbuilding of esprit de corps than by merely shouldering a rifle or squinting behind a machine gun."

Mulcahy's induction cost him more than the five prime pitching years he devoted to military service. For years, Gerry Nugent, the owner of the Phillies, had made ends meet by selling his best players. After the 1940 season, Nugent let it be known that his two workhorse pitchers, Mulcahy and Kirby Higbe, were for sale. Mulcahy, retired from a long career as an instructor of minor league pitchers in the Chicago White Sox farm system, recalled the situation:

You never know what the background music is, but supposedly I was the next fellow to be sold. I know the Dodgers were after me, and Cincinnati and the Cubs were trying to get me. Any move would be a move upstairs; you'd have a better chance. But of course being single, my draft status was worse. Higbe was married and supported his mother. He went to the Dodgers in '41.

They had a bowl [Mulcahy recalled of the draft lottery] and they picked the numbers out of the bowl like they did in World War I. So they picked my number out. I had heard that people were getting as much as a year's deferment to get things squared away, so I tried to get a six-month delay but they wouldn't give it to me. And then they said—of course, everything was kind of mixed up then—that they wouldn't catch me until September. I was already packed, ready to go to spring training at Miami Beach the next day, when I got the notice. So I was in; it was March 8th when I went in, about nine months before Pearl Harbor, and everyone's attitude was, "What's going on?" There was a song, "Goodbye Dear, I'll Be Back in a Year." Then Pearl Harbor hit and everybody whipped into trying to get the job done.

Bad luck? I don't know. I might have got hit with a line drive if I spent six more months with the Phillies [laughs]. Seriously, I never felt really bad about it. It never shook me up; I never think back on what might have been. I'm very thankful that I came back.

Although apprehension among club owners remained high, the only major leaguers who spent the 1941 season in military service were Mulcahy, Greenberg, and three players so obscure that their departures were barely mentioned: Washington pitcher Lou Thuman, Brooklyn outfielder Joe (Muscles) Gallagher, and Pittsburgh pitcher Oad Swigart. Pitcher John Rigney of the Chicago White Sox was summoned, but deferred because of a perforated eardrum. Morris Arnovich, an outfielder with the New York Giants, volunteered but was not taken because he lacked a pair of occluding molars, a fact he proved to reporters by removing his false teeth.

By August of 1941, 193 minor league players were in service. The minor leagues were then so vast, with forty-three leagues and nearly 5,000 players, that the loss averaged less than one man from each of the 287 teams, but of course some clubs were hurt worse than others. The Snow Hill (North Carolina) Billies of the Coastal Plain League lost three players to the Army. Lloyd (Clugger) Rice, a .360 hitter the year before, was drafted from the Wilmington (Delaware) Blue Rocks of the Inter-State League, and Tommy Flynn, who hit .328 and stole thirty bases in 1940, was taken from the Lima Pandas of the Ohio State League. Joseph (Izzy) Caradona, who sold tickets for New Orleans of the Southern Association, became paymaster at Camp Polk, Louisiana. An early enlistee, pitcher Johnnie Wilbourne of Greenville (South Carolina) in the South Atlantic League, got perhaps the first medical discharge conferred upon a baseball player. "Fort Jackson doctors discovered he was ruptured, so he's to be mustered out," reported the *Sporting News*.

Greenberg's induction made Detroit the first team to be harmed by World War II. From first place in 1940, the Tigers sank to a fourth-place tie with Cleveland in 1941, twenty-six games behind the champion Yankees. But even with Greenberg, Detroit would have been hard pressed to catch the Yanks. Early that season, Joe DiMaggio hit safely in fifty-six straight games, still a record. After being blanked in one game on July 17, he then hit safely in the next sixteen. DiMaggio led the American League in runs batted in with 125, three more than teammate Charlie Keller, and was voted the league's Most Valuable Player. His .357 batting average ranked him third; Ted Williams hit .406, and Cecil Travis of Washington celebrated his draft deferment by batting .359.

Although the Phillies finished last again, Mulcahy's induction may have affected the National League pennant race. Kirby Higbe, Brooklyn's $100,000 acquisition from the Phils, won twenty-two games as the Dodgers edged the Cardinals for the pennant. Mulcahy, who might have been in Higbe's shoes were it not for the draft, meantime learned the artillery trade in Massachusetts.

Dolf Camilli, a first baseman whom the Dodgers had purchased from the Phillies three years before, led the National League in home runs with thirty-four and runs batted in with 120, and was voted the league's Most Valuable Player. Pete Reiser, Brooklyn's sensational rookie outfielder, hit .343 to win the batting championship. To the embarrassment of the sportswriting fraternity, only one of the 262 members of the Baseball Writers Association of America had correctly predicted, before the season, that the Yankees would win in the American League, and that the Dodgers, Cardinals, and Reds would finish in that order in the National League. This seer was Charles Dexter of the New York *Daily Worker*, a newspaper identified with the Communist Party.

The Yankees won the World Series four games to one, taking the fourth game with a ninth-inning rally that began when Mickey Owen, the Brooklyn catcher, dropped a third strike on what would have been the final out.

CHAPTER 4

Pearl Harbor

Bob Feller joined the Cleveland Indians in 1936 at the age of 17, so young and so spectacular as a pitcher that he became an instant celebrity. His graduation from high school in Van Meter, Iowa, was broadcast live on NBC radio. In 1939, 1940, and 1941, he led the American League in victories with twenty-four, twenty-seven, and twenty-five, respectively, and in strikeouts with 246, 261, and 260. By the winter of 1941, Feller was one of the most famous men in America. He had achieved more by the age of 23 than any other pitcher in baseball, before or since. In an era when $15,000 was considered an excellent baseball salary, Feller was paid more than $50,000 a year by the Cleveland Indians. In the off season, he lived on the Iowa family farm where, as a boy, he had learned to pitch under his father's tutelage. Thirty-five years later, Feller, an executive with Hilton Hotels in Cleveland, recalled his attitude about military service:

My dad had had cancer since 1936, so I was classified as 2-C or 3-C. Food production was the name of it, and it meant I was a farmer. In fact, Tris Speaker was on my draft board, right here in Cleveland. I took care of my mother, who wasn't particularly well, and my sister Marguerite, who was a young thing. I could have stayed out of the service; I would have had to work as a farmer. But I told my mother and sister and dad that I was not going to take advantage of this. I said, "When it's time for me to do the job I'm ready to do the job. When they want me I'll go."

Why? Because of my position in public life. Besides, I didn't think it was right. I'd been talking to Gene Tunney during the summer. He was running the Navy physical fitness program, and he wanted me to go into his program. Jack Dempsey had the same job in the Coast Guard; they still weren't very great friends, even then.

So I was driving to Chicago for the major league meetings; had nothing else to do, and I was going to go in and see all the guys at the Palmer House. It was Sunday, about 12 noon or early afternoon, and I was crossing the Mississippi River at Moline, driving by myself, and just as I landed on the other side of the bridge I heard the thing on the car radio—"Attack on Pearl Harbor."

I drove into Chicago and Monday morning, eight o'clock, I called Tunney. He said, "I can't get there today, Bob, but I'll be on the last plane out tonight and I'll sign you up at the courthouse." So the next morning at eight o'clock, December ninth, I was there at the courthouse and I signed up with the Navy. They took pictures. [In fact, they did more than that; Feller's enlistment was recorded by newsreel cameras and was broadcast live, nationwide.] At that time, anybody that was going to war from public life, it was a big thing. We needed some heroes, right now. That's why Doolittle bombed Tokyo. There were all these stunts. Like Colin Kelly; whether he really dove his plane in the stack of that Jap ship or was shot down. . . . But we needed heroes. That's right; at that point we were losing the war.

Feller was not baseball's only Pearl Harbor hero. On December 5, Greenberg, 30 years old, had been discharged from the Army under a new law permitting draftees 28 or older to cut short their year of military training. Two days later, Pearl Harbor was attacked; Greenberg promptly reenlisted, regaining his rank as a sergeant and his salary of $60 a month. He had been making about $50,000 a year in baseball. "We are in trouble and there is only one thing for me to do—return to the service," Greenberg said. ". . . This doubtless means I am finished with baseball, and it would be silly for me to say I do not leave it without a pang. But all of us are confronted with a terrible task—the defense of our country and the fight for our lives." The *Sporting News* splashed Greenberg's picture across three columns and praised him as "the Hank Gowdy of 1941." Gowdy, a catcher with the Boston Braves, was the first major leaguer to enlist in the armed forces during World War I.

While the patriotic glow from Feller's enlistment and Greenberg's reenlistment helped Americans warm themselves for the long war ahead, two men were suffering in the shadows of that December, 1941, major league convention. Donald Barnes and William O. DeWitt, respectively the president and general manager of the St. Louis Browns, had come up with an idea a decade ahead of its time. Drained by financial losses caused by their inability to draw fans in St. Louis, Barnes and DeWitt had decided to move the Browns to Los Angeles in time for the 1942 season. Such a notion was then unheard of; the two major leagues had maintained the same sixteen teams in the same cities since 1903. On the major league map, St. Louis was at the extreme southwestern corner of the United States. Nevertheless, Barnes and DeWitt had negotiated the move and had come to Chicago anticipating formal ratification.

The details had been excruciating. Philip K. Wrigley, owner of the Chicago Cubs, had to be persuaded to sell his franchise rights and his ball park in Los Angeles, where the Cubs operated a farm club in the Pacific Coast League. A schedule had to be drawn up that would take the teams to and from Los Angeles by train, since air travel was still considered dangerous and impractical. Owners of the other seven American League teams had to be convinced that they should subordinate their distaste for change to their relish for profits; larger crowds in Los Angeles would mean larger gate receipts for visiting teams as well as for the Browns. To provide the Browns with a stake, Sam Breadon, the notoriously thrifty owner of the St. Louis Cardinals, had to be talked into paying his Brownie competition to get out of town.

DeWitt, still genial and active sixty years after taking his first baseball job as office boy for Branch Rickey, recalled the details in conversations during 1975 and 1976 at his homes in North Palm Beach, Florida, and Cincinnati, Ohio:

This went on in the summer of 1941. It was kept very quiet. In fact, the Browns' directors didn't even know about it; Barnes and I were the only ones who knew at first. Barnes worked out a deal with Sam Breadon; if Breadon would pay him $350,000, he would vacate St. Louis. And he went to Chicago and made a deal with Phil Wrigley to buy Wrigley Field in Los Angeles—a nice ball park, the same as Wrigley Field in Chicago, only a little smaller—and the franchise. I think the price was a million dollars. We talked to Will Harridge, the president of the league, and he talked to the other club owners, confidentially.

The clubs were working on a three-trip schedule at that time, two four-game series and a three-game series in each city. I sat down in the New Yorker Hotel with the guy who wrote the American League schedules for fifty years, an old man who was in charge of the safe-deposit department of a bank in Boston. He had these long sheets and wide sheets; we had to get a card table in there to spread the things out. We'd try it this way and that way, trying to work it out so the other clubs could get out to the Coast and get back again. On the train; there was no flying then. We figured that we'd open up out there and play about four clubs, and we'd only have them make two trips out there. They'd take the Super Chief out of Chicago. We had the schedules made out.

December 7th, 1941, screwed up the whole thing. We were in Comiskey Park watching the Bears and the Cardinals play football that d y, and it was cold as the devil. Somebody came in and said, "Gee, they just had a flash on the radio that the Japs have bombed Pearl Harbor." Me, I didn't know where the hell Pearl Harbor was; I never heard of Pearl Harbor. Everybody started, "Buzz, buzz. . . ."

Well, we had the meeting the·next day, and that killed the whole thing.

With trains needed to move troops and supplies and with baseball men fearing that the sport's continued operation was uncertain, the idea of a franchise move appeared to be out of the question. To put the matter to rest, Barnes arose when the American League meeting began and told his colleagues—who, of course, already knew it—that Los Angeles interests had asked him to move the Browns there. The league's club owners immediately voted the idea down, with even Barnes casting a negative ballot, to make it unanimous. Pearl Harbor had temporarily cost the Indians and Tigers their best players. The Browns, bombed back into St. Louis by the Japanese, had lost their whole future. It appeared that the fortunes of wartime, like those of peacetime, were going against the Browns.

Organized baseball wasted no time in joining the war effort. Ford Frick, president of the National League, quickly sent President Roosevelt a telegram of support. "Individually and collectively, we are yours to command," it said. Philip K. Wrigley announced that he had planned to install baseball's finest lighting system at Wrigley Field in Chicago so Cub fans could enjoy night games in 1942, but was instead turning in the electrical equipment for defense use. (Three decades later, Wrigley Field was still without lights. Mr. Wrigley had decided that night games might bother residents of the neighborhood.) Ed Barrow, president of the New York Yankees, offered civil defense authorities the use of Yankee Stadium as a bomb shelter, saying that citizens would be safe under the stands.

In its first issue after Pearl Harbor, the *Sporting News* said baseball was even ready to close down if asked to do so by President Roosevelt, although an editorial emphasized the importance of sports in building morale and of baseball in carrying forward American traditions. "Born in America, propagated in America and recognized as the National Game, baseball and all those engaged in the sport are Americans first, last and always," the editorial said. ". . . In all the history of baseball there never was a conscientious objector, or a slacker in its ranks." (Actually, the *Sporting News* itself had already reported the case of one minor league player, pitcher Tom Ananicz of Kansas City, who was a pacifist by religion and had applied for combat exemption as a conscientious objector.)

On January 15, 1942, President Roosevelt laid baseball's fears to rest. In a letter to Judge Landis, Roosevelt wrote:

"I honestly feel that it would be best for the country to keep baseball going. There will be fewer people unemployed and everybody will work longer hours and harder than ever before. And that means that they ought to have a chance for recreation and for taking their minds off their work even more than before.

"Baseball provides a recreation which does not last over two hours or two hours and a half, and which can be got for very little cost. And, incidentally, I hope that night games can be extended because it gives an opportunity to the day shift to see a game occasionally."

Roosevelt's letter was front-page news; it was baseball's green light to continue operating in wartime. The *Sporting News* said that Roosevelt should be named player of the year. Newspapers reported that the president was replying to a handwritten note from Landis asking what organized baseball should do. In fact, Roosevelt's letter was a coup engineered behind the scenes by two astute baseball lobbyists. One was the Old Fox, Clark Griffith, owner of the Washington Senators. The other was Robert E. Hannegan, postmaster general in Roosevelt's cabinet, chairman of the Democratic National Committee, and confidant of the president. By happy coincidence, Hannegan, a St. Louisan, was also a sports buff. He starred in football at St. Louis University and maintained close ties with St. Louis sports figures, including Sam Breadon of the Cardinals and Don Barnes and Bill DeWitt of the Browns. After the war, Hannegan became a part owner of the Cardinals.

Griffith's role was recalled by Shirley Povich, the retired sports editor and columnist of the Washington *Post*, who covered the Senators for thirty years:

Whereas Landis got the green light from Roosevelt, it was all inspired by Clark Griffith. The fact is that Landis despised Roosevelt and Roosevelt didn't care much for Landis. I don't think Roosevelt knew Landis, but he'd heard that Landis had spouted off against him from the start; Landis was very, very conservative.

I remember shortly after the war broke out, Bob Considine and I were then covering the Senators and we were in Clearwater, where Landis spent every winter, and we wandered by Judge Landis's hotel to see him. He knew who we were, that we were from Washington. Landis was almost violent. He grabbed us by the lapels, both of us, and he said, "Listen, young fellows, don't you let that man in the White House send you to war!" Did he really hate FDR? He sure did. Landis was not welcome at the White House. That is why he wanted no representation in Washington, and Griffith had to carry the ball.

Griffith always talked to the president because he automatically went to the White House every opening day to present him with his pass, and the president always came out to the opening game. Roosevelt, as you know, had four terms. Griffith had a lot of chances to see him, a lot of opening days, so they knew each other. Griffith was the one who persuaded Roosevelt to take this action.

Bill DeWitt:

Another fellow that had a lot to do with it was Robert Hannegan. Don Barnes and Hannegan were very close. I went to high school with Hannegan, and so of course I knew him all through the years. He was chairman of the Democratic National Committee, and he was in great shape with the president. Did he talk to Roosevelt about the green light? Yeah, absolutely. Griffith helped, but the guy who really put it over was Hannegan. No, the newspapers didn't know that. Hannegan wasn't going to tell them, and we weren't going to tell them, so how were they going to know? That's a dead man's secret.

Hannegan died in 1949.

Landis, who no doubt wrote to Roosevelt at the suggestion of Griffith or Barnes, said nothing in his note about night games; Roosevelt's suggestion that more of them be played appeared to be gratuitous. It startled many baseball officials, not including Griffith or Hannegan, who had made night baseball part of their pitch to the president. Night baseball had been played in the minor leagues since 1930 and began spreading to the majors in 1938. By 1939, 70 percent of minor league games were being played at night, and Robert J. Swackhamer, an engineer for the General Electric Company, predicted that baseball eventually would be played in roofed stadiums with indirect lighting.

But many baseball executives, including Judge Landis, still viewed night baseball with suspicion. It was variously feared that players would lose their keen eyesight or their morals, that the wrong kind of fan would be attracted, that a new generation of fans would not be developed because children could not stay out so late, and that the novelty attraction of night games would soon wear off, turning fans sour on the National Pastime itself. Even Griffith had once proclaimed that "baseball is made to be played in God's own sunshine."

The only virtue of night games was that fans paid to see them. In

1939, the Browns drew as many fans in fourteen night games as in sixty-three day games. But in 1940 and 1941 the ration was cut in half; with the support of Landis, night ball opponents among the major league club owners enacted a rule limiting each team to seven home night games a season. At the major league meeting that followed Pearl Harbor, Barnes and Griffith, the latter a convert to the night ball cause, urged their colleagues to let the Senators and Browns, at least, play more than seven night games so they could stay afloat financially. American League club owners voted to let them play fourteen, but the National League voted against it and Landis broke the tie in favor of daylight. Some executives, including Ed Barrow of the Yankees, thought seven night games were too many. Yankee Stadium had no lights and Barrow had no intention of installing any; he thought night baseball was a fad. "If night ball is stopped, I will not be the one to cry," Barrow said. "It's a wart on the nose of the game."

But as Griffith, Barnes, and DeWitt had gleefully anticipated, baseball officials could not gracefully deny Roosevelt's request that more night games be played. The ration was raised to twenty-one night games for Washington, which was considered a special case as a city of day-shift bureaucrats, and to fourteen for all other teams. "Maybe our luck is changing," said Barnes. Fourteen night games, predicted Sam Breadon, owner of the Cardinals, would be "all the traffic will bear." "One thing we want understood," said Frick, the National League president: "This war measure is not to be regarded as precedent." Lest anyone accuse baseball of squandering energy, the Westinghouse Electric Company produced figures proving that fans would burn more electricity reading individually in their homes than gathering under the arc lights of a baseball stadium.

One thing remained to gird baseball for war. The Japanese, who for years had embraced baseball as their national sport and had waxed delirious at barnstorming visits by the likes of Babe Ruth and Lou Gehrig, had to be drummed out of the game. The *Sporting News* undertook this task, although acknowledging in an editorial that baseball was so popular in Japan that "every bit of vacant space, even on the sea coast, was crowded with yellow-skinned, almond-eyed players.

"It was introduced by American missionaries, who wanted to wean their boy pupils away from such native sports as the stupid Japanese wrestling, fencing with crude broadswords and jujitsu," the editorial explained. "Having a natural catlike agility, the Japanese took naturally to the diamond pastime. They became first-class fielders and made some progress in pitching, but because of their smallness of stature, they remained feeble hitters. In their games with visiting American teams, it always was a sore spot with this cocky race that their batsmen were so outclassed by the stronger, more powerful American sluggers. For, despite the brusqueness and braggadocio of the militarists, Japanese cockiness hid a national inferiority complex.

". . . After looking at the 70 years of Japanese baseball in retrospect, this treacherous Asiatic land was really never converted to baseball," the editorial said. "Japanese fans, in the past, have expressed surprise at our American custom of 'riding' the umpire and the often good-natured jockeying from bench and coaching line. They argued: 'After all, the umpire is the official in charge; he should command respect.' As to the jockeying, the comment was: 'It is discourteous, impolite to speak to an opponent so he will lose his natural ability.' American baseball does not breed a punctilious politeness, saying 'so sorry' behind a grimacing yellow mask, but through our great game runs an inherent decency, fair dealing, love of the game and respect for one's opponents. That is the very soul of baseball. We may cut a few corners on the playing area, but we do not stab an 'honorable opponent' in the back, nor do we crush out his brains with a bat while he is asleep, before even challenging him to a match.

". . . So, we repeat, Japan never was converted to baseball. They may have acquired a little skill at the game, but the soul of our National Game never touched them. No nation which has had as intimate contact with baseball as the Japanese could have committed the vicious, infamous deed of the early morning of December 7, 1941, if the spirit of the game ever had penetrated their yellow hides."

J. G. Taylor Spink, editor and publisher of the *Sporting News*, followed that editorial with a 1942 New Year's resolution asking that the major leagues somehow "withdraw from Japan the gift of baseball which we made to that misguided and ill-begotten country." The Japanese government seemed to bow. It abolished baseball by decree as an American influence, and ordered that Japanese translations replace those American baseball expressions that had come into common usage in Japan. The war was on.

CHAPTER 5

Branch Rickey:
Championships on the Cheap

With the United States mobilizing for war on two fronts, the 1942 baseball season was expected to be one of steady decline in the quality of play. In fact, draft calls were surprisingly light, and that first wartime season is remembered instead for producing one of the finest teams in baseball history, the 1942 St. Louis Cardinals. It was the last of Branch Rickey's twenty-five seasons as Cardinal vice-president and business manager, and the team he fielded that year exemplified the peculiar combination of vision and avarice that Rickey applied to his work.

Starting with a second-division team so poor that it had to conduct spring training at home in 1919, with players riding public streetcars to and from a chilly St. Louis practice field, Rickey had built up the Cardinals by developing baseball's first farm system. In 1942, the Cardinals owned fourteen minor league teams and had working agreements with nine others, for a total of twenty-three; the next largest farm system had ten clubs in all. (Today, most major league clubs, including the Cardinals, get by with four or five farm teams.)

There was no draft of amateur players then, and bonuses of

more than a few hundred dollars were rarely paid. The Cardinals had the largest scouting staff in the major leagues, conducted more tryout camps than any other team, and often were able to sign skillful young players at very low salaries. That system produced Cardinal teams that frequently contended for the pennant, winning in 1926, 1928, 1930, 1931, and 1934, and farm teams that helped pay their way by winning consistently and thus attracting local fans.

It also produced a surplus of players good enough to be sold to other clubs at high prices. The latter consideration was of more than secondary interest to Rickey, whose contract provided him with a salary plus 20 percent of the Cardinal profits, and to Sam Breadon, who owned 78 percent of the team's stock. "Rickey was always profit-minded," recalled Bill DeWitt, who worked for the Cardinals under Rickey from 1916 until he, DeWitt, moved to the Browns in late 1936. "Rickey had the idea that when a player got to the point where he was making top salary, he didn't have the incentive to really put out. He was replacing them with younger players at lower salaries, and he picked up that cash."

In 1938, Breadon sold Dizzy Dean, the hero of the 1934 Cardinal Gashouse Gang, to the Chicago Cubs for $185,000 and three players. (Dean had a sore arm.) In 1940, Rickey sold Joe Medwick, who for three seasons had led the National League in runs batted in, to the Brooklyn Dodgers for $125,000. (Medwick's best years were behind him.) Between the 1940 and 1941 seasons, Rickey sold catcher Mickey Owen to Brooklyn for $60,000 and two players. Following the 1941 season, he dealt first baseman Johnny Mize, perhaps the National League's most feared slugger, to the New York Giants for $50,000 and three players. At the same time, Don Padgett, a utility man who could catch and play the outfield, was sold to Brooklyn for $20,000. Padgett entered the Navy before he played a game for the Dodgers, who sought a refund without success.

Adding in the sale of respectable but lesser known players such as Curt Davis, Clyde Shoun, Tuck Stainback, Danny Murtaugh, Herman Franks, Johnny Rizzo, Bob Bowman, Joe Orengo, Mike Ryba, Stu Martin, Ernie Koy, and Fiddler Bill McGee, the Cardinals' take from player sales between 1938 and 1942 was in the neighborhood of $600,000. "How can we sell so many players and still come up with a winning team? I'll tell you," Rickey said in a 1941 interview. "It's mass production! And by that I mean mass production primarily in tryout camps, and mass production primarily of pitchers."

Not coincidentally, many of the players selected for sale were drawing salaries that the Cardinal management considered excessive. For example, Lon Warneke, "The Arkansas Humming Bird," a veteran pitcher whose seventeen wins the season before included a no-hitter, reportedly was the highest paid member of that superb 1942 Cardinal team, drawing all of about $15,000. Too much; at mid-season, Warneke was sold to the Cubs for $15,000. That same year J.G. Taylor Spink wrote in the *Sporting News* that Breadon, as Cardinal owner, was paying himself a reported $100,000, and Rickey was drawing $80,000.

Marty Marion, a star shortstop for the Cardinals from 1940 through 1950, now manages the Stadium Club, a glassed-in bar and restaurant at Busch Stadium in St. Louis where members can watch a baseball or football game while they dine. Working close to athletes who earn many times what he made as a baseball player, Marion recalled the working conditions under Rickey and Breadon:

Mr. Rickey would be sure you weren't paid much. When I first signed with the Cardinals back in 1936 I had a four-year contract, one of the first contracts that was ever written for a long term. I think I got $500 to sign. The first year I was to make $125 a month and the second year I was to make $175 a month, no matter where I played. That's for five months a year. The third year, no matter where I played, I was to make $3,000, and the fourth year I was to make $5,000. It was a pretty good contract for its time. So I made $5,000 the last year I was in Rochester, and $5,000 when I came up to St. Louis. They said I was overpaid already.

When I got to the big leagues, you had to have a break to get here in the first place. Today, the talent's just not around to draw from like it used to be; if a guy can't play here he can play someplace else in the big leagues. Back in those days, hell, if you didn't play real good ball they'd send you back to Rochester or somewhere, and they could bring up somebody just as good. They had them. They didn't ask you whether you liked it or not; they sent you right back. The break I got was that I was a pretty good fielder, and at that time the Cardinals had been searching for a shortstop since Durocher left. So I came at the right time. I did all right or I wouldn't have been here. Suppose they had a real good shortstop at that time. I would have stayed in the minor leagues a long time. Maybe I'd never have gotten up. Who knows?

Mr. Rickey and Mr. Breadon were very tough bosses. You knew they owned the ballclub but that was it. They didn't even talk to you; the only time you ever saw them to talk to was at contract time. I had quite the conversations with Mr. Rickey. He was a great orator, Mr. Rickey was, and a great writer. No matter what you did, he would always send you a nice three-page letter, and he would explain to you in no uncertain terms that although you may have fielded well, you didn't do this right or that right. There was always something you didn't do right; you were not the complete ballplayer.

Mr. Rickey was a genius at selling you just after you passed your peak. He didn't believe in sentiment. Take a player these days like Bob Gibson, who hung on too long; Rickey would have sold him a long time ago. Gibson, Lou Brock, those kind of ballplayers, he'd have sold them. Probably would have sold Musial, too.

Although a man of religious conviction so deep that he would rarely attend a baseball game on Sunday, Rickey was not above sharp practice. Rickey's difficulties with Commissioner Landis and subsequent fallout with Sam Breadon, the Cardinal owner, were recalled by Bob Broeg, the veteran sports editor of the St. Louis *Post-Dispatch:*

Breadon was a good, convivial, barber-shop singing Democrat, whereas Rickey was a hymn-singing, teetotaling Republican. You say Rickey is remembered now as a symbol of rectitude? Well, he wasn't. He always had an angle. In 1938, Landis caught Rickey in some circumventions of baseball law involving the contracts of almost 100 minor league players, including Pete Reiser. Landis declared them all free agents; otherwise Reiser would have been a Cardinal. Breadon was really embarrassed by that. Very embarrassed. Breadon was a very honorable man.

For freeing so many players from Cardinal bondage, sportswriters nicknamed Landis "The Great Emancipator."

As a result of this incident, Rickey's contract with the Cardinals was allowed to expire in 1942. The Dodgers signed him as general manager. Rickey quickly built up the Brooklyn farm system and got a head start on other clubs by taking the courageous and pioneering step of signing black players. By the late 1940s, the Dodgers were dominating the National League.

Despite their sale of prominent Cardinal players in the 1930s and 1940s, Rickey and Breadon could say with some justification that they had to make room on the roster for outstanding young players who were overdue for promotion from the minor leagues. When Howard Pollet was promoted from Houston during the 1941 season, his record was twenty wins, three losses, and an earned run average of 1.09; Rickey apologized to the Houston fans for taking Pollet so soon. In 1942, the Cardinals' most promising rookie pitcher, John Grodzicki, was inducted into the Army. The Cardinals settled instead for rookies John Beazley, who won twenty-one games and lost six that year, and Murry Dickson, a later twenty-game winner. Among those pitching for Cardinal farm teams in 1942 were Harry Brecheen, George Munger, Ted Wilks, Elwin (Preacher) Roe, and Al Brazle. Roe, in fact, could not quite crack the starting rotation for the Columbus Red Birds of the American Association. All five pitchers became stars when they finally made it to the major leagues.

Nor were pitchers the only bright young Cardinal prospects in 1942. One rookie, Stanley Musial, edged another, Harry Walker, for the left field job. Both went on to become National League batting champions, Musial seven times. Third baseman Whitey Kurowski was a rookie, and catcher Walker Cooper was playing his second season in the major leagues. Among the regulars, the oldest players were second baseman Jimmy Brown, 32, and center fielder Terry Moore, 30. Enos Slaughter, the team's top hitter with a .318 batting average and ninety-eight runs batted in, was relatively old at 26.

Among eight Cardinal pitchers who shared most of the work that season, Harry Gumbert, 32, was the only man 30 or older, and the only one who yielded as many as three earned runs per nine innings pitched; Gumbert's earned run average was a very respectable 3.26. Walker Cooper's elder brother, Mort, pitched ten shutouts, had a league-leading ERA of 1.77, and won twenty-two games against seven losses. Beazley's ERA was 2.14. Howie Krist, the top reliever, had an ERA of 2.52 and a won-loss record of thirteen and three, following a record of ten and zero the season before. Max Lanier, who became a left-hander when he broke his right arm as a youngster, was thirteen and eight with a 2.96 ERA.

Even so, the Cardinals appeared to be beaten. Brooklyn won seventy-one of its first 100 games, the second fastest pace in National League history. "As the situation now stands," the *Sporting News* reported on August 6, "the Cardinal death notice is likely to be released around September 15." On August 15, the Cardinals were nine and a half games behind. They won thirty of their next thirty-six games, an .833 pace, and won the pennant with 106 wins and 48 losses, the best record in the National League since 1909. "That '42 Cardinal team was the best team I ever played on, better than all the Yankee teams and everything else," recalled Enos Slaughter, who later played for Casey Stengel's Yankee champions of the 1950s. "We had a young team, and it was a great ballclub. We had desire."

Agreeing with Slaughter and Marion, baseball historians often have cited the 1942 Cardinals as a team of poor, unspoiled country boys who worked extra hard. At the time, however, Manager Billy Southworth saw them much as today's managers see their players. "You can't drive players anymore, the way they were driven in McGraw's heyday," Southworth told an interviewer in September of 1942. "We have college boys, young men who have been pampered. Baseball is handed to them on a silver platter."

The Dodgers did not cave in, winning 104 games, although they were weakened when Pete Reiser ran into the center field wall at Sportsman's Park in St. Louis while chasing a drive by Slaughter in the eleventh inning of a July game. Both the ball and Reiser caromed off the wall, giving Slaughter an inside-the-park home run and Reiser a concussion that affected his hitting for the rest of the season.

The Yankees, managed by Joe McCarthy, won the American

League pennant by nine games and were heavily favored to win the World Series, having won the last eight in which they had played. Joe DiMaggio, Charlie Keller, and Joe Gordon drove in more than 100 runs each for the Yankees that season. Bill Dickey starred behind the plate, Phil Rizzuto at shortstop, and Red Rolfe at third base. Ernie Bonham won twenty-one games and lost only five; Spud Chandler was sixteen and five, Hank Borowy fifteen and four, Charley (Red) Ruffing fourteen and seven, and Atley Donald eleven and three. To start against Mort Cooper in the first World Series game, McCarthy chose Ruffing, 38, who had won six Series games starting in 1932. At his home in Cleveland, Ruffing recalled his attitude about World Series pitching, and his performance in the 1942 Series:

It was easier for me to pitch a World Series game than a regular season game. The crowd would get me all whooped up. It's just like giving you a shot or something, you know? I could get so pepped up with a big crowd out there. So keyed up! My arm felt good and my whole body felt good. I remember telling my wife one time, it was against Cincinnati, first game of the 1939 World Series. She says, "I wish you luck today, Charles." I says, "Don't worry. It's in the bag." She kind of laughed. She says, "Don't be too cocky." I says, "It's in the bag." I was figuring, well, first game, big crowd, and they're all for me. Sure enough, I beat Paul Derringer, good pitcher, 2 to 1.

The best Series game I pitched? That first one in St. Louis, 1942. I had a no-hit, no-run ball game up until the eighth inning. Then things flew up in the ninth. Well, I got a little careless. Frank Crosetti used to say, "I hope we don't get you a lot of runs, because all you'll do is be a Thomas Edison out there—experimenting."

I got to clowning around a little, you know. It was 7 to 2, I think, and Dickey comes out to the mound. He says, "You better start pitching, boy." I says, "OK, Bill." Then when I tried to pitch, I got wild, see. Lost my control. I had the bases filled. I think Chandler came in to relieve, and a guy hits one to the first baseman. If he'd hit it out of the park, we'd probably got beat.

The guy was Musial. The Yankees won that game, 7 to 4, but the Cardinals won the next four, with rookie Beazley beating Ruffing in the finale on a ninth-inning home run by Kurowski.

The 1942 Series was the first one to be broadcast live to U.S.

servicemen overseas. After the fourth game, Slaughter was asked to address the soldiers by radio. "Hi, fellows," he said. "We played a great game today and we won again. And we are going to finish this thing tomorrow. Then I'm going to report for duty in the Army Air Corps and join you."

Although the 1942 Series marked the last games of prewar quality, Dan Daniel of the New York *World-Telegram* found a wartime explanation for the outcome, saying that the Yankee players suffered from "vagueness" about their proper role. "It was quite patent that many of the Bombers went into the classic fighting the war and not the Cardinals," Daniel wrote in the *Sporting News*. ". . . The Cardinals conceivably were not bothered as yet by wartime considerations." Thus dismissed, the Cardinal players returned to St. Louis; the next day, a number of them were photographed as they lined up to give blood to the Red Cross.

The Cardinals lost only Grodzicki to military service for the 1942 season. Among their regulars, the Yankees lost only first baseman Johnny Sturm, a .239 hitter in 1941 who gained the distinction of becoming the first married major league player to be drafted. Besides Padgett, the Dodgers lost third baseman Cookie Lavagetto, whom they replaced with a better player, veteran Arky Vaughan. (Vaughan is still the last National Leaguer to bat .380 or higher, a feat he achieved with Pittsburgh in 1935.) Mulcahy was joined in service by another Phillie pitcher, Lee Grissom, 2 and 13 in 1941, and by journeyman outfielder Joe Marty. The Boston Braves lost their second baseman, Carvel ('Bama) Rowell, and the Pittsburgh Pirates lost theirs, Burgess Whitehead. The Giants lost Morrie Arnovich, accepted for service this time despite his missing molars, and another second-line player, infielder John Davis.

Detroit, Cleveland, Washington, Boston, and Philadelphia were hurt the most in the American League in 1942. Besides Greenberg, the Tigers gave up Pat Mullin, who hit .345 in fifty-one games as a rookie in 1941, and Fred Hutchinson, a pitcher who was the Most Valuable Player of 1941 in the International League. Cleveland lost Feller and his roommate, outfielder Clarence (Soup) Campbell. Washington gave up Cecil Travis and Buddy Lewis, whose deferments expired.

From the Boston Red Sox, the armed forces took catcher Frank Pytlak and pitchers Mickey Harris and Earl Johnson. The *Sporting News* pictured Harris with a rifle, and, in a typically bellicose wartime caption, said he was alertly manning an antiaircraft gun in the Panama Canal Zone. "Mickey is ready to pitch, too—pitch lead skyward," the caption said. As things turned out, the war did not reach the Canal Zone and Harris spent much of his service time pitching baseballs plateward.

The Red Sox finished second in 1942, but the armed forces were poised to gut the team. After being classified 1-A in January of 1942, Ted Williams, 23, who had hit an electrifying .406 in 1941, was reclassified 3-A in February because he supported his mother. (1-A meant physically and mentally fit and with no grounds for deferment. 3-A meant fit but with dependents.) Some people complained that Williams' deferment was unjust, although there was no evidence that he was getting preferential treatment. "Why does the boy's prominence as a ballplayer strip him of his rights?" Frank Graham asked in the New York *Sun*. The *Sporting News* called Williams' critics "snipers from behind typewriters and microphones."

In March, Williams announced that he would enlist after the 1942 season. "I am going to play ball this season," he said. "My conscience is clear. I have as much right to be exempted as anybody else. I have my mother to support. Before my status was changed to 1-A, I made commitments which I must go through with. I can do so by playing ball this year. When the season is over, I'll get into the Navy as fast as I can." Praising Williams for prevailing "against the boos of thoughtless fans," the *Sporting News* added: "When the season is over, Ted will enter Naval aviation, ready to see if he can smash out hits against enemy strongholds."

The Red Sox' second best hitter, shortstop Johnny Pesky, was classified 1-A although he, too, contributed to the support of his parents and three ailing siblings. Draft regulations permitted only one such deferment for any family; Johnny's elder brother, Tony, who worked as a stockman for a casket company and earned a quarter as much as John did, was deferred as the first of three Pesky boys to register for the draft. In their farewell season of

1942, Williams led the American League in batting with .356 and Pesky was second with .331. In August of 1942, Dom DiMaggio, the outstanding center fielder of the Red Sox, enlisted in the Navy for call to active duty following the season.

The Athletics, a last place team that could hardly afford it, lost three regulars for the 1942 season. Outfielder Sam Chapman was the club's best hitter; the other two players who entered service were second baseman Benny McCoy and shortstop Al Brancato. Brancato's induction was witnessed by Connie Mack, the A's owner and manager, who was then 79 years old.

With these men gone, the Athletics provided a glimpse of things to come in the major leagues by fielding an atrocious 1942 infield. Pete Suder, the only competent fielder, was moved from second to third to short, but could play only one position at a time. Lawrence (Crash) Davis was shuttled between second and short; he could play neither. The other participants were first baseman Dick Siebert, third baseman Buddy Blair, and second baseman Bill Knickerbocker. All of them are remembered well by Phil Marchildon, a hard-throwing right-handed pitcher who, against all odds, won seventeen and lost fourteen for the 1942 Athletics. A wry Canadian, Marchildon lives in Etobicoke, Ontario, a suburb of Toronto. Marchildon:

That team was a bad one. They couldn't make a double play if you hit a line drive. Dick Siebert, he had a brace on his knee, and the other guy on third base, Buddy Blair, he had a brace on his knee. They couldn't move very far, either one of them. There was a fellow playing shortstop by the name of Davis; he wasn't too much of a player either. Oh, boy. There was a challenge. You got quite a kick out of being able to win.

In a piece of postseason doggerel, the *Sporting News* anticipated military inroads on the Cardinals. Entitled "The Saga of Southworth," the poem concluded:

His team was superb—so the sports writers said.
But next year they'll play for the Army instead.
That is Billy's reward for the life he has led.

CHAPTER 6

The Browns Become Beggars

The Browns had an unexpected renaissance in 1942, finishing third with eighty-two wins and sixty-nine losses. Aided by the seven additional night games—Thank You, Mr. President—attendance at home reached 256,000, more than had turned out to see the Browns in any of the past twelve seasons. The 1942 Browns no doubt would have attracted many more fans had their third-place season not coincided with the exciting pennant chase by the Cardinals, whose attendance for the year was more than twice that of the Browns. It was an old story: Cardinal success begetting Brownie misfortune. Each Cardinal player got a World Series share of $5,573.78 plus War Bonds with a value at maturity of $825. For finishing third, each Brownie got $637.64 plus a $100 War Bond.

Long ago, the original St. Louis Browns had been successful, playing in the American Association, a major league of the 1880s. They won pennants in 1885, 1886, 1887, and 1888 under the ownership of Chris von der Ahe, a bibulous grocer and saloonkeeper who agreed to finance the team in exchange for the beer concession. To catch the crowds coming and going as well as while there, von der Ahe built a saloon adjacent to the ball park. He sold beer for a nickel and baseball tickets for a quarter, and soon was basking in prosperity. After a game, the day's gate receipts would be heaped in a wheelbarrow. A porter would wheel the cash down the street to von der Ahe's office, with the Brownie owner walking behind and a larger man, carrying a musket, bringing up the rear.

Von der Ahe became expansive with his team's success. He wore diamonds and fashionable clothes, and was seen in the best saloons with women of varying reputation. Making fun of von der Ahe's heavy German accent as if he were the buffoonish captain in the Katzenjammer Kids comic strip, newspapers of the day said that he proudly referred to himself as "der poss bresident" and to his team as "my Brown vonder poys." Ensuring his position as a solid civic figure, von der Ahe had a life-sized marble statue of himself erected so local citizens could admire him at their leisure; the statue now stands over his grave.

According to a later account in the *Sporting News*, the word "fan" to describe a follower of a team or a sport resulted from von der Ahe's description of his patrons as "fanatics," a word that sportswriters of the day shortened. The Brownie owner appreciated his fanatics. In 1888 he chartered a special train to take the team and its followers to New York for the World Series against the Giants, paying not only the train fare of everyone on board but also their hotel and meal expenses in New York. The train was festooned with banners proclaiming: "St. Louis Browns—Four Time Pennant Winners." Von der Ahe provided lots of champagne en route, and in a final gesture he sent the passengers to a New York tailor and bought each one a new suit.

In 1890, the Browns were ruined when several of their best players jumped to the Players Brotherhood, a new league that was called a cooperative by the players who formed it and communistic by the club owners, who opposed it. The players were rebelling against the low salaries they were being paid and against a contract provision that bound a player to one team unless released, sold, or traded by its owner. The Players Brotherhood collapsed after one year. The controversial contract provision, called the "reserve clause," was finally altered in 1976.

The Browns played poorly in the 1890s. As baseball attendance declined, von der Ahe tried to attract fans with showmanship, a notion that was considered sinful by most club owners then and by most club owners sixty years later when Bill Veeck tried it. In many ways, von der Ahe's shows were more flamboyant than Veeck's. Fans could ride a chute-the-chute in center field. Von der Ahe also offered horse races, boxing matches, a wild west show, a glamorous all-girl cornet band, and, in 1896, the Democratic presidential candidate, William Jennings Bryan, whose campaign manager rented use of the ball park and was outraged when von der Ahe charged admission for the event.

Adherents of the Browns have always contended that the team was bewitched. If so, the jinx may have first flared on April 16, 1898, when a fire broke out under the grandstand during a game attended by about 6,000 people. About 100 were burned or otherwise injured. That night, Brownie players helped workmen clear the debris. Circus seats were erected, and the next day the Browns reaped the reward of their hard night's work. With 7,000 looking on, the exhausted St. Louisans were drubbed by Chicago, 14 to 1.

Lawsuits resulting from the fire forced von der Ahe to sell the club; in fact, the Browns were auctioned off on the courthouse steps like a herd of livestock. The National League moved the Cleveland Spiders to St. Louis in 1899, brushing aside the remnants of the old Browns. The Spiders were known as a scrappy bunch. During a game in Louisville in 1896, the whole team was arrested and charged with precipitating a riot.

The Spiders wore uniforms with red piping, and after a while a St. Louis sportswriter named Willie McHale began calling the team the Cardinals. The new name was formally adopted in 1900. In 1902, the Browns were reincarnated as part of the American League when the Milwaukee Brewers were moved to St. Louis, giving the city two major league teams. Since the new Browns could not trace their ancestry to von der Ahe's champions, the twentieth-century Browns were never credited with those four pennants. Indeed, some historical accounts have traced the Cardinals to von der Ahe's club.

This spiriting away of the family tree was only the first of many shell games performed by the Cardinals at the Browns' expense. Neither St. Louis team did well during the first two decades of the twentieth century, but the Browns were beginning to look up under Branch Rickey. Once a mediocre Brownie catcher himself, Rickey signed on as the team's manager in 1913 after finishing law school at the University of Michigan, where he paid his tuition by coaching the baseball team.

In 1917, the Cardinals hired Rickey away from the Browns, who by then were owned by Philip de Catesby Ball, a mercurial millionaire who made his fortune in the ice business. His baseball playing career had been ruined by a barroom knife fight that incapacitated his left hand. Ball sued Rickey for breaking his contract, and publicly insulted him for disloyalty. Rickey sued Ball for slander. The two lawsuits canceled each other.

With the Cardinals, Rickey was soon joined by Sam Breadon, a poor boy from New York's Greenwich Village who made money as an automobile dealer. The Cardinals were impoverished. Unable to afford the usual trip to Florida, they trained at home in the spring of 1919. Rickey's office was so barren that he brought a rug from home when impressionable visitors were expected. The Cardinal ball park, Robinson Field, was so ramshackle that firemen had to circulate during games to keep the old, wooden stands from igniting.

The Browns looked comparatively affluent. Before leaving, Rickey had acquired some excellent players, including George Sisler, the star of his Michigan college team. The Browns were the local favorites. Like a fat lamb in a pool hall, Ball was set up for a hustle; when Breadon came begging in 1920, Ball magnanimously agreed to let the Cardinals rent the use of Sportsman's Park, the stadium owned by the Browns. That enabled the Cardinals to sell their own wreck of a ball park to the city, which wanted the site for a new high school. They were paid $350,000, which Rickey used to found the Cardinal farm system.

Still, Ball was blind to the future. With Sisler batting .420, his 1922 team fought the Yankees tooth and nail for the pennant and drew 713,000 fans. A Brownie outfielder, Ken Williams, edged Babe Ruth for the home run championship, thirty-nine to thirty-five. A Brownie pitcher, Hubert (Shucks) Pruett, who played baseball during the summer to pay his way through medical school, struck out Ruth ten of the first eleven times he faced him. On September 16, a Brownie fan made the best throw in a crucial game against the Yankees, beaning New York outfielder Whitey Witt with a pop bottle as Witt camped under a fly ball. But the Yankees won two of three games in that series and took the pennant by one game.

Sportsman's Park then held 18,000 fans. Those three games with New York drew 26,000, 28,000, and 29,000; many of them, including the unknown hero with the accurate throwing arm, stood behind ropes in the outfield. After the 1925 season, Ball expanded the park's seating capacity to 36,000. Believing the Browns were on the rise, he envisioned a St. Louis pennant in 1926. Ball was right, but he had the wrong team. In 1926, the Cardinals won a thrilling pennant race under the playing managership of Rogers Hornsby, and beat the Yankees in a World Series that is still remembered for Grover Cleveland Alexander's strikeout of Tony Lazzeri with the bases filled in the seventh inning of the final game. The Cardinals, who paid for none of the stadium expansion, had immediately cashed its benefits. The Browns finished seventh in 1926 and dropped from local favor, drawing fewer than half as many fans as the Cardinals.

Ball's bad judgment was matched only by his bad luck. Sportsman's Park was a curse. By June of 1930, Brownie pitching had sunk to such depths that the team was becoming shellshocked from the effects of opponents' home runs into the right field pavilion, only 310 feet from home plate. Ball had a screen erected that would limit most such drives to doubles. The screen worked, particularly bedeviling a left-handed slugger named Heinie Manush, who, unfortunately, played for the Browns.

Ball's player transactions turned out no better. After rookie pitcher Charlie Root failed to win a game in 1923, Ball dealt him to the Chicago Cubs, where he became the pitching ace of the team that won the 1929 pennant. By 1933, Clark Griffith had outfoxed Ball on so many trades that Griffith's Washington Senators won the American League pennant. The Senators' excellent, hard-hitting outfield of Manush, Leon (Goose) Goslin, and Fred Schulte all came from the Browns. So did Washington pitchers Alvin (General) Crowder, who won twenty-four and lost fifteen, and Walter (Lefty) Stewart, who won fifteen and lost six. The Browns, fortified with the players they had received in exchange, finished last. They drew 88,000 fans, an average of a little over 1,000 a game. It was in 1933 that the Browns one day played before thirty-four fans, each of whom could have had a thousand seats to himself.

Ball died in 1933 after losing about $300,000 during eighteen years as owner of the Browns. Even his death was ill-timed. The Depression was at its worst; even blue chip investments were considered dubious. No one came forward to buy the Browns, and the team reverted to Ball's estate. Rogers Hornsby was named manager in hopes that his skills would rub off on the Brownie players and his fame would attract St. Louis fans. Neither event occurred.

In 1935, the Browns finished seventh and attendance declined to 81,000. In desperation, Louis B. von Weise, who as executor of Ball's estate had been forced into the torment of running the Browns, turned to Branch Rickey, who by then was puffing cigars and otherwise living baronially as vice-president and business manager of the successful Cardinals. If Rickey could find a buyer for the Browns, he would get a nice commission.

Von Weise could not have chosen a better broker. Rickey was an artist at selling damaged and inferior goods, as he was later to prove when he peddled Dizzy Dean with a sore arm and talked Pittsburgh into taking an outfielder named Johnny Rizzo when, for the same price, the Pirates could have had Enos Slaughter instead. Rickey's search for a new Brownie owner took him all the way to the next office, where sat his executive assistant, William O. DeWitt. DeWitt was not wealthy enough to buy a baseball team, even a cheap one like the Browns, but Cupid intervened in his behalf. On March 21, 1936, DeWitt married Margaret Holekamp, a socially prominent St. Louis horsewoman whose best friend and frequent riding companion was the daughter of Donald L. Barnes, wealthy president of American Investment Company, a small-loan firm listed on the New York Stock Exchange. DeWitt and Barnes became friends; through DeWitt, Barnes gradually became interested in buying the Browns. The price was $325,000. DeWitt:

I talked to Don Barnes and got him interested, and he said, "Well, why don't we let the public own it. That's the way to build up interest." So Barnes got clearance from the Missouri Securities Commission to sell stock to the people of St. Louis at $5 a share. Barnes had connections with all the brokerage houses; he had a meeting with all the brokers and told them what he wanted to do—a civic thing. The brokers got about 1,300 shareholders and raised about $100,000. So Barnes put up $50,000, a guy named Al Curtis put up $50,000, I put up $25,000, we got International Shoe to put up money, and the American League loaned us $50,000. We raised $375,000 altogether to have $50,000 for working capital, and in November of 1936 we bought the Browns and the farm system—two or three clubs, including San Antonio—for $325,000. Rickey got $25,000 for putting the deal together. I became the general manager. Barnes was the president. We leased the ball park from the Ball estate.

In 1936, the attendance was only 93,000. So first thing, we had a terrific buildup. We did everything we thought could be done. We ran a contest to get an emblem for the Browns. We did everything to get the fan interest. We worked, and we tried to sell season tickets, and we had people out speaking to the Chamber of Commerce and all, and we got lots of publicity. And you know how many we drew in 1937? 123,000. Big deal! With all that work and all that money we spent. We knocked ourselves out and we drew only 123,000.

We operated close to the belt. We had to. Once we ran out of cash, and Barnes tried to get the board of directors to put up some money. They said, "No, that's money down the rathole." A lot of wealthy guys, too! So Barnes went to the bank and borrowed the money for the ballclub to pay the bills, and he personally guaranteed the loan.

Hornsby was the manager; we were paying him about $20,000 or $25,000. Hornsby would be a good manager with good ballplayers, but he was a lousy manager with lousy players. He couldn't stand mediocrity. We had a ballclub that was, oh, Jesus, it was brutal.

Hornsby used to bet on the horses a lot. Judge Landis was against anybody betting on the horses or anything else; he thought you might become involved in some kind of scheme or subject yourself to some bribe. Barnes talked to Hornsby about gambling before he ever went to spring training in 1937. He said, "Look, you can't gamble, you can't bet on the horses and have your mind on the ball game at the same time. There's no way you can do it. Why don't you go one season and not bet on the horses at all. Just forget it." Hornsby said, "All right, sure, I'll do it."

Hornsby was about through as a player then, although on opening day, 1937, he hit a ball into the bleachers. He would go to the park in the morning very early, something like nine or ten o'clock, and the ball game wasn't until around 2:30. He would always go into one of the phone booths in the ball park. Then during the game, the clubhouse boy would go out two or three times and spend ten or fifteen minutes away. We couldn't figure what he was doing. So we finally checked around and found out that he was running bets for Hornsby to a saloon across the street, where they used to make book on the horses and the ball games and everything else. He'd come down and give Hornsby the results on the bench. Jesus, here he is supposed to be running the ballclub. Isn't that something?

Barnes got the idea of tapping the telephone, and we hired some Pinkerton's guy to get on the other end of the line to see what was going on. The guy gave us a report every day; we had all Hornsby's bets, what he lost, what he won, everything. Listen, he was a big bettor. He'd bet $50 across the board or $100 across the board. Sometimes he'd bet $1,500 on a race. He'd bet eight or nine different races. And he was placing bets all over the country.

I think he owed us something like $4,800; as an incentive to invest in something besides horses, Barnes had loaned him the money to buy stock in Barnes' company, American Investment Company. And one day Hornsby had a hell of a day at the tracks, won about $3,000 or $3,500. So he came in the office and he said, "I want to pay off some of that money, about $2,000." Barnes said, "You must have had a windfall." Hornsby said, "Well, a guy owed me some money and paid me." Of course, we knew where he got it, so he and Barnes got into an argument. Barnes wound up firing him, right then. We made Jim Bottomley manager. He had been sort of a player-coach with the Browns.

Bottomley, a first baseman, was another former Cardinal hero. He was named the Most Valuable Player in the National League for the Cardinal pennant year of 1928, and was awarded a sack filled with $1,000 in gold. (The next year and ever after, a more dignified award was chosen for the Most Valuable Player: a plaque.) Hornsby and Bottomley were the first in a succession of former Cardinal stars hired by the Browns in a pitiable attempt to attract Cardinal fans. In 1937, the Browns won twenty-five and lost fifty under Hornsby; under Bottomley, they won twenty-one and lost fifty-eight. They finished last.

Barnes and DeWitt were not the only ones investigating Hornsby's gambling habits. Thirty-nine years later, at his retirement home outside Milan, Missouri, Cal Hubbard, a former American League umpire, recalled his own brush with the investigation. Hubbard used to umpire in the summer and play on the line of the Green Bay Packers and New York Giants in the fall. He is the only person elected to both the Baseball Hall of Fame at Cooperstown, New York, and the Football Hall of Fame at Canton, Ohio. Hubbard:

Bill Dinneen and Lou Kolls and I were umpiring in St. Louis, and Rogers Hornsby was the manager. Rogers liked to bet on the horse races and of course Judge Landis hated that. He hated anything that pertained to gambling. Bill Dinneen, he always bet on those horses, and I never did bet them. Only a couple of times, and this was one of them.

Bill got this tip from Hornsby. Bill bet $10 or $15 on the horse and I bet $5 and Lou Kolls bet $5. I didn't know a thing in the world about the horse. Hornsby had a guy who worked for him, a clubhouse man who was really Hornsby's runner. They called him Alabam—he was from Alabama—and he took the bets and placed them with some bookie. I don't know where in the hell he bet them, but of course Landis was after Hornsby and he had a tail on Alabam when he placed those bets.

This guy, the tail, finally had to tell Landis that he bet for Dinneen, Hubbard, and Kolls. Later, we were working in Chicago and we had a day off on Monday. Mr. Harridge called us and said, "Come in the office on Monday." So we got up in the morning and went over to Mr. Harridge's office. He got his hat and said, "We're going up to Judge Landis's office."

I didn't know what the hell was going on. We didn't know Judge Landis had found out about us placing those bets, see. So we went up there. Old Judge, he's sitting at that desk, Christ, I don't know how in hell he ever found anything, that desk was so cluttered up. He's sitting there. Boy, he was a mean old devil. I finally got so I was pretty friendly with him but that was later on; this was my second year in the league, 1937. He let us talk just one at a time, and he talked to Lou Kolls first. We didn't tell him a damned thing. We weren't going to tell him anything about Hornsby because Hornsby was a good fellow and a good friend of ours.

But he found out what it was all about. He finally said to me, "Young man, don't you know it's wrong to be gambling on horse races?" I said, "Well, Judge, it's legal." Christ, he hit the ceiling. Oh, Christ, he raised hell. He ranted and raved for ten minutes. Then he started talking to Dinneen and Dinneen said he bet on horse racing, always had, and his family did, and so that's all there was to it. I never heard any more about it but it kept me out of the World Series that year. Mr. Harridge told me, "You were going to work the '37 World Series but Judge Landis kept you out." Because of me popping off to him, see. I was in the Series the next year, '38, so it didn't make any difference.

Did the horse win? I don't even remember; only bet five bucks.

Hornsby was not the only baseball celebrity who, for reasons known only to themselves, wanted to manage the woebegone Browns. DeWitt:

Then in 1938 or 1939, Babe Ruth called me up. Out of the blue; I didn't know him. Never met him. He said, "Hey, kid, this is Babe Ruth. I know you haven't got a good ballclub, but I'd like to be your manager. I can't get a job managing anyplace else so I'd like to be the manager of the Browns." I said, "Now, let me think about it. We've just about made up our minds on a guy. Let me talk to some people." I took his phone number and so forth. We decided fine, he would be a great attraction for a year. But we'd probably have to pay him a pretty good salary, and at the end of a year his attractiveness is gone. We had a lousy ballclub, and you know he's not going to be a good manager, and we were going to try to develop some young players. So we decided not to do it.

We picked up Toledo, expanding our farm system, and we hired a lot of scouts. We signed Al Zarilla, Vern Stephens, Jack Kramer, all the good ballplayers who helped us later on.

The Browns' new management really was trying. After the 1937 season, the Browns tried to buy first baseman George McQuinn from the Yankees' farm club at Newark, New Jersey. The Yankees, like the Cardinals, had a large farm system stocked with excellent players, many of whom were good enough to have played regularly for lesser major league teams. At his home in Alexandria, Virginia, McQuinn recalled his frustration and his eventual promotion to the majors:

I was owned by the Yankees for eight years. Actually, I should have been in the major leagues at least four years sooner. But they had Lou Gehrig there; Gehrig wanted to play. He wouldn't even sit out an exhibition game. My second year I played at Scranton, hit .316, and drove in over 100 runs to lead the league. The next year I played with Albany and Binghamton. I hit around .340 and drove in around 100 runs. The next year I was back at Binghamton and led the league in hitting. The following year, 1934, I went to Toronto and hit .331.

Still, the Yankees never even took me to spring training with them. I thought after the great years that I had they would at least say, "Well, let's give him a chance in spring training." But they didn't bother.

The Yankees finally sold me to Cincinnati on a look-see basis. Charlie Dressen was the manager at Cincinnati and he almost ruined my career. We trained in Puerto Rico in 1936. He must have known I was not a pull hitter; I hit balls down the left-field line, left-center and right-center, but I seldom pulled the ball. You'd think with all the success I'd had hitting that way he'd let me alone. But from the first day in camp, the first time I walked up to the batter's box, Charlie and a coach yelled at me, "Pull the ball, pull the ball!"

They changed my whole stance, made me square around, made me try to pull everything. I went along with them. But after a couple of weeks of the season I still wasn't doing anything, and Charlie came to me one day when we had a morning workout. He says, "George, show me how you used to hit. You're not doing it my way." I says, "Charlie, I'm so fouled up I don't even know how I used to hit or used to stand." That's the way it went for the next month or so. I was playing every day, but I was in such a slump that I couldn't do anything right.

So they returned me to the Yankees, who in turn sent me back to Toronto. The first two weeks at Toronto I was just as bad as I was at Cincinnati. But nobody was bothering me then, and I gradually worked my way around and wound up hitting around .330 again. So they sent me back to Newark in 1937.

That was the year Newark had the great ballclub. We won the pennant by twenty-five and a half games. Won the play-offs in eight straight. Everybody on the ballclub went to the big leagues except one man. We had Buddy Rosar, Babe Dahlgren, Spud Chandler, Marius Russo, Atley Donald, Joe Gordon, and Charlie Keller. I played first, hit around .330.

I was 28 years old. I said, "If I don't go to the big leagues after this year I'm giving it up. I'm not going to bum around the minor leagues all my life."

In those days, the major leagues could only draft one player off a minor league ballclub. The Yankees wound up letting me be drafted by the Browns. I was grateful to get a chance to play, even with the Browns, just to play in the big leagues.

But later, I found out it wasn't all on the up and up; it wasn't a straight draft like it should have been. I found out that the Yanks made the Browns pay more than the draft price for me. This was the first year I was with the Browns. I was having a great year. I hit .324 and I hit in thirty-four straight ball games that spring. If Judge Landis would have found out what happened, he would have declared me a free agent; I could have signed on with the highest bidder.

I wrote Landis a letter and then I walked into his office. He paced up and down his office like a madman. He tried to get me to say where my information came from. And I said I couldn't possibly reveal that, because the guy would be blacklisted in baseball, probably forever. He told me, "You go on and join your ballclub. You'll hear from me." They had covered it up, so I never heard from him. I've never been able to find out exactly what happened, but it was an undercover deal and it wasn't fair.

Bill DeWitt:

We finished last in '37 so we had the first draft choice, and I talked to George Weiss of the Yankees about buying McQuinn. He said, "I won't sell him to you, but I tell you what I'll do. If you'll draft him as your number one choice, why, I'll let him sit on that roster and you can draft him for $7,500." That was the draft price. At that point you could draft only one man off a double-A club like Newark. So that gave him the opportunity to load everybody else that was any good onto the Newark team, and by drafting McQuinn I protected the rest of the ballplayers for him. Was there anything under the table? Yeah, we had to sell Harry Davis, our first baseman, to the Yanks for $2,500. We had to give them Davis plus the draft price to get McQuinn. Illegal? Of course; it was even illegal to prearrange a draft choice. But we were that anxious to get McQuinn.

McQuinn:

So that was it; I knew something was wrong. No question that if Landis had known that he would have turned me loose from the Browns. Thanks for your sympathy, but I don't think I can buy a hamburger with it.

Davis, who batted .276 as a Brownie regular in 1937, found himself assigned to McQuinn's old job at Newark in 1938. He never reappeared in the major leagues.

In 1939, the Detroit Tigers, needing an ace pitcher to bring their fine team to championship caliber, dealt outfielder Chet Laabs, third baseman Mark Christman, and four pitchers to the Browns for Buck (Bobo) Newsom, who in 1938 won twenty games for the seventh-place Browns and led the league in innings pitched. The Browns threw in three other players, including outfielder Roy (Beau) Bell, who for two years had been one of the best hitters in the American League. In 1936, at the age of 29, Bell hit .344 and in 1937 he hit .340. In no other season, before or after, did he hit as high as .280.

Newsom, a free spirit, had been feuding with Fred Haney, the Brownie manager. Besides, the Browns had so many holes to fill that it appeared worthwhile to yield Newsom for a half dozen serviceable players. Christman, 25, was a native of St. Louis; his younger brother, Paul, was an All-American quarterback at the University of Missouri who later starred for the Chicago Cardinals of the National Football League and became a network sportscaster. In July of 1976, only a few months before he suffered a fatal heart attack, Mark Christman recalled the trade that brought him home:

I'll never forget it. My heart was broken. See, with Detroit I knew we were going to win in a couple of years, because we had all these good ballplayers. When I was traded to the Browns, oh, I was ready to quit baseball. I wasn't worried about the way they treated me, or the money; heck, you never made much over $7,000 or $8,000 in those days anyway. I was worried about going to a ballclub that couldn't win. They had a ballclub that practically set a record for losses in 1939.

That pitching staff we had then was just the worst in the business. It was a terrible pitching staff; if we don't get ten runs we don't win. You would try to get yourself up, to key yourself up. But when you know you're going to be eight runs behind after the first couple of innings, there's just no way you could pull yourself up to really go out there and bear down 100 percent. We were playing in this heat all summer long; day games, doubleheaders on Sunday.

Playing the infield, you get a pitcher out there that's three and two on every hitter. You get ready, on your toes, and it's called a strike; you relax. Then you get ready and it's a ball. Then you get ready again and it's another ball. And the first thing you know you're back on your heels, you can't help yourself, and finally when somebody does hit one you're not ready.

Bob Feller remembered Laabs, the outfielder acquired by the Browns, for his role with Detroit on October 2, 1938, the day Feller set a record by striking out eighteen batters:

I struck out Laabs five times, including the last out of the game that gave me the record. The last pitch was a fast ball, a called third strike. Laabs was stocky and muscular, strong. He had a lot of power for a little guy. If he ever got one low he'd hit it. But he couldn't hit a high fast ball; he had a blind spot two feet high.

Cal Hubbard, who umpired that game:

Chet was a nice guy. They used to pitch up here to him, see. Way high; bad pitches. The higher the pitch, seemed like, the harder he'd swing. If he ever got a ball down he'd hit it out of the park; he could hit it a long ways. The pitchers of course were wise to it. Hell, they just kept going up with it and he kept swinging.

The Browns finished seventh in 1938. In 1939 they finished last, losing 111 games and winning forty-three for a .279 percentage. Nelson Potter, then a pitcher for the Philadelphia Athletics, recalled the crowds that would turn out in St. Louis to see the last-place Browns play the seventh-place A's:

One day we sat there in the bullpen and counted them. The announced attendance was about 154, and we thought that was an exaggeration. We said, "Well, half of them must have been out for hot dogs." Because we only counted about seventy-five people in the stands.

The Browns employed twenty-two pitchers that season. Among the four acquired from Detroit in the Newsom deal, veteran Vern Kennedy led the league in losses with twenty, George Gill won one game against thirteen losses, Bob Harris won four and lost thirteen, and Roxie Lawson, the ace of the bunch, won four and lost eight. Newsom won twenty games; the next year he was twenty-one and five as Detroit won the pennant. It appeared that the deal, like so many others, was hardly a Brownie coup.

That winter, the Browns became beggars. Losses since the Barnes-DeWitt combine bought the club were averaging about $100,000 a year, a lot of money in those days. In December of

1939, William Harridge, league president, urged the other American League teams to help the Browns, without saying exactly what they should do. "Harridge, like all others connected with the league, realizes that visiting clubs cannot endure indefinitely the long trip to St. Louis without at least collecting railroad fares and hotel bills," the *Sporting News* reported, adding that Harridge would "suggest that the boys go a little socialistic for their own benefit." Bill DeWitt:

The Browns had a hell of a time because the Cardinals were so popular, and the Browns couldn't do a damned thing. We didn't have any attendance money to build up the ballclub with. Most of the other clubs had players in the minors that were better than some of the players we had on the Browns. So Barnes made a plea to the league, and every club in the American League agreed to sell a player to the Browns for $7,500. We had the option to buy them. Only two or three clubs offered us anybody that was worth a damn. We got Eldon Auker, and we got Walt Judnich.

In Auker, the Browns acquired the only underhand pitcher outside of softball. Auker had developed the unusual delivery as the result of a shoulder injury, suffered while playing blocking back for Kansas State, that prevented him from lifting his right arm above shoulder height. With Detroit in 1935, Auker led the American League in winning percentage with .720 on eighteen wins and seven losses. But Walter O. Briggs, the Tigers' owner, could not stand to watch Auker's strange pitching style and traded him to the Boston Red Sox, where too many of his underhand serves were volleyed over the short left-field wall. Auker won only nine and lost ten for Boston in 1939, and the Red Sox considered him expendable. Judnich, an outfielder, was an excellent minor league hitter whom the Yankees simply did not need. From Cincinnati, the Browns acquired pitcher Johnny Niggeling, 36.

Barnes and DeWitt were not the only Brownies seeking charity. To the team's embarrassment, a newspaper story revealed that shortstop Johnny Berardino, catcher-outfielder Joe Glenn, and pitcher Ed Cole were getting off-season unemployment relief checks of $15 a week. (Berardino, who has since dropped the second "r" in his surname, no longer has need for the dole. An aspiring actor even in his baseball days, when he would direct his team-mates in skits and Shakespearean dramas during long train trips, Beradino in the mid-1970s was earning some $250,000 a year as Dr. Steve Hardy, the leading character in the network television soap opera *General Hospital.* His experience with the Browns may have helped Beradino express the pathos and tragedy that Dr. Hardy so often encounters during the daily dramas.)

That winter, the Browns and Cardinals agreed to share the cost of a $150,000 lighting system for Sportsman's Park. With his usual foresight, Ball in 1932 had rejected Sam Breadon's suggestion that St. Louis become the first major league city to offer night baseball. For the 1940 season, the American League made two concessions to the Browns' poverty. They allowed the Browns to play fourteen night games at home, double the number allowed other teams. And they scheduled the Browns away from home every holiday of the summer so no team would have to waste the crowd-drawing potential of a holiday playing before empty seats in St. Louis.

On May 24, the Browns hosted Cleveland in the first night game played in St. Louis, and 24,827 fans paid their way to watch, the Browns' biggest crowd since 1928. Bob Feller hit a home run and outdueled Auker, 3 to 2. The *Sporting News* was impressed with the new lighting system, reporting that "illuminating engineers still are making great strides toward rivaling the sun." Even Philip K. Wrigley of the Chicago Cubs expressed interest in lights, saying that he would install them at Wrigley Field if they could be disguised to look like trees.

In June of 1940, Barnes turned down Detroit's offer of $200,000 for McQuinn, third baseman Harlond Clift, and pitcher Emil Bildilli. With Auker winning sixteen games and Judnich batting .303 with twenty-four home runs, the Browns climbed past Washington and Philadelphia into sixth place. More important, they drew 240,000 fans, half of them for the fourteen night games, and almost broke even financially. That winter, Barnes purchased veteran pitchers George Caster, Johnny Allen, Denny Galehouse, and Fritz Ostermueller, the latter two from the Boston Red Sox for

$30,000. Galehouse, a major league scout in northeastern Ohio since his playing days, recalled the circumstances:

I got a note through the mail that I was traded to the Browns. I didn't like it, knowing that they weren't drawing and weren't doing too well on the field or financially. I was living in Sarasota where the Red Sox trained, and I didn't like having to go clear across to San Antonio to train with the Browns. Did I have to take a salary cut? Yes, sure. That's the way things were in those days.

I never knew how that sale came about until long, long afterward. A writer who was there when it happened told me. They were at the Coca-Cola Company's final party, you know, where they serve more than Coca-Cola, after the annual baseball meetings, and a St. Louis guy, Don Barnes, was crying on Joe Cronin's shoulder that he hadn't been able to make any deals to improve his club. He mentioned myself and Ostermueller. "How much will you take for them?" Cronin made what he thought was an unreasonable request. and Barnes said, "OK, I'll take 'em."

In the *Sporting News*, Bing Miller, a Detroit coach, complimented the Browns on their acquisitions. "The Browns have been strengthening," he said. "They might sneak into the first division." A third of the way into the 1941 season, the Browns had instead sneaked into seventh place, only a half game out of the cellar. Fred Haney was fired as manager and Luke Sewell, a former catcher who had been coaching for the Cleveland Indians, was named to succeed him.

"Luke Sewell has had as many condolences from friends as he has received congratulations since replacing Fred Haney as manager of the Browns," the *Sporting News* reported. Unable to afford the usual practice of paying a dismissed manager without requiring him to work, the Browns sent Haney to their Toledo farm club and assigned him three jobs—manager, vice-president, and business manager. Zack Taylor, the Toledo manager, was promoted to the Browns as a coach.

Sewell was born in 1901. After attending a one-room schoolhouse in his hometown of Titus, Alabama, he enrolled at the age of 15 at the University of Alabama, where he quarterbacked the football team, preceding Joe Namath and Ken Stabler by two generations. Sewell and his elder brother, Joe, a third baseman who was inducted into the Hall of Fame in 1977, were two of seven players on the 1920 and 1921 Alabama baseball team who eventually played major league baseball.

Luke Sewell's baseball career spanned thirty-five years as player, coach, manager, and minor league executive. He then became a successful business entrepreneur. Even in baseball, Sewell had an eye for business. As a player in the 1930s, he worked mornings and days off selling tires to dealers. As manager of the Cincinnati Reds· from 1949 to 1952, he introduced the practice of having grounds keepers drag the infield in the middle of the game. This provided the players with a smooth surface and, more important, provided a long break that enhanced hot dog and beer sales.

In 1972, Sewell was persuaded to accept the Ohio chairmanship of President Richard M. Nixon's reelection campaign. The fall from grace of Nixon and Vice-President Spiro T. Agnew left Sewell somewhat embittered toward politicians. When interviewed during the summer of 1976 at his comfortable home outside Akron, Ohio, Sewell, at the age of 75, was just home from a round of golf, apologizing to a partner for a score in the low 80s, some eight to ten strokes above Sewell's usual game. Sewell:

I was coaching at Cleveland in 1941, and one day Alva Bradley, who owned the team, called me and said, "Don Barnes is going to call you and wants to talk to you about managing the Browns." I said, "Mr. Bradley, I don't want to go to St. Louis. I don't want to manage the Browns." It was probably the lowest job in the majors. They were on the bottom of the league and didn't have much of a ballclub; had no money. After having gone through the experience in Cleveland with Ossie Vitt I knew that managing was no bed of roses with any team.

Bradley said, "You've been in baseball now for twenty years. You owe it to yourself to go over and listen to them."

I rode the train over to St. Louis, and went over to the hotel where they had an airline ticket office and I made a reservation for the plane back to Cleveland; I'd get back to Cleveland at 5 o'clock, in time for the night game. I met Barnes at his apartment with Bill DeWitt. We talked about the job for a while. Barnes was a pretty persuasive little fellow. No question, he's a salesman.

I told him I'd like to have a voice in running the club, how mucn money

I wanted, a contract to finish that year and the next year. They excused themselves and went back into a bedroom. They came out and Barnes came up and shook my hand and said, "You're the manager of the Browns, starting tomorrow."

I came out of it with a pretty good agreement. I could shake that ball-club up any way I wanted to. Trade them, hire them, fire them, do anything I wanted to. When your team is on the bottom, you might as well take chances; you can't go wrong much.

When I went over there, the old Brownies had a defeatist attitude. I think they had gotten a lot of criticism from the management, and the press and the public. They were afraid everything they were going to do would be a mistake. Some of them came out of it. Some of them didn't, and you just had to pass those players on to someone else. Barnes didn't have any money. We'd trade even and hope to pick up some minor leaguers.

Under Sewell, the Browns played .500 baseball for the remainder of the 1941 season, finishing sixth. McQuinn, Laabs, and Judnich hit well. Veterans Auker, Galehouse, Niggeling, and Caster pitched respectably, and rookie Bob Muncrief won thirteen games against nine losses. Muncrief, a serious pitcher who developed a curve ball by pitching into pillows in his hotel room, came from an athletic family. His sisters, twins Dora and Nora, starred for the Amicos of Galveston, Texas, who won the National Girls Amateur Basketball Championship.

But St. Louis fans stuck with the Cardinals, who finished just short of Brooklyn in the National League pennant race. The Browns drew only 176,000 fans. Crowds of fewer than 500 were not unusual. The Cardinals drew 646,000. The more fans the Cardinals drew and the fewer the Browns drew, the greater the Browns' financial distress. Under terms of their stadium leases, the two teams divided all ushering and cleanup costs. As a result, the Browns wound up subsidizing the wealthier Cardinals, who had to hire more ushers and sweepers to accommodate their larger crowds.

The Brownie stock that citizens had purchased for five dollars a share went begging at two dollars. Losses for the season topped $100,000. To save money, the Browns dropped five farm clubs.

The American League, which had helped create the financial crisis by cutting the Browns back to seven home night games in 1941, had to help solve it by lending the team $25,000.

In February of 1942, an angel suddenly appeared in Richard D. Muckerman, who bought about $300,000 worth of a new stock issue and became a Brownie vice-president. Muckerman, heir to the St. Louis City Ice & Fuel Company fortune, later was to take over the team and run it down as skillfully as had the previous ice millionaire, Phil Ball. But in the early 1940s, Muckerman's money allowed Barnes, DeWitt, and Sewell to maintain their policy of keeping the Browns' most promising players while trying to acquire others on the cheap.

For the 1942 season, Sewell acquired a new second-base combination, and in doing so learned to question the advice of his Brownie colleagues. Vernon (Junior) Stephens, 21, had impressive statistics in 1941 at shortstop for the Toledo Mud Hens, the Browns' top farm club. Don Gutteridge, 30, who had been sent back to the minors after five mediocre years as a Cardinal third baseman, hit .309 with Sacramento in 1941, scored 113 runs and led the Pacific Coast League with forty-six stolen bases. Gutteridge was nevertheless passed up in the major league draft. Discouraged, he said he would quit baseball rather than spend another year in the minor leagues. The Cardinals offered him for sale on a consignment basis. Considering the alternatives, Sewell saw no reason to be finicky about the skills of either man. Sewell:

When the 1941 season was over we called our minor league managers and scouts in for a review, and they got to talking about Stephens. Fred Haney told me, these were his exact words, "Stephens will never play shortstop in the major leagues as long as he's got a hole in his ass." I said, "Doesn't take too much to do better than the man we've got at shortstop." Rickey offered us Gutteridge on a look-see basis. We could keep him all through spring training. We could have him for $7,500, or if we didn't want him we could ship him back. I told Bill DeWitt, "Bring him in here and we'll make a second baseman out of him." Bill told me, "Mr. Rickey said Don couldn't play second." I said, "Well, the man we've got can't play second." So we got Gutteridge.

They also bought another discard, Al (Boots) Hollingsworth, a left-handed pitcher who had spent 1941 with Sacramento after being cuffed around the National League for five years.

Continuing to trade players that he considered losers, Sewell in June swapped Roy Cullenbine, a .317 hitter the year before, to Washington for pitcher Steve Sundra and outfielder-first baseman Mike Chartak. "Cullenbine wouldn't swing the bat," DeWitt recalled. "Sewell would give him the hit sign and he'd take it, trying to get the base on balls. Laziest human being you ever saw." During his ten years in the major leagues, Cullenbine got 1,072 hits and 852 walks, an astounding number of walks for a man who was neither a lead-off batter nor the kind of power hitter who frightened pitchers.

Playing in a league that was still strong despite the departure into military service of a few stars like Greenberg and Feller, Sewell's patchwork Browns performed magnificently in 1942. They won their first four games, two of them with the help of ninth-inning home runs by Stephens. After slumping, the Browns began moving up in July. Stephens was superb, both at bat and in the field; Gutteridge was significantly better than the second basemen he replaced, Johnny Lucadello and Don Heffner. Most surprising was Laabs, who in July arose from six seasons of mediocrity and hit seven homers in eight games, including a grand slam. "This morning three reporters walked into my room before breakfast to ask me all about myself," Laabs told a *Sporting News* correspondent. "They're making me feel famous, and I love it."

Spink, the *Sporting News'* publisher, called Sewell a sorcerer. "His entire pitching staff is haunted!" Spink wrote. "Graybeards like Al Hollingsworth, Eldon Auker, Johnny Niggeling, Denny Galehouse, George Caster live in a bygone day, but pitch decidedly in the present."

In late July, the Browns climbed into the first division. In September, they passed Cleveland and took third place, finishing eight and a half games ahead of the Indians. The Browns had not finished so high since 1928; home attendance of 256,000 was the Brownies' highest since 1929. Laabs, in by far the best season of his career, hit twenty-seven home runs, second only to Ted Williams in the American League, and drove in ninety-nine runs. Stephens batted .294, hit fourteen homers, drove in ninety-two runs, and finished second to Johnny Pesky of Boston in balloting for Rookie of the Year. Judnich batted .313 with seventeen homers. Niggeling was fifteen and eleven, Auker fourteen and thirteen, Hollingsworth ten and six, Galehouse twelve and twelve, Sundra eight and three, and Caster, pitching in relief, was eight and two. Inspired by an excellent manager, the Browns played over their heads. For the Browns to progress further, the rest of the league had to decline. The next step was up to the Germans, the Japanese, and the U.S. Selective Service System.

CHAPTER 7

Hardships on the Home Front

In baseball, nothing is more traditional than spring training in Florida. In wartime, nothing would more conspicuously flout the national mood of self-sacrifice than the sight of professional athletes basking in the sun. In January of 1943, Judge Landis pulled the prickliest hair shirt of all onto every player lucky enough to escape the draft. He ordered the sixteen major league teams to conduct their spring training north of the Mason-Dixon Line.

The move was not entirely of Landis's own making. A month before, Joseph B. Eastman, director of the Office of Defense Transportation, had asked the commissioner and the presidents of the two major leagues to meet baseball's travel requirements "without waste in space or mileage"; war needs threatened to tax the railroads' capacity. Among other things, Eastman suggested less travel for preseason exhibition games.

Wisely doing the government one better, Landis journeyed to Washington and told Eastman that baseball teams would train in the North and revise their playing schedules so a team would visit each of its seven competitors three times during the season rather than four. Multiplying the number of travel miles eliminated by the number of people involved—players, coaches, sportswriters, and so forth—the major leagues claimed that they reduced their travel in 1943 by five million "man miles."

The program was not immediately made public; Landis let Eastman have the first word so baseball could bask in official praise. "Judge Landis came to me with certain proposals which I approve," Eastman said. "I approve of baseball's cooperation with the war effort, and I'd say baseball's cooperation with us might serve as a pattern for the nation." Indeed, the agreement was a public relations coup for both men. Landis had the government's blessing; Eastman had a well-publicized example of civilian restraint in use of the railroads.

Teams immediately began scrambling for training sites. Arthur Daley of the *New York Times* reported that Midwestern clubs had an advantage. "The baseball fathers have been searching throughout the East for colleges with field houses which may be available for spring training," Daley wrote. "Although no self-respecting Midwest school would think of doing without a field house, the Atlantic seaboard has mighty few of them."

The Florida "Grapefruit League" was replaced by the Indiana "Limestone League," with the Chicago Cubs and White Sox at the resort community of French Lick, the Cincinnati Reds at Indiana University in Bloomington, the Detroit Tigers at Evansville, the Pittsburgh Pirates at Muncie, the Cleveland Indians at Purdue University in Lafayette, and the Minneapolis Millers of the American Association at Terre Haute. "The wind is cold tonight along the Wabash," commented the *Sporting News*.

The Boston Braves chose Choate, an exclusive prep school for young men at Wallingford, Connecticut; the Red Sox selected Tufts College in Medford, Massachusetts. The Brooklyn Dodgers trained at Bear Mountain, New York, the New York Giants at Lakewood, New Jersey, and the Yankees at Asbury Park, New Jersey. The Philadelphia Athletics chose Wilmington, Delaware, the Phillies picked Hershey, Pennsylvania, and the Washington Senators trained at the University of Maryland in College Park, bedding down in fraternity houses.

Although Landis had ruled out training camps south of the Ohio or Potomac rivers, the St. Louis teams were allowed more southerly sites so long as they stayed close to home. The Cardinals selected Cairo (pronounced *Kay*-row) at the southern tip of Illinois. The Cardinals' trainer, Harrison J. Weaver, ordered long underwear for all hands. The Browns found an excellent site, considering the circumstances, at Cape Girardeau, Missouri, a small town on the Mississippi River 120 miles downstream from St. Louis. The two St. Louis teams were on opposite sides of the Mississippi, about sixty miles apart. Serving both was a gambling casino, just north of Cairo, that flourished with the blessing of hospitable Illinois authorities.

There was optimistic talk among baseball officials about the prospects for decent weather that spring, but a fan, W. G. Wolf of Delaware, Ohio, looked up the spring training sites in the 1941 *Yearbook of Agriculture* and reported through the *Sporting News* that every team could expect some freezing weather. They encountered worse than that. In French Lick, the White Sox found their field under four feet of muddy water; the Cubs' field, laid out on a golf course, was covered with water three feet deep.

Some teams, including the Red Sox, Indians, Cardinals, and Browns, had good indoor training facilities to use during bad weather. The Dodgers were allowed to use the field house of the nearby U.S. Military Academy at West Point, but only when Army cadets did not need it. In contrast to the gentlemanly mid-morning drill schedules of previous springs, Brooklyn players were summoned to the field house at night or early in the morning. Dodger drills were occasionally interrupted when cadets preempted the facilities.

The managers of the 1942 championship teams had differing attitudes that exemplified the ability of some teams, and the refusal of others, to adapt to wartime conditions.

"That occasional indoor drill is a good break, rather than an interruption in our routine," said Billy Southworth, manager of the Cardinals, whose upbeat attitude included this medical explanation: "You see, the early outdoor work makes the muscles sore and the indoor work warms them up and takes out the soreness. I believe we have hit upon an excellent way of getting into condition."

"I am getting ready a club for play in sunlight, on a field," said Joe McCarthy, the Yankee manager. "I am not training a basketball team or a track squad. ... I am dead set against training indoors, and while I recognize that some clubs cannot help themselves, I want none of it for the Yankees." McCarthy, too, had an explanation. He said players might strain their eyes in artificial light, get accustomed to sneakers rather than spiked shoes, and forget how to throw against the wind.

Thus committed to the great outdoors, the Yankees encountered the New York and New Jersey area's coldest and windiest spring in a decade. The Giants endured the same weather; their training camp was a former Rockefeller enclave with a diamond laid out on the first fairway of the estate's private golf course. Carl Hubbell, the great Giant pitcher, was by then 40 years old and felt no compulsion to brave the elements. "Hubbell did nothing in Lakewood but play Ping-Pong," the *Sporting News* reported. The next fall, Hubbell announced that he was retiring so he would not have to train in the North again. He was not alone. Joe Gordon of the Yankees asked permission to train at his Oregon home in 1944. "I am not going to subject myself again to the freeze we suffered at Asbury Park last March," Gordon said.

The war imposed other hardships as well. Accustomed to private railroad cars and lower berths, baseball players sometimes had to mix on trains with soldiers and common citizens, sleep in upper berths, and ride on day coaches when an overnight trip was not involved. On more fortunate occasions, recalls Joe Cronin, who was then the playing manager of the Boston Red Sox, players found themselves assigned to railroad staterooms, which the armed forces considered too expensive.

Other aspects of baseball's life-style also were crimped by wartime shortages, which of course affected the entire civilian population. Cracker Jacks, a ball park staple in fact as well as in song, had to give up prizes made in Japan and turn to domestic substitutes. Rationing was imposed (in this order) on tires, cars, sugar, gasoline, bicycles, men's rubber boots and work shoes, fuel oil, coffee, heating stoves, shoes, processed foods, and meats and fats. A popular song included this line: "Take it easy, take it easy. Don't you know you only get three pairs of shoes a year?"

Automobile factories began converting to weapons production even before the United States entered the war. Few cars were made for civilian use; 1942 models were the latest thing until 1946 models came out. Turning this impending shortage to its advantage, General Motors ran this advertisement in October of 1941:

"We had to have a real and representative Buick, one we could be proud of, one *able* enough, *durable* enough to serve until annual new models are the rule again.

"We resolved on a 1942 automobile of such merit as would carry the Buick reputation without fault until other new Buicks, however far off, could come along to refresh it.

". . . It would be a shame, for you and for us, to have you miss the dreadnought Buick we've built to stand up successfully to the toughest job in years."

Food shortages caused perhaps the most pervasive rationing nuisance. Traveling baseball teams often encountered beefless menus; athletes accustomed to their nightly steak settled for fish instead. The wives of four Philadelphia Phillies seized on their husbands' yearning for beef as a spur to their own desire for slimmer figures; they dieted to save ration points. "A good T-bone steak takes about sixteen points," said Mrs. Merrill May, whose husband, nicknamed "Pinky," played third base for the Phils. "I go on a liquid diet and can lose three pounds in three days when my husband's away." She was joined by the wives of outfielders Danny Litwhiler and Ron Northey, and of pitcher Si Johnson.

In the same constructive and patriotic spirit, Dr. Harry P. Nimphius, chief veterinarian and dietician at the Central Park Zoo in New York, imposed horsemeat rationing on the zoo's lions and tigers, although horsemeat was not rationed. "This reduced diet will probably be beneficial to the animals," he said, "because they're all fat."

Even for materials that were not rationed, consumption was held down by government restrictions. For example, a man's suit could not be made with pleats, a vest, or a second pair of trousers.

In 1943, wartime restrictions threatened the very heart of baseball—the ball itself. Before the war, baseball covers were made of horsehide imported from Belgium and rural France, where horses were slaughtered while young for their meat. The German occupation cut off this supply, so horsehide from Bolivia was substituted. By 1943, Bolivian horsehide was no longer available for the cover, nor cork for the core. With some qualms, a domestic grade of horsehide was substituted. More than a dozen tanning formulas were tried before one passed muster.

Two cores were considered. Thousands of golf ball cores had been orphaned when the government banned wartime production of golf balls. The National League thought that these could be used in baseballs. The American League preferred a core made of granulated cork, a variety that was available, with a double shell of balata, the hard rubberlike material used for golf ball covers.

On the basis of comparative testing, this "balata ball" was chosen for major league play. Commissioner Landis ordered the A. G. Spalding Company to make the 1943 ball as resilient as the ball used in 1939; batting averages had declined since then, and the fans were thought to prefer a lustier game.

Instead, the new ball was as dead as a rock. In a four-game series at Cincinnati opening the 1943 season, the Cardinals and Reds scored six runs between them. No home runs were hit in the first eleven major league games; of the first twenty-nine games, eleven were shutouts. Stan Musial was on a batting tear, but his best drives were being caught short of the fences. He said that the experience made him understand the plight of old-time players who complained of the dead ball that was used in the major leagues before Babe Ruth glamorized the home run.

Spalding at first defended the new ball, but no one was convinced. Warren Giles, general manager of the Reds, threatened to have an outlaw ball made for his team. The New York *Daily News* had the balata ball tested by Cooper Union Institute of Technology, which reported that it was 25.9 percent less resilient than the 1942 baseball. Spalding ruefully acknowledged similar results from its own tests; it said that the cause was a wartime cement made of re-processed rubber.

While balls with a better cement were rushed into production, baseballs left over from 1942 were used. The next winter, the War Production Board took Spalding off the hook; cork and synthetic rubber were made available. "With these new materials, we will be in a position to produce balls that will have a degree of liveliness to meet league requirements," the Spalding firm announced.

Spalding has made every major league baseball for a century, starting in 1877, and the dead ball of 1943 was not the firm's proudest achievement. If you ask, Spalding will mail you a four-page mimeographed description of the way baseballs are made. It includes a little history, but there is no mention of World War II or the balata ball.

The United States produced enough oil during World War II to supply both the armed forces and the civilian population, but driving and gasoline use were restricted nevertheless. There were two reasons—a nationwide rubber shortage and a regional oil shortage.

Most of the world's rubber plantations had fallen into Japanese hands. In the Eastern United States, an oil shortage developed in 1942 because German submarines were sinking tankers that carried oil from the Gulf Coast to New York and other Eastern ports. There was no pipeline between the Southwestern oil fields and the Eastern states; railroads and trucks could carry only half as much oil as the region needed. When the Socony-Vacuum Oil Company's *China Arrow* went down 100 miles off New York on February 8, 1942, it was the fourteenth vessel sunk by U-boats off the U.S. coast in less than a month. Six others had been sunk off Canada.

In early 1942, gasoline rationing was imposed in seventeen Eastern states. Businesses and families that used oil heat were urged to turn their thermostats down to 68 degrees, and fuel oil was rationed on that basis. Many of the tanker sinkings were at night, and military authorities believed that the vessels might be silhouetted by the bright lights on shore, making them easy targets for U-boats. In April of 1942, a coastal "dim-out" was ordered to prevent this. The huge neon signs of Times Square were darkened for the first time since 1917, when a severe winter caused a coal shortage.

As part of the dim-out, only one hour of artificial light was allowed at the Polo Grounds and Ebbets Field, homes respectively of the Giants and the Dodgers. "Army officials decided that the glare would invite trouble at sea and perhaps guide some suicide flier bearing a grim message from Dizzy Adolf, and ordered the two ball parks blacked out," the *Sporting News* reported. This dim-out rule imposed another innovation on baseball; evening games that started in daylight and ended under the lights. At first called "twights" or "dusk" games, these contests eventually became known as "twilight" or "twi-night" games.

"Twi-night" games were first tried at coastal minor league parks that also were covered by the dim-out rule. The Sally League started games at 7:15 P.M. and ordered the umpires to speed up play. Infielders were not allowed to throw the ball around after an out. On May 26, 1942, Savannah, Georgia, beat Jacksonville, Florida, 12 to 3, in one hour and forty-four minutes.

The International League could have used a similar speed-up rule. In a game at Jersey City between the Jersey City Giants and the Montreal Royals, the Giants finished the eighth inning with a 3 to 2 lead and plenty of time remaining before the lights-out deadline of 9:24 P.M. The Royals pulled ahead in the ninth, and the Giants began stalling so the ninth inning would not finish before the lights went out, and hence would not count. Hugh East, the Jersey City pitcher, walked four batters in a row, although they swung at every pitch within reach. The Royals scored eight runs, but the Giants' ploy worked. The lights went out during the home half of the ninth, and the game reverted to the end of the eighth inning, giving Jersey City a 3 to 2 victory.

The New York Giants and Brooklyn Dodgers rescheduled their night games as twi-night affairs. Although other major league parks were not affected by the blackout order—Yankee Stadium had no lights, and the Army said it had checked Shibe Park in Philadelphia and decided that night games there entailed no risk—twi-night games caught on in other cities as well.

In Washington, Clark Griffith, limited to twenty-one night games, decided that the Senators would play their other weekday games as twi-nighters, starting at 7 P.M. To Griffith's chagrin, William Harridge, president of the American League, ruled that such games would count against the Senators' night game quota.

In St. Louis, a sportswriter was inspired to compose these lyrics for the *Post-Dispatch*:

> Take me out to the ball game,
> Half past five is the time.
> I'll have some peanuts and Cracker Jacks
> Don't hold up dinner—I may not be back;
> I'll just take a look in the icebox
> If the shelves are bare it's a shame.
> I'll waive soup, shortcake and all to be out
> At the old ball game.

For the last six weeks of the 1942 season and the entire 1943 season, night baseball was banned on the Pacific Coast as well. Attendance declined initially but recovered; the Los Angeles Angels drew 234,000 in 1942, their best attendance record in twelve years.

The dim-out cast a pall on the 1943 New Year's celebration in Times Square. The New York *Times* reported that about 400,000 celebrants tooted second-hand horns but lacked the usual verve. Seven days later, all pleasure driving was banned along the Eastern seaboard. Government inspectors from the Office of Price Administration were posted at Madison Square Garden, Carnegie Hall, the Waldorf Astoria and Roosevelt hotels, and at night spots such as Leon and Eddie's and the Stork Club. Others rode around the city in the sidecars of police motorcycles. The first people stopped on suspicion of driving for fun turned out to be a doctor finishing his rounds and a man who said he was stopping to eat on his way to a war plant job.

Many people wrote to the Office of Price Administration for permission to make motoring trips of various kinds. An Italian family living in a Jewish neighborhood was granted permission to drive to an Italian market once weekly, public transportation not being available. A soldier on leave was told he could use a car for social calls, soldiers being a special case, but only if he did the driving.

An elderly couple asked if their chauffeur could continue driving them to the opera; it was their only means of recreation, and they otherwise would lay off their chauffeur. They were turned down. A bride and groom were told that they could drive to the church for their wedding. But the guests could not, and the newlyweds could not use a car for their honeymoon.

The shortage of rubber posed a serious problem. The public was urged to walk or use public transportation so their tires would not wear out. "Each time a motorist turns a wheel in unnecessary driving, he must realize that it is a turn of the wheel against our soldiers and in favor of Hitler," Leon Henderson, head of the Office of Price Administration, said in September of 1942.

But voluntary conservation was not enough. To save rubber, gasoline rationing was imposed nationwide in October of 1942. To prevent hoarding, motorists were allowed to own only five tires per car; the government bought the rest. The basic gasoline ration was enough to drive about 240 miles a month, less than one-third of the average norm for most families. To get a more generous ration, a driver had to show a real need, such as a job in a defense plant far from home and not served by public transportation. Since faster driving is harder on tires, a nationwide speed limit of thirty-five miles per hour was imposed.

Driving to baseball games was out in the East. Most families could not afford to squander their meager gasoline ration on trips to the ball park. Nor was baseball as much of an attraction as it had been before the war; the casual fan who had bought a ticket to watch Bob Feller or Joe DiMaggio would not as readily pay to watch drab replacements such as Jack Salveson and Bud Metheny.

But there were counterbalancing forces. Fortunately, suburban stadiums were not yet in vogue. All the major league baseball parks were well served by public transportation. In some ways, baseball and other forms of entertainment benefited from the war. The demand for munitions pulled the economy from depression to prosperity, and virtually halted the production of cars, appliances, and many other consumer products. People had more money than before and less to spend it on.

This created inflationary trends, prompting the government to impose strict controls on wages and prices. In early 1943, the Office of Price Administration estimated that consumer income would total $130 billion that year, and that there would be only $77 billion worth of goods available to buy. To sop up some of this money and thus lessen inflationary pressures, the OPA considered a plan under which automobile dealers, appliance stores, and other merchants would sell "postwar delivery certificates." The buyer would pay advance installments during the war, and be first in line for a new car, refrigerator, sofa, or what have you after the war. Merchants and consumer finance companies enthusiastically endorsed the plan, but it was not adopted.

That left the public with more money to spend on movies and baseball. In addition, the war was continuing to promote night baseball, dim-outs aside. In July of 1943, Commissioner Landis yielded to Griffith's continuing requests that the Senators be allowed to play as many night games as they chose. "Wartime conditions of employment in Washington make it worthwhile to have more night games," Landis said. Attendance in Washington was so good that the Senators cut the price of a hot dog from fifteen cents to a dime. The dim-outs ended after the 1943 season. In April of 1944, George W. McMurphey, chief of the War Production Board's division of recreation and amusement, recommended more night baseball, citing attendance figures and a *Sporting News* poll of fans, which came out two and a half to one in favor of more night games. "In some of the big league cities, night games outdrew weekday games in the afternoon by as much as three to one," McMurphey said, adding that the government should have a voice since baseball was important to wartime morale.

McMurphey's department even suggested that the Yankees, Red Sox, Braves, Cubs, and Tigers apply to the government for steel and wiring to light their ball parks so every big league stadium could offer night baseball. He was overruled by higher authority, but in July of 1944, the major leagues approved unlimited night ball despite the opposition of several officials, none of whom were prophets. "I am more convinced than ever that there is absolutely no future in electric-lighted play," said Ed Barrow, president of the Yankees. "It killed the minors. It has ruined thousands of fine prospects. It has chased our youngsters out of our parks. It has deteriorated the living habits of players and spectators."

Branch Rickey, by then general manager of the Dodgers, expressed fear that night games, once commonplace, would draw no more than day games. Rickey had not lost his sense of thrift. "You don't have to pay for sunshine," he said.

Babe Ruth, who hit all of his 714 home runs in daylight and spent his evenings drinking and whoring, warned that night games would ruin players' eyes, give them colds, and deprive them of sleep. He was supported by Bill Terry, who once batted .401 for the Giants in daylight but more recently had been an administrator in the minor leagues, where most games were played at night.

Terry was sensitive to nocturnal dampness. "The players are always wet, with soggy socks, soggy shoes, uncomfortable conditions," he said. Vince DiMaggio of the Pirates, elder brother of Joe and Dominic, raised an unexpected economic issue when he ordered a $9.60 meal following a night game in Cincinnati, and charged it to his employers. Traveling players were then limited to about four dollars a day for meals, but DiMaggio explained that no restaurant was open at midnight except an expensive one with a floor show and a 20 percent service charge.

In 1941, the last prewar season, major league attendance totaled 9,689,000. It declined to 8,620,000 in 1942, and to 7,148,000 in 1943, when there was no real pennant race in either league. By 1944, the number of night games was up and so was the level of prosperity; attendance climbed to 8,697,000. In 1945, the war was ending, many more night games were played, and the public had still more money. Major league attendance reached 10,842,000.

Following the war, night ball opponents among the club owners tried to reimpose a limit on the number of night games, but were outvoted. World War II had forced baseball to accept a change that would help to enrich everyone connected with the game, including the club owners who had opposed it.

CHAPTER 8

Sergeant DiMaggio
and Other Baseball Patriots

In September of 1942, J.G. Taylor Spink, editor and publisher of the *Sporting News*, put angelic wings and organic tone to his typewriter. "LOOK WELL AT THESE HEROES, FOR THEY GO," read the headline. Then this:

"Hail, and farewell! As the days roll along into this wartime autumn, many ball players are chanting their valedictories with their bats, while their spikes make final trails along the dirt of our infields. A goodly number—who knows how many?—are going into battle. Look well at these heroes of our diamonds. Let their pictures become indelible in your minds. For they go, nobody knows where, and nobody knows when once again you will see them in their habiliments of the diamond, scorching the infield, poised on the mound, tearing across the outer reaches, swinging the sticks of baseball valor.

". . . While you enjoy yourself with the recreation of the diamond, be not given to harsh outburst or too captious view. These men whom you watch are doing the best they can in an atmosphere of tremendous strain, enveloped in a psychology which does not conduce to the best in artistic result.

"If your shortstop makes a couple of boots—well, he is married, but has been told to report to his draft board for early induction into the Army.

"If your outfielder fans twice or thrice, don't strain your vocal chords into vociferous displeasure. He is supporting his aged parents, but the Army has sent its call to the colors. He goes—and he knows not where, nor whether he will once again gaze into that packed grandstand, whether he will peer into those shirt-sleeved bleachers in 1943, 1944, or ever.

"Look well at these heroes, for they go. Examine their physical lineaments so that you forget them not. Examine them with a new mental attitude. Cheer them on in their daily tasks of difficulty . . .

"Think of these men who now play, but soon will fight, and remember that they will take Baseball with them, in their hearts—that, if through the fortunes of war and the will of God, they fall, that spot where they will lie will be forever American, and Baseball.

"Look well at these heroes, for they go . . . They go to fight and they go to come back. But if they don't return, theirs will be the Valhalla of Eddie Grant . . .

"Look well at these heroes, for they go."

Eddie Grant, the first major league player killed in World War I, had been enjoying quite a revival. Judge Landis even recommended his election to the Hall of Fame, an honor that would have been based on his death rather than his lifetime batting average of .249.

Hank Gowdy, the first player to enlist during World War I, also became a hero once again. Not yet consigned to Valhalla, Gowdy was coaching for the Cincinnati Reds and extolling the virtues of military service. "I have been the recipient of many honors in my lengthy baseball career, and also have been in receipt of honors outside the realm of baseball," Gowdy said in an interview of lofty tone, as quoted in the *Sporting News.* "But the highest honor of my entire life came through being privileged to wear the United States Army uniform and serve my country in the last war in which it was engaged."

Gowdy meant it; in early 1943, at the age of 53, he enlisted again and was commissioned as an Army captain.

Two weeks after Pearl Harbor, Congress enacted a new draft law calling for the conscription of men 20 through 45 years of age. Men 18 and 19 years old were required to register, but could not be drafted; Congress and the Administration feared the wrath of mothers. Men from 45 to 64 years old also had to register, but could not be called.

Inductions accelerated swiftly during 1942 and 1943, and the law and regulations under which men were drafted changed just as rapidly. In June of 1942, Congress enacted a law providing monthly allowances for the wives and children of men in service. Military manpower authorities pointed out that the allowances should ᴾreclude the need to exempt husbands and fathers from the draft, but Congress did not agree. The same law stipulated that draft deferments were to be based on the number of dependents a man had and the extent to which his civilian job contributed to the war effort. In figuring dependents, weddings and conceptions that occurred after Pearl Harbor did not count.

The pecking order worked out by the Selective Service System to implement this law was complicated. Single men with no dependents were to be drafted first. Second to go were single men with "collateral" dependents, such as parents, but without a job that contributed to the war effort. Third were single men with collateral dependents and with a job that did contribute. Fourth came married men without children and without a contributing job. Fifth were married men without children but with a contributing job. Sixth were married men with children but without a contributing job. Seventh and last to be called were married men with children and with a job that contributed to the war effort.

The complications did not end there. Selective Service headquarters issued long lists of jobs that it considered important to the war effort. For example, in October of 1942 local draft boards received from headquarters a list of ninety-two jobs in the field of communications, ranging from newspaper editor to telephone office repairman. But these were only recommendations; local draft boards decided for themselves which jobs were important and which were not, and whether a man with an important job could be replaced by a woman or by someone else exempt from the draft.

Standards varied from community to community. So did the number of men available to meet local draft quotas. Some local boards could fill their quotas with single men; others could not. Rural areas had a harder time meeting their draft quotas, so a married man in a city was less likely to be called than one living in the country.

There was nothing in the law or regulations to make a 21-year-old any more liable for induction than a man of 45, and the Army soon found itself burdened with too many old soldiers. Many of them could not endure the rigors of training. In September of 1942, Senator Robert Taft of Ohio, an influential Republican, called for the induction of men 18 and 19 years old, and accused President Roosevelt of planning to postpone such a move until after the congressional elections that November.

On October 12, Roosevelt asked Congress to lower the draft age to 18. Secretary of War Henry L. Stimson revealed that the goal was an armed force of 7.5 million men by the end of 1943. The armed forces then numbered 4,250,000; too few, Stimson said, and "too old." As 18- and 19-year-olds were inducted, an Army spokesman said, men in their 40s and late 30s would be discharged.

Congress seemed disposed to approve the induction of 18- and 19-year-olds. But even in wartime, Congress often was distracted by side issues. This time it was prohibition. The drys had been looking for an opportunity to revive their cause ever since the humiliation of 1933, when federal prohibition of the sale of alcoholic beverages was repealed. The prohibition groups that had pushed the Volstead Act through Congress during World War I were still strong; the Anti-Saloon League, the Women's Christian Temperance Union, the Methodist Board of Temperance, and the Prohibitionist Party were united under the lobbying tent of the National Temperance and Prohibition Council. The Council had a budget of $10 million, a headquarters just east of the Capitol, and as the New York *Times* said, an opportunity for the dry camel to push its nose under the tent. Who wanted innocent teenage soldiers exposed to the evils of alcohol?

When the bill to draft 18- and 19-year-olds came up, Senator Josh Lee, Democrat of Oklahoma, proposed an amendment to bar the sale of beer and liquor in the vicinity of military establishments. As interpreted by Lee and his allies, the government had already listed liquor as unnecessary during wartime by ordering U.S. distilleries to make nothing but alcohol, which was needed for munitions. (A four-year supply of liquor was in storage.) The *Times* described the dry lobby much as newspapers of today describe the National Rifle Association—smooth, well organized, well financed—while the drinking majority, like the majority that favors gun control, was in disarray.

The 1942 election was only a week off, and senators on both sides of the issue told reporters privately that Lee's amendment was sure to pass if senators were forced to vote on it. But the prohibitionists failed. Senate leaders crept around the issue by referring Lee's amendment to a subcommittee for study. On November 12, Congress approved the conscription of men aged 18 and 19; those still in high school were given six months to finish up. The bill also deferred agricultural workers.

Baseball club owners who had been hoarding young players turned to older ones, and particularly to married players with children. But in early 1943, Manpower Commissioner Paul V. McNutt moved to narrow the grounds for deferments based on dependents. To be deferred, he said, a man should work at something that contributed to the war effort. McNutt issued a list of twenty-nine occupations—astrologer, bartender, dancing teacher, soda jerk, waiter—and said that men in those jobs should be drafted regardless of their families. So, he said, should men working at any job in thirty-six businesses, including antiques, turkish baths, florist shops, and social-escort services. Most jobs, including baseball player, made neither the nonessential list nor any of the government's lists of essential positions. Groundskeepers were listed as nonessential and subject to the draft regardless of their families, but older men could be found to care for the playing fields.

Without deferments of one kind or another, baseball would be in trouble. The draft was taking men 18 through 38 years old. On the sixteen major league rosters, there were only ten players older than 38 and none younger than 18. McNutt's position was ambiguous; his agency said that baseball's contribution to national morale might be considered. On the other hand, baseball players could not expect an occupational deferment. "The usefulness of the sport is a separate question from the 'essentiality' of individuals who play it," McNutt explained. "Thus it may well be that it is desirable that Blankville have a ball team. But Blankville may lose certain members of that team to higher priority industries—even members that might be 'essential' to winning the pennant. The pennant is not 'essential.'"

The Associated Press reported that horse racing was in the best position among major sports, because many jockeys were under 18 and many former jocks could work as exercise boys although older than 38. Boxing had been severely curtailed; 2,700 fighters were in service, including thirty-one past or present world champions. Professional baseball and football planned to continue as long as they could.

Baseball officials interpreted McNutt's rulings optimistically. "McNutt's intent is obvious," said Ford Frick, president of the National League. "He wants able-bodied men whose work could be done by older males or women to get into war industry or the Army. I don't believe anybody in Washington thinks the major leagues could be manned by old veterans and girls."

Branch Rickey agreed. "If Bob Hope and Fred Allen and Jack Benny and others can do a better job carrying a rifle than they are doing right now, then, of course, essentiality compels them to change their jobs overnight," Rickey said. "And if these 400 players now classed as 3-A [meaning with dependents] can do a better job for our 130 million people at anything other than playing this game this coming summer, then we want to know the way to do it and we are anxious to do it. By and large these men do not have any specialized skills in any other field of work, and neither women nor men past 38 can take over their present jobs. If there is a morale job to be done by baseball, these particular men must do it."

Rickey's reference to entertainers was not accidental. The movie industry, unlike baseball, had petitioned the government for deferment of essential employees, and got it. On February 8, 1942, General Hershey ruled that movie production was "an activity essential in certain instances to the national health, safety and interest, and in other instances to war production." He told Selective Service boards in California to defer "actors, directors, writers, producers, cameramen, sound engineers and other technicians" who could not be replaced. The idea was that in addition to entertaining everyone, movies would help persuade the public to support the war effort in various ways.

Congress was less enthusiastic about that. A few days after Hershey's ruling, the House of Representatives voted down an $80,000 appropriation to pay for a Walt Disney film entitled "The New Spirit," in which Disney's animated characters tried to make Americans cheerfully accept wartime income tax rates, which increased the taxes paid by some lower-income families sevenfold. "Not a buck for Donald Duck!" proclaimed one Congressional wag.

The movie and baseball industries were by no means the only groups that saw their personnel as essential to national morale, propaganda, or some other noble objective. Students studying for the ministry were deferred through most of the war. So were various kinds of technicians and government employees. Deferments were sought—and in some instances, granted—for, among many other occupations, state legislators, farmers, chemists, chemical engineers, medical and pre-medical students, policemen, firemen, public utility employees, aliens, members of Moral Rearmament, longshoremen, commercial fishermen, merchant seamen, food processing workers, tobacco workers, automobile mechanics, copper and coal miners, metals workers, loggers, dairy and livestock workers, prison employees, draft board members, candidates for elective office, teachers, law students, engineering and science students, and musicians 29 or older.

No wonder baseball did not quite know where it stood!

One effect of the uncertainty was to inhibit trading of players between the 1942 and 1943 seasons. "Would I like to trade? Yes," said Mel Ott, manager of the New York Giants. "But whom would I trade, and whom would the other clubs trade to me? And if I made a trade, how sure would I be that the man I got would report to me around March 1?"

At the Waldorf Astoria in New York, the Circus Saints and Sinners, a social organization, inducted Billy Southworth, the Cardinal manager, and looked forward to the next baseball season with a skit entitled "World Series of 1943." As portrayed in the skit, Commissioner Landis had ruled that no team could carry more than four players, and none of them could be physically able. Four aged players hobbled onstage with the help of canes, crutches, and nurses administering vitamin hypodermics.

In fact, the skit was as close to the truth as were the statements by Frick and Rickey. Although a local draft board here or there might consider the game's contribution to morale, it could not be a major consideration. Baseball players clearly had no grounds for occupational deferment. Many citizens felt that athletes should be the first to go. "If your next door neighbor were deferred on account of pyorrhea, you'd think nothing of it," wrote Ed McAuley of the Cleveland *News*. "If a ball player were deferred on the same grounds, you'd write to your congressman."

One victim of this discrimination was Red Ruffing, the Yankee pitcher, who was drafted after the 1942 World Series. Ruffing:

I was living in Long Beach, California, at the time, and I was 38 years old. I've got four toes missing on my left foot, from a coal mine accident when I was young. I had a wife and kids. I had a mother-in-law, she was my responsibility. But there it was: "Greetings from the President." A lot of people thought I wouldn't be taken. Matter of fact, I talked to some lady on the draft board out there in California. One night we had a party and happened to be talking. I told her about my induction notice. She said, "How old are you?" I told her. She said, "Oh, they won't take you." I told her about my foot, and I showed it to her. "Oh my God," she says, "they'll never take you."

I had to report at Los Angeles, for induction. Some sergeant called out my name over the loudspeaker; "Red Ruffing in this group? Step forward!" So I went up to him. He says, "I'm from Detroit; I'm a baseball nut. Will you talk baseball with me?" I says, "Sure, why not?" He says, "They're not going to take you." I says, "That I find hard to believe. With my name in the papers, for the World Series and all, they aren't going to take me? Huh!" He says, "Nope. I talked to several doctors." And he was right in a way. The regular doctors examined me. They turned me down; 4-F. The last doctor I came to was an Army doctor. He put on his report that what I could do on the outside I could do on the inside. He would have drafted any ballplayer. So that's how I got in.

Ruffing's case to the contrary, deferments based on dependency were keeping baseball alive. The United States was the only country engaged in the war that deferred men because of family responsibilities. These dependency deferments were almost wiped out during 1943. With the Army, Navy, and various war industries needing more men, McNutt repeatedly urged local draft boards to give more weight to a man's occupation and less to his status as a family man. He finally issued a ruling to eliminate fatherhood as grounds for deferment unless induction would subject the man's family to extreme hardship, a case that most major league players would have been hard pressed to prove.

The "father draft" was scheduled to begin on October 1, 1943. But it aroused a storm of public protest and became a tender political issue. Some citizens called for the induction of Japanese-Americans, 17-year-olds, and "moral undesirables" so fathers could stay home. Most soldiers were not engaged in combat, and some people believed that single women should be conscripted; a Gallup Poll reported that the drafting of women was favored by a majority of women but opposed by a majority of men. It was never seriously considered by Congress.

Others suspected that the draft was overlooking able-bodied men without children. Widely publicized errors fed public skepticism about the efficiency of the draft classification process. J.W. Keene of Caribou, Maine, was classified 1-A at the age of 90. O.D. Meyer of Newark, New Jersey, passed his physical exam although deaf and missing his trigger finger. Pitcher Tom Sunkel of the New York Giants was classified 1-A although blind in his left eye.

Nearly one third of the men called for induction were being re-

jected as physically, mentally, or morally unfit, and many citizens
thought that some of these rejects should serve. A podiatrist testi-
fied that foot troubles accounted for 30 percent of the physical re-
jections; couldn't men with flat feet serve some military purpose?
In Tennessee, where 5,000 men had been rejected because of il-
literacy, former Sergeant Alvin C. York, 54, a renowned World
War I combat hero, offered to organize a battalion of Tennessee il-
literates under his command. "They are crack shots," York said.
"They are the best soldiers in the world." The Army politely declined.

To head off the "father draft," Senator Burton K. Wheeler of
Montana introduced legislation that put fathers at the bottom of
the draft list, whatever their job, so long as the child was conceived
before Pearl Harbor and the parents were still married. Congress
passed the bill, and President Roosevelt signed it on December 19,
1943. "Pre-Pearl fathers," as the shorthand of the day put it, were
to be taken only when a local draft board could find no one else.
Purely by accident, Congress had saved baseball from a draft policy that might have endangered continuation of the game.

In addition to their worries about the draft, baseball club owners
had to cope with the patriotism of many of their employees. Following the example set by Feller and Greenberg, a great many
baseball figures enlisted in military service during World War II.
Some could have stayed out altogether; others could have postponed induction by awaiting the draft. Since an athletic career is
short, their financial sacrifice was greater than most. They also set
an important example for other young men, and helped to glamor-
ize military service. That was important; World War II had to be
won, and to win it the United States had to raise an armed force of
nearly sixteen million men. The situation bore little resemblance to
the Vietnam War, which many Americans considered unwise to
begin with and for which only a fraction of the country's able young
men were needed.

Perhaps the most glamorous military reputation owned by a
baseball man was that of Larry MacPhail, general manager of the
Brooklyn Dodgers, who gave up a $70,000 salary in late 1942 for a
commission as an Army lieutenant colonel. MacPhail had been a

daring and ingenious soldier in World War I. On January 6, 1919, shortly after the Armistice was declared, MacPhail and seven other soldiers set out on an unauthorized mission of their own making. They decided to kidnap Kaiser Wilhelm, Germany's wartime leader, who was then a refugee living at the castle of Count von Bentinck at Amerongen, Holland. The Americans disarmed a guard and made their way into the Kaiser's drawing room, but were scared away by German soldiers. On his way out, MacPhail grabbed the Kaiser's ashtray, a souvenir he proudly displayed thereafter.

Also enlisting in late 1942 was Ted Lyons, 41, who surely knew that he was sacrificing the last years of his outstanding career. Despite his age, Lyons was not over the hill as a pitcher. In 1942, he won fourteen and lost six for the Chicago White Sox, finishing all twenty games that he started.

Lyons joined the Marines. Eldon Auker, the underhand pitcher, could not qualify for military service because of his arm injury, but retired from baseball to work year round in a Detroit war factory. Auker won fourteen and lost thirteen for the 1942 Browns; he was then traded to Washington. "Whereas my decision to quit baseball and retain my position in war work will certainly not win the war, a different attitude by too many other ballplayers might lose it for us," Auker wrote to Clark Griffith, owner of the Senators. Pitcher Harry Eisenstat of Cleveland also stuck with a defense plant job, citing it as his patriotic duty.

Hal Weafer, 42, a minor league umpire who had finally won promotion to the American League for the 1943 season, joined the Navy instead. Connie Mack's daughter, Mrs. Mary Mack Riley, joined the WAACS.

Birdie Tebbetts, Detroit's catcher, joined the Army Air Corps. He was ordered to organize an athletic program at Waco, Texas, and did so with a flare. At Tebbetts' urging, a number of major and minor league players joined the Air Corps at Waco. They included pitcher Sid Hudson and outfielder Bruce Campbell of Washington, who were recruited by Tebbetts independently of one another and were surprised to meet at Waco.

Another recruiter was sportscaster Jack Starr of station KXOK in St. Louis. Starr extolled sea service on his radio programs and finally joined the Navy in an enlistment ceremony that was broadcast live under the sponsorship of Griesedieck Brothers beer. Roy A. Shannon, the brewery's advertising manager, and J. G. Taylor Spink of the *Sporting News* participated in the ceremony.

Right fielder Tommy Henrich of the Yankees joined the Coast Guard. So did Hank Majeski, the 1942 batting champion of the International League, whom the Yankees had expected to play at third base, veteran Red Rolfe having retired to coach baseball at Yale. Although deferred, Yankee veteran George (Twinkletoes) Selkirk, 34, joined the Navy, as did Buddy Hassett, the Yankee first baseman.

Hassett, who was an average player on the field but an outstanding Irish tenor in the clubhouse, was 30 years old and sportswriter Dan Daniel speculated that he might be washed up as a player by the time the war ended. "It will be a long time before we are rid of the menace of the sneaks from Nippon," Daniel wrote.

Ted Williams, 24, carried out his promise to enlist, entering the Navy for pilot training. Like Williams, Joe DiMaggio had been criticized for accepting a deferment. For example, in a column of letters to the sports editor published on January 31, 1942, the New York *Times* included this from one M. M. Caretti of New York:

"Men have been drafted into the Army who never have earned more than a small salary in civilian life, who had no sideline returns to fall back on, and who had wives and children to support. On the other hand, especially in baseball, there are quite a few, too many, high-salaried players, some of them with businesses on the side, who have been exempted from the service. A case in point is Joe DiMaggio of the Yankees. Why he ever was exempted from service is beyond comprehension. Not that he is the only one, however. It seems to me that men well known in sport should take the lead in volunteering for their country in time of need and not wait to be drafted, much less accept exemption."

DiMaggio's military plans were mixed up with his marital difficulties, at least in public speculation. In December of 1942, Mrs. Dorothy Arnold DiMaggio, who before their marriage had been a movie actress, went to Reno seeking a divorce. The DiMaggios had a baby; being a father could postpone DiMaggio's induction if the couple stayed together. The *Sporting News* said that Ed Barrow, the Yankee president, might act as a marriage counselor.

Whether he did or not, the DiMaggios patched up their difficulties for a little while, and DiMaggio, 28, was given a 3-A draft classification. But in February of 1943 he joined the Army, not bothering to notify the Yankees, who had sent him a 1943 contract that called for a pay cut from $43,750 to $40,000.

DiMaggio even refused the furlough that soldiers were allowed to take before beginning their service. Dan Daniel was moved. "He is built for the soldier," Daniel wrote. "He has the temperament for the soldier. He has gone into the Army looking for no favors, searching for no job as a coach. He wants to fight, and when he gets his chance, he will prove a credit to himself and his game and the Yanks and his family. This DiMaggio guy really has it." Mrs. DiMaggio divorced Sergeant DiMaggio the following May.

Branch Rickey became so carried away with the succession of patriotic enlistments that he suggested that baseball use only players who would otherwise be idle. A sportswriter, J. Roy Stockton of the St. Louis *Post-Dispatch*, noted that such a policy wouldn't make for much of a game. "A man so helpless physically that he would be idle if it were not for baseball, with a nation at war and workers needed in all fields, could not find a place on a class E minor league club, unless perhaps as a ticket-taker," Stockton wrote.

Although soldiers groused enough about military life, baseball players were rarely quoted on the subject unless their comments were positive. The *Sporting News* carried a letter from Myril Hoag, a Chicago White Sox outfielder who had joined the Army Air Corps. "Living in the barracks with so many swell fellows reminds me of my cutup days in the major leagues," Hoag wrote.

Ted Williams and Johnny Beazley, who also had enlisted following the 1942 season, were quoted as expressing interest in a military career. "If I can make a success of flying, I'd just as soon stay in service—provided I could get a month off once in a while to go hunting," Williams said. "I'm going to make a career of the Army, and the game is a thing of the past for me," said Beazley, according to the Fort Oglethorpe post newspaper. Jack Malaney of the Boston *Post* suggested that fans take Williams' comment with a grain of salt, since the slugger received "more pay than a half-dozen admirals." Beazley personally wrote off prospects for his military career in a speech while accepting the Rookie of the Year award at a Chicago banquet in December of 1942. "This stuff about never coming back to baseball is a lot of bull," he said.

The popular buildup of military life no doubt made service more tolerable; servicemen were portrayed as dashing figures. Buddy Lewis, the Washington Senators' star, who served nearly four years as an Army Air Force transport pilot:

The Air Corps was probably more glamorous in World War II than baseball, and flying to me was the most wonderful thing in the world. Oh, my God almighty, I just wouldn't take anything for my years of flying. You could say my record in baseball might have been better otherwise. But fate injected me into this thing, and I liked it.

Before we went overseas, us transport pilots were stationed at Lawson Field in Georgia. As part of our training, they'd say, "Take a crew and go to any city you want to on the weekends. Let us know what you're doing and when you're going to be back, but go." I guess I spent every weekend away.

I took a planeload into Washington on one of these trips in 1943, and I went out to Griffith Stadium and I spoke to everybody I knew. I told them I was coming by with my plane; I had landed at Andrews Air Base, and I had to leave to go back to Georgia late in the afternoon. I broke every rule in the book. I knew where Griffith Stadium was. There was a game on, and I flew straight there and made a dive over the stadium. I was down low enough so I could almost read the letters on the uniforms. George Case told me later that he was the batter, and he threw his bat in the air. I took off. I knew I was in the wrong, and I expected to be reprimanded. We were under a strict command, almost like West Point. But there were no repercussions. I was surprised the people in the Pentagon didn't read about it in the paper and get in touch with my commanding officer.

CHAPTER 9

The 1943 Runaways

Altogether, 219 players listed on major league rosters spent all or most of the 1943 season in military service. Many of them were front-line players.

Of the major league all-star team selected after the 1942 season by the *Sporting News*, five were in service in 1943—Johnny Mize, Johnny Pesky, Ted Williams, Joe DiMaggio, and Enos Slaughter. Six were not—second baseman Joe Gordon of the Yankees, third baseman Stan Hack of the Cubs, catcher Mickey Owen of the Dodgers, and pitchers Tex Hughson of the Red Sox, Ernie Bonham of the Yankees, and Mort Cooper of the Cardinals. Two players selected on the 1941 postseason all-star team, Bob Feller and Cecil Travis, had missed the 1942 season and were still in service. So was Hank Greenberg, a member of the 1940 major league all-star team.

The Yankees were missing DiMaggio, Henrich, Hassett, Rizzuto, and Ruffing; in addition, Rolfe had retired. The Red Sox, second in 1942, had lost Williams, Pesky, Dom DiMaggio, catcher Frankie Pytlak, and pitcher Charley Wagner. Dave (Boo) Ferris, a promising pitcher in the Red Sox farm system, also had entered service.

The Browns, third in 1942, were more fortunate, losing only out-fielder Walt Judnich and pitcher Jack Kramer from among their starters. Second baseman Johnny Lucadello and shortstop Johnnie Berardino had entered service, but they had lost their jobs the year before to Don Gutteridge and Vern Stephens, respectively. Brownie part-timers in service included outfielders Joe Grace and Glenn (Red) McQuillen, and pitcher Pete Appleton.

Besides Feller and outfielder Soup Campbell, the Cleveland Indians started 1943 without catcher Jim Hegan and two promising youngsters, first baseman Eddie Robinson and third baseman Bob Lemon, who later won election in 1976 to the Hall of Fame as a pitcher. Cleveland pitcher Red Embree stayed on his farm in 1943.

From Detroit, outfielders Greenberg, Barney McCosky, and Pat Mullin, all excellent hitters, were in service. So was Hoot Evers, a potential outfield replacement who had starred for the Tigers' Beaumont, Texas, farm club in 1942. The Tigers also had lost catcher Birdie Tebbetts, pitchers Fred Hutchinson and Al Benton, and second baseman Charlie Gehringer.

The White Sox entered the 1943 season without their best pitcher, Ted Lyons, their best hitter, outfielder Taft Wright, and two other regulars, third baseman Bob Kennedy and outfielder Myril Hoag.

The Senators were missing Lewis, Travis, outfielder Bruce Campbell, and two starting pitchers, Sid Hudson and Walt Masterson. From the Athletics, the armed forces had taken four starters—outfielder Sam Chapman and infielders Benny McCoy, Crash Davis, and Buddy Blair. The Athletics' top pitcher, Phil Marchildon, and another starting pitcher, Dick Fowler, had entered the armed forces of Canada, their native country.

The Cardinals lost two of their fine outfielders, Slaughter and Terry Moore, plus pitchers John Beazley and John Grodzicki. From the Dodgers, Pete Reiser was drafted; shortstop Pee Wee Reese and pitchers Larry French and Hugh Casey joined the Navy. Outfielder Johnny Rizzo was inducted. So were pitcher Joe Hatten and outfielder Carl Furillo, promising Brooklyn farmhands. The

Dodgers led the league in catchers in service with three—Don Padgett, Herman Franks, and Cliff Dapper—but starter Owen was spared.

The Dodgers almost lost veterans Dolf Camilli and Arky Vaughan, both of whom expressed a desire to work their ranches during the summer, but Branch Rickey finally coaxed them back to Brooklyn. With Cookie Lavagetto already in service, Brooklyn's infield was further weakened by the induction of reserves Lew Riggs and Stan Rojek.

The New York Giants were badly hurt. Slugger Mize joined the Navy. His sub, Babe Young, also was inducted, as was Clint Hartung, a highly regarded prospect. Other Giants who entered military service included outfielder Willard Marshall, catcher Harry (the Horse) Danning, infielder Buddy Blattner, and pitchers Hal (Prince) Schumacher, Dave Koslo (real name Koslowski), and Bob Carpenter. Fiddler Bill McGee, another pitcher, was deferred as a farmer and worked his farm all summer. So did outfielder Hank Leiber, who raised chickens in Arizona.

The Cincinnati Reds lost catcher Ray Lamanno, outfielders Mike McCormick and Clyde Vollmer, infield prospects Bobby Adams and Benny Zientara, and a promising young pitcher, Ewell (The Whip) Blackwell. Pittsburgh was without pitchers Ken Heintzelman and Lefty Wilkie, and infielder Billy Cox. Pirate catcher Babe (Blimp) Phelps, a power hitter, quit baseball because he preferred his job as a baggagemaster at the Odenton, Maryland, railroad depot.

The Chicago Cubs' service roster included second baseman Lou Stringer, first baseman Eddie Waitkus, catcher Bob Scheffing, shortstop Bob Sturgeon, and pitchers Johnny Schmitz and Vern Olsen.

The Boston Braves' top relief pitcher, young Johnny Sain, joined the Navy Air Corps, and a rookie pitching prospect, Warren Spahn, entered the Army. The service also took pitcher Lou Tost, third baseman Nanny Fernandez, first baseman Buddy Gremp, outfielder Max West, and second baseman Sibby Sisti, who had replaced 'Bama Rowell, drafted a year before.

The Phillies lost outfielder Ernie (Chief) Koy and pitchers Tommy Hughes and Frank Hoerst. Two other Phil starters, Hugh Mulcahy and Lee Grissom, were still in service, as was outfielder Joe Marty. "If the Phillies suffer losses through injuries, sore arms or further loss to the service, the team is going to look like the cat that was machine-gunned on the back fence," Stan Baumgartner wrote in the *Sporting News*.

As teams cast about for replacements, some players were suddenly lifted from plodding careers as if touched by a magic wand. The Yankees acquired Roy (Stormy) Weatherly from Cleveland to play center field and Nick Etten from the Phillies to play first base. "I don't have to tell you my reaction when told I belonged to New York," Weatherly told an interviewer at the time. "I don't have to tell you that every ballplayer's prayers are directed toward New York and a job with the Yankees." Etten had played lackadaisically in 1942 as the Phils lost 109 games. "Imagine a man in that environment hearing that he had been sold to the Yankees!" he said. Etten played to the new role, suddenly becoming a power hitter.

The Cardinals resurrected Debs Garms, 35, who had won the 1940 National League batting championship for Pittsburgh but had been consigned to the minor leagues when his batting average dropped ninety-one points the following year. After about one third of the 1943 season, the Cardinals got outfielder Danny Litwhiler from the Phillies for outfielders Buster Adams and Coaker Triplett.

Triplett started well, but soon adapted to the Phils as deftly as Etten had to the Yankees. Trailing the Reds 6 to 0 one day, the Phils loaded the bases with no one out. Triplett was on second base and set out to steal third, forcing Ron Northey to run for home, where he was tagged out. As Triplett stood off third base, kicking the dirt and hanging his head in shame, he failed to see the third baseman gesture for the ball, catch it and turn toward him. But he felt the tag; double play.

Playing talent was getting so short in 1943 that James T. Gallagher, general manager of the Chicago Cubs, proposed that the clubs pool their players to equalize strength, and warned that there might be a scarcity of players after the war. "That, then, might be the time for a reconstruction of baseball law which would eliminate the reserve clause," Gallagher said. Sam Breadon, owner of the Cardinals, called Gallagher's suggestions "unthinkable, unworkable . . . an offspring of socialism that has no business in baseball."

Shortly before the 1943 season began, some of the lesser teams began to get their hopes up. Lou Boudreau, Cleveland's playing manager, said the Indians were the "team to beat" in the American League. "Our team should be better than last season, and the rest of the league is coming back to us," said Clark Griffith of the Senators. Frankie Frisch, manager of the Pittsburgh Pirates, expressed similar sentiments about the National League.

The Yankees and Cardinals were favored to repeat as pennant winners, but toward the end of May, the Indians and Dodgers were in front. Rookies, old men, and career journeymen were suddenly stars. Outfielder Oris Hockett, a veteran who had never before distinguished himself, was Cleveland's best hitter. Paul Waner, 40, the former Pittsburgh star, was playing in the Brooklyn outfield, wearing glasses for the first time in his career, and batting around .400. Johnny Allen, 38, who had once starred for Cleveland, won three straight games in relief for the Dodgers, but was then suspended thirty days for charging and shaking umpire George Barr. Manager Leo Durocher finally tackled Allen to keep him from the umpire.

The Phillies got off to a fast start and were running fourth. Danny Litwhiler, Earl Naylor, Babe Dahlgren, and Jimmy Wasdell were hitting well. Schoolboy Rowe, 33, the former Tiger star, was making a comeback after winning only two games in 1942. He became the Phils' pitching ace and hit a grand slam home run as a pinch hitter. One Phillie fan ordered World Series tickets, and 31,176 came to Shibe Park for a doubleheader against Pittsburgh.

"Nobody is intimidating anybody," said Steve O'Neill, manager of the Tigers. "The two leagues are leveled off, and as we go along, the tendency toward that process will increase. . . . The top clubs

lose five players and have to take on five who are about on a level
with the five the cellar team acquired to fill in. You lose a DiMaggio and get a Weatherly. It is going to be a grand race."

O'Neill was wrong. By the All-Star break in mid-July, the Yankees and Cardinals were on top, largely because their farm systems
were providing excellent young players.

Joe Gordon and Charlie Keller were not hitting up to their usual
standards, but the Yankees were getting plenty of punch from Nick
Etten and two rookies. One, Johnny Lindell, had flunked his trial
as a pitcher but was given a chance in the outfield because of his
power hitting. The other, Billy Johnson, inherited the third base
job when Rolfe retired and Majeski entered military service.

Playing superb deferment baseball, the Yankees had sold infielder Gerry Priddy to Washington, apparently because he had no
children and was likely to be drafted. The only bachelors on the
1943 Yankees were pitcher Atley Donald, who was 4-F because of
eye and back ailments, and rookie infielder Snuffy Stirnweiss, who
supported his mother and sister and had a stomach ulcer besides.

Detroit, in second place, was being paced by rookie outfielder
Dick Wakefield, who had been signed off the University of Michigan campus for the largest bonus ever paid to an amateur—
$52,000 and a new Packard. Joe Hoover, a rookie at 28, was play-
ing shortstop so smoothly that he was nicknamed "The Carpet
Sweeper." Dizzy Trout was pitching well, and lefty Hal Newhouser
was showing signs of stardom after three mediocre seasons. He
struck out fourteen Yankees in one game. Newhouser was 4-F be
cause of a heart ailment. He neither smoked nor drank but was an
impressive trencherman; Trout said he once saw him consume a
five-pound roast.

Superb pitching had moved Washington into third place. Milo
Candini, a rookie, won his first seven games. Dutch Leonard, Early
Wynn, and Alex Carrasquel also were winning. The Senators
lacked batting strength, but stole sixty-two bases in the first two
months of the season. George Case was leading the league in stolen
bases and Mickey Vernon was second.

The White Sox were fourth. Rookie Guy Curtright, 30, who

had earned a master's degree at the University of Missouri while playing nine years in the minor leagues, hit safely in twenty-six straight games and became Chicago's cleanup hitter. Gordon Maltzberger, 31, another rookie, was pitching well in relief.

After a poor start, the Browns had climbed to fifth place, seven and a half games out of first. As a good omen for the future, Vern Stephens and George McQuinn flunked Army physical examinations. Stephens was leading the league in runs batted in. While winning eighteen of twenty-six games during June, the Browns also had been getting good hitting from Chet Laabs, Don Gutteridge, rookie Al Zarilla, and Mike Chartak, whom the *Sporting News* called "The Volga Batman" because of his Russian heritage.

Cleveland had fallen to sixth place, largely because of injuries to Hockett, third baseman Ken Keltner, rookie center fielder Hank Edwards, and veteran pitcher Mel Harder. Lou Boudreau, the Indians' manager and shortstop, caught one game because he had no healthy catchers.

The Red Sox were seventh despite the pinch-hitting of their manager, Joe Cronin, 37. In successive doubleheaders against the Athletics in June, Cronin pinch-hit four times and slammed three home runs, all with two men on base. But the Red Sox had not found adequate replacements for Williams, DiMaggio, or Pesky. Al Simmons, 41, the great Philadelphia Athletics outfielder of the 1920s and 1930s, was restored to playing status by the Red Sox, but could no longer hit very well. His only home run of the season tied a game at Yankee Stadium in the ninth inning, but the Yankees won it in their half.

Just as Simmons was too old, a rookie Red Sox outfielder, George (Catfish) Metkovich, was too young. He had flunked a spring training trial with the Boston Braves in 1940 because of a bizarre fishing accident that gave him his nickname. Metkovich caught a three-foot catfish off a bridge, put his foot on its back while trying to extricate the hook, and was badly hurt when the catfish raised a sharp fin that cut through the crepe sole of Metkovich's shoe and through most of his foot. The fin was removed by surgery.

"I've got a young first baseman by the name of Metkovich who's in the hospital," Casey Stengel, manager of the Braves, said at the time. "Do you know how? He was attacked by a catfish!"

(As a spring training accident, Metkovich's mishap rivaled that of Fat Freddie Fitzsimmons, the Giant pitcher. While rocking on a hotel veranda, Fitzsimmons let a hand droop and rocked on his fingers.)

The Cardinals closed an Eastern trip in early July with six straight wins, and led Brooklyn by five and a half games at the All-Star break. On July 15, Howard Pollet pitched his fifth shutout, and was called into the Army Air Corps. Ernie White, another left-handed pitcher, had a sore arm. But Harry Brecheen had finally made the team. He was 28. When Pollet left, the Cardinals called up another 28-year-old rookie southpaw, Al Brazle, from Sacramento. Jimmy Brown also was drafted, but he had already lost his second base job to rookie Lou Klein, a superior hitter. Another youngster, Ray Sanders, had won the first base job from Johnny Hopp. Outdoing each other, Stan Musial hit safely in seventeen straight games, Klein and Harry Walker in twenty-one, and George Kurowski in twenty-two.

The Dodgers could not find a shortstop to replace Pee Wee Reese. One candidate, Alban Glossop, chased a pop fly in practice with such abandon that he stepped on Paul Waner's foot, inflicting a cut that required eleven stitches. Catcher Mickey Owen was tried at short, and catcher Dee Moore at third base. Manager Durocher, 38, who had not played since 1941, started six games at short without convincing himself that he could handle the job.

Durocher was testy to the point of hurting his team. He and pitcher Buck Newsom, neither of whom were diplomats by nature, argued angrily about the manner of pitching to various hitters. Durocher suspended Newsom, who with nine wins was Brooklyn's best pitcher. Other players threatened to strike in support of Newsom. In a tense clubhouse meeting on July 10, Durocher called out the starting lineup, player by player. Only Arky Vaughan refused to play, and he skipped only one game. To gain peace, Rickey traded Newsom to the Browns for pitchers Archie McKain and Fritz

Ostermueller, who between them had one victory. "The dirtiest deal I ever got," said Newsom, who knew whereof he spoke, having been with the Browns twice before.

The Pittsburgh Pirates were third. They had one of baseball's leading gate attractions in pitcher Rip Sewell, who about once an inning threw his "blooper ball," a pitch that arched about twenty feet high. Sewell won ten of his first twelve decisions. Vince Di-Maggio hit six home runs in ten days. But two effective pitchers, Johnny Lanning and Jack Hallett, were drafted in late June. Rookie shortstop Huck Geary could not shake his homesickness and repeatedly left the team to visit his wife and children in Buffalo.

Cincinnati was fourth at the All-Star break. The Phillies were fifth, the Boston Braves sixth, the Cubs seventh, and the Giants last. The Cubs' farm team at Los Angeles was leading the Pacific Coast League, and the Los Angeles manager, Lefty O'Doul, suggested that the Cubs would improve if the two teams swapped rosters. Eddie Stanky, a Cub rookie, was playing well; he angered Dodger veteran Arky Vaughan by bowling him over with a hard slide.

The Giants were dreadful. Neither Joe Orengo nor Nap Reyes could adequately replace Mize at first base, and manager Mel Ott was having an off year at bat. Carl Hubbell, 40, pitched a one-hitter against Pittsburgh June 5, but it was his first win of the year.

In the All-Star game, played in Philadelphia the night of July 6, the American League won, 5 to 3, on a three-run homer in the second by Bobby Doerr of the Red Sox. Doerr connected off Mort Cooper, who had yielded the decisive home runs in the American League's 1942 All-Star victory. Fourteen of the fifty players on the 1942 All-Star squads were in military service. Flaunting the American League's superiority, manager Joe McCarthy did not play any of the six Yankees named to the All-Star team.

By early August, the Cardinals were eleven and a half games ahead and the Yankees were nine ahead. Stan Musial was leading the National League in batting. Nick Etten and Bill Johnson were first and second in the American League in runs batted in. The Cards won fifteen of seventeen games, including four straight from Brooklyn. The methodical Yankees won a majority of the games in each of thirteen straight series before the Senators stopped them by sweeping a doubleheader September 2.

The hopes of other teams had faded. As the Phils dropped to seventh place, owner William D. Cox fired manager Bucky Harris, complaining that he called his players "jerks" and failed to inspire them. Freddie Fitzsimmons, the pitcher, was hired to replace him.

At Brooklyn, Branch Rickey adopted the same youth policy that had served him so well in St. Louis. He sold Joe Medwick and Johnny Allen to the Giants. Rex Barney, 18, a wild fast-ball pitcher just out of high school, joined the Dodgers. So did Howie Schultz, 21, a first baseman who was too tall for the Army at 6 feet 6½ inches. The *Sporting News* called him "The Leaning Tower of Flatbush."

The Cardinals finished with 105 wins; Cincinnati was second, eighteen games behind. Musial led the league in batting with .357 and Cooper in pitching with twenty-one wins and eight losses. The Yankees won ninety-eight games and finished thirteen and a half games ahead of Washington. Etten drove in 107 runs, Johnson ninety-four, and Keller eighty-six; Spud Chandler won twenty games and lost four.

The World Series matched the only two really good teams left in baseball, the Cardinals and Yankees having been sustained by player acquisitions and, most of all, by their superior farm systems. Not counting pitchers, the only men in the Yankee starting lineups of both the 1942 and 1943 World Series were Joe Gordon, Charlie Keller, and Bill Dickey. The only Cardinal starters both years were Musial, Marion, Whitey Kurowski, and Walker Cooper.

To reduce travel, the first three Series games were played in New York, the remainder in St. Louis. Chandler stopped the Cardinals in the first game, 4 to 2, with the help of a home run by Gordon and a wild pitch by Max Lanier, the Cardinal pitcher. Shortly before the second game, Mort and Walker Cooper of the Cardinals received word that their father had died. Mort pitched anyway and Walker caught; the Cardinals won, 4 to 3, on home runs by Marion and Sanders.

The Yankees won the third game, 6 to 2, with five runs in the eighth, three of them driven home by Johnson's triple. They won the fourth, 2 to 1, as pitcher Marius Russo doubled and scored the winning run in the eighth. In the fifth and last game, Bill Dickey's homer, only the second Yankee home run of the Series, provided the only runs as Chandler beat Cooper, 2 to 0. Superb Yankee pitching had reversed the outcome of the 1942 Series.

CHAPTER 10

Patching a Brown
Purse with Sows' Ears

The Browns finished sixth in 1943. Laabs's home run output dropped to seventeen and he led the league in strikeouts with 105. McQuinn hit only .243 and Frankie Hayes, a catcher from whom much had been expected, hit .188 and grumped continually about having to play for the Browns. But adversity had its constructive side. The Browns were building for 1944.

The new Brownies were of the usual kind. As important as any was Mike Kreevich, a veteran center fielder who still shares a major league hitting record: most double plays hit into in one game—four. Kreevich had been released by the lowly Philadelphia Athletics after the 1942 season because he drank too much. Luke Sewell, the Brownie manager, had played with Kreevich on the Chicago White Sox in the late 1930s and thought he was worth reclaiming. Sewell:

Mike had had this drinking problem before, but I was in Chicago with him for four years and I never knew it. I never saw Mike take as much as a bottle of beer. Then he went over to Philadelphia, and they got him rooming with Al Simmons. Mike is a witty little fellow, funny, and Al got to taking him around as a good sidekick. That got Mike back on liquor, and Connie Mack released him, because he couldn't sober him up.

So I went out to Springfield, Illinois, where Mike lived, that winter. I called him up, and he was going to meet me at the Abraham Lincoln Hotel at 11 o'clock on Sunday morning. I went there to meet him, and he just reeled in. I said, "Mike, we can use you, but only if you're sober. If you don't stay sober I'm going to have to release you." He said, "You don't have to worry about it.", I said, "How much do you want?" He told me what salary he wanted, and I said, "Now, I'm going to give you another $2,000." I think it came to $14,000, a good salary in those days. He was worth it; Mike Kreevich was a great outfielder.

So he signed the contract. I had a friend, one of the originators of Alcoholics Anonymous. I got hold of him, and he helped me get hold of a fellow who got hold of Mike, down in Springfield, and he got straightened out.

Kreevich also had two children born before Pearl Harbor, providing him with a draft deferment.

Milt (Skippy) Byrnes, another outfielder, was brought up from Toledo. Byrnes was 4-F because of a bronchial condition, and had difficulty judging fly balls. Sewell:

To show you how the scouting was, the reports on Byrnes were that he was one of the better center fielders in the minor leagues but he couldn't hit. When he got to the majors, we found it was just reversed. He was a good hitter but couldn't field.

In the annual draft of minor league players, the Browns picked up Nelson Potter, a screwball pitcher, who had won nineteen games for Louisville in 1942 but, like Kreevich, was considered a has-been by other major league clubs. Potter had an undistinguished record during four seasons with the Athletics and Red Sox. A surgeon's error sent him to the minor leagues, which in turn made him available to the Browns, and eventually provided him with a 4-F draft classification. Potter:

I had a torn cartilage in my right knee, and I had two knee operations— one in Philadelphia in '38 and then another one in Chicago. I had a bad experience my first operation. The doctor removed the wrong cartilage, so then I had to go back in and have another operation.

I had had that second operation in 1940, and I didn't recover right away. I was with the Boston Red Sox and they sent me to Louisville. My knee came around pretty good then, and I was sold to the Browns from there, in 1943.

The team was nothing outstanding in '43. I started relieving, and then I started. The club got going pretty good; they thought we had a chance to really do something that year, and remember? They bought Buck Newsom that year, from Brooklyn. He called himself Bobo, you know.

When they bought Buck, I went back to the bullpen for a while. But Buck, he just didn't materialize for us. They hit him hard, time after time. They knocked him out nine straight times. It seemed like anywhere from the second to the fifth inning he'd be gone. He'd start, and I'd relieve him. He'd start, and I'd relieve him. I came out to the clubhouse one day and I said, "Say, Buck, when are you and I pitching again?"

He had a few run-ins with some sportswriters there. Buck was having some family troubles and someone was suing him for some unpaid bills or something. After he'd been knocked out so many times he finally finished a ball game, and one of the writers said the reason he did it was because he saw the sheriff in the stands and was afraid to leave the field. Buck got mad about that. Anyway, after he'd been knocked out nine or ten times the Browns got rid of him. Sold him to Washington.

Throwing on the sidelines there in St. Louis in 1943, I came up with a slider that made the difference in my pitching. Before that, I had just a screwball and a curve ball; my fast ball was never too outstanding. I picked up that slider real quick, and it just happened to fit in nice, and it was easy for me to throw. The batters used to start leaning out over the plate for the screwball; now I could move that slider in on their fists. It made a tremendous difference. There were just a few pitchers using the slider then.

Pitcher Jack Kramer, who had lost sixteen games as a Brownie rookie in 1939 and had not improved much the following two years, skipped the 1942 season in favor of a war plant job. He then joined the Seabees but was given a medical discharge during the summer of 1943 because he suffered from asthma. The Browns sent Kramer to Toledo, where he suddenly blossomed, winning eight straight games including a no-hitter.

During the 1943 season, the Browns traded Harlond Clift to Washington for Ellis Clary; both were third basemen. The trade exemplified Sewell's determination to rid the team of players with a losing attitude and his willingness to shepherd ne'er-do-wells. Clary was popular among the players because of his wit, but he had a reputation for precipitating fights. "Clary was real good with his fists," recalled Red Hayworth, a catcher and teammate of Clary's in

St. Louis. "He was a street fighter. He was a fellow who could smile and hit you at the same time."

Clift had developed from humble beginnings. During a tryout in 1931, he scuttled to his left after a ground ball, stepped on his own outstretched glove, somersaulted, and broke his collarbone. Perhaps sensing that they had found one of their own, the Browns signed him.

Clift developed into a power hitter, driving in 118 runs in 1937 and again in 1938. But by 1943 his hitting had tailed off, and after nine straight seasons with the Browns he was accustomed to losing. "Clift had dropped to .230 in hitting, and according to New York critics, acted like a man in a fog," reported the *Sporting News*. Nevertheless, Clift was coveted by Clark Griffith of the Senators. Sewell:

One day Don Barnes called me. He said, "How well do you like Clift?" I said, "Don, he's a pretty good ballplayer, but we can't win with him." You see, when it came down to the clinches, Clift didn't field or hit. He said, "Well, Griff just keeps hounding me to death to buy him." I said, "You tell Griff that we're going to let him have Clift, but I don't want him to blame us for what he gets." We sold him; I think we got $35,000 and a ballplayer.

So Clift comes into St. Louis with the Senators, and one of his children has the mumps. Clift has never had the mumps. He gets the mumps, and finally this mumps gets down into his testicles. He was in the hospital, and he didn't play any more that year. He went home to his farm out in the state of Washington. He was riding a horse, and damned if this horse didn't throw him. He fell on his right shoulder, and do you know I don't think he played fifty ball games for Griff after Griff had put out this money for him. Every time I saw Griff after that—he always had a cigar in his mouth—he'd say to me, "You owe me a ballplayer." Well, Jeez. That was a tough break for Griff.

But not for the Browns. While awaiting Clary's arrival from Washington, Sewell put Mark Christman, a utility player, at third base. By the time Clary arrived, the job was taken. Christman:

Clary called the Browns and told them that he wouldn't be able to get into St. Louis for about two weeks because he had to go home and pick up his family and drive them to St. Louis and make arrangements for a house.

So I had to play [laughs]. The first night I hit two triples. I hit well, and I never got out of the lineup the rest of the year or the next three years. I didn't dare get out of the lineup, because there were three or four kids sitting on the bench who could play as good as me or better [laughs].

Between the 1943 and 1944 seasons, the Browns put more patches on their patchwork team. Frankie Hayes, the disappointing catcher, was traded to the Athletics for rookies Barney Lutz, an outfielder who soon was drafted, and Sad Sam Zoldak, a pitcher who was 4-F. Another veteran catcher, Rick Ferrell, was traded to Washington for catcher Angelo Giuliani. When Giuliani decided to retire rather than play for the Browns, the Senators sent in his place Gene Moore, 34, a journeyman outfielder whose ranch in Texas adjoined that of Dizzy Dean. Moore's ailing knees had dropped him from the Boston Braves to the minor leagues in 1942.

From Minneapolis, the Browns drafted catcher Hank Helf, whose only distinction during a brief trial with the Indians in 1938 was the catching of a baseball dropped from the 700-foot-high Terminal Tower in Cleveland. Before he could report, the Army drafted Helf from the Browns. That left the Browns without a single catcher, an embarrassing circumstance for a team whose manager, Luke Sewell, and coaches, Zack Taylor and Fred (Bootnose) Hofmann, were all former catchers.

In fact, Brownie catching had been a problem ever since Sewell took over the team. In 1942, Sewell himself creaked through six games behind the plate at the age of 41. Having gained both years and poundage since then, Sewell did not want to repeat the experience. He and Bill DeWitt began searching for catchers.

They found two of them, Myron (Red) Hayworth, 29, and Frank Mancuso, 26. The two rookies had much in common. Hayworth was the younger and less talented brother of Ray Hayworth, a major league catcher for fifteen years. Mancuso was the younger and less talented brother of Gus Mancuso, a major league catcher for seventeen years.

Red Hayworth was a poor hitter but a good receiver, although he had some difficulty catching pop flies. Frank Mancuso was, in a way, a gift from heaven. He joined the Army in 1942, was commissioned a lieutenant, and volunteered for the paratroops. After four successful jumps, Mancuso was almost ready for combat duty. On his fifth jump, however, he fell from the airplane head first by mistake. His legs caught in the lines, and when he landed he broke a leg and wrenched his back. The back injury was so bad that Mancuso could neither stay in the Army nor, as the Browns soon discovered, look straight up for a pop fly.

The Brownie pitching, too, looked questionable. Steve Sundra, the team's best pitcher in 1943, was told that he would be drafted, although he was 34 years old. Bob Muncrief, another starter, was inclined to stick with his shipyard job in Houston. Denny Galehouse was deferred from induction because of his essential job at a Goodyear Aircraft factory in Akron, Ohio. His job, ironically, was to work with Selective Service in deciding which employees at the plant warranted deferment from the draft. Like a couple of dozen other major leaguers, Galehouse's war plant job was not in the same city as his baseball team. DeWitt said that if worse came to worst, he might use Galehouse as a weekend pitcher. The commissioner's office said that would be all right.

Desperately casting about for pitching help, DeWitt signed two long shots. One was Alvis (Tex) Shirley, 26, of Birthright, Texas, who had been released by the Athletics after losing his only decision in 1942. Shirley drank a lot and had a hot temper, characteristics that may not have endeared him to Connie Mack. But as a drunkard and brawler he could not hold a candle to the Browns' other pitching acquisition, Sigmund (Jack) Jakucki.

Jakucki played his first baseball with the Polish Citizens Club of Camden, New Jersey, his hometown. In 1927, he joined the Army, and became a star slugger and occasional pitcher for the Schofield Barracks Army baseball team in Hawaii. The Army discharged Jakucki in 1931. But he stayed in Hawaii to play semipro baseball, first with the Honolulu Braves and later with Asahi, a team made up of Hawaiians of Japanese descent, Hawaiians of Portuguese descent, and one hefty towhead of Polish descent named Jakucki.

Jakucki became such a star in Hawaii that fans paid his way to

San Francisco in 1934 for a tryout with the San Francisco Seals of the Pacific Coast League. The Seals sent Jakucki to Galveston of the Texas League, where manager Billy Webb converted him to a full-time pitcher. For Galveston in 1936, Jakucki had lost nineteen games by late August, and caught the Browns' eye; they brought him up. He lost three games, won none, and failed to impress manager Rogers Hornsby. Bill DeWitt:

Hornsby didn't like the guy, so in spring training of 1937 we sent him back to the minors. He bounced around from one club to another, and he'd get drunk all the time, so he got released. Then he started pitching for these semi-pro clubs in Galveston and Houston. He was a paperhanger and painter during the week and then he'd pitch on weekends.

We had forgotten all about him. Then in the spring of '44 we were short of pitchers, and this fellow down in Texas told us about him. He says, "You better get this guy. He can win some games for you." So we got him.

When the Browns surprised Jakucki with a contract, the big right-hander was 34 years old and had been out of organized baseball for six years. But he had become something of a legend in semi-pro ranks. Bob Broeg of the St. Louis *Post-Dispatch:*

Jakucki would get drunk. He pitched in the National Semi-pro Tournament in 1940 for Houston Grand Prize Beer. They won third place. Jakucki got stiff, and he got angry at an umpire, and he accosted him crossing the Arkansas River right outside Lawrence Stadium in Wichita, and he dangled the umpire over the rail by his heels. Oh, he was something, that Jakucki. Luke Sewell had some real cutthroats to handle.

Although the Browns had been naturally favored by the Army's preference for healthy men, the team had not yet fully benefited from the age of its players. The war took care of that in early 1944. Younger soldiers were doing so well that, for the first time, the Selective Service System began taking men 26 or younger in preference to older men. Advanced age was not a guarantee of deferment, but it helped.

Most major league teams were already listing toward age, older men being more likely to have fathered children before Pearl Harbor, but the Browns were particularly long in the tooth. McQuinn was 35, Gutteridge 32, and Christman 30. In the outfield, Kreevich was 36, Moore 34, Laabs 32, and Byrnes 27. Among the pitchers, Al Hollingsworth and George Caster were 36, Steve Sundra 34, Potter and Galehouse 32, and Muncrief 28.

Like a succession of lucky cards in poker, that and other changes in draft policy fell in the Browns' favor. Chet Laabs:

I was working in a Dodge Brothers defense plant in Detroit in the employment office. On April 4, 1944, I got my draft notice; I was ordered to report on the 15th. I was saved five days later. On the ninth of April, they came out with a ruling that anyone 27 or older, married, and working in a defense plant was deferred.

Mark Christman:

I went in and took my physical and passed, and they told me that within about two or three weeks I'd go. But I had two kids, and within that two weeks they passed a ruling that anybody over 26, married, with kids, wouldn't have to go in. I missed it by two weeks.

By the start of the 1944 season, about 340 major league players were in military service, not to mention more than 3,000 from the minor leagues. But not a single player of even the faintest reputation was inducted from the Browns between the 1943 and 1944 seasons, although pitcher Sundra was drafted shortly after the 1944 season began. The team listed fifteen players in the armed forces in 1944, but Sundra and Walt Judnich were the only regulars among them. Considering that Kramer, Mancuso, and Jakucki had been discharged, the Browns had gained more front-line players from the service than they had surrendered. The Army did not have an overt policy of rejecting Brownies; it just seemed that way.

The draft was meantime completing the destruction of other teams. The *Sporting News* suggested in an editorial that baseball players should get occupational deferments on the same footing as workers in war industries, but the government failed to take heed.

From the Yankees, Marius Russo and Roy Weatherly were inducted; Billy Johnson and Charlie Keller joined the Merchant Marine. During the Yankees' 1944 spring training at Atlantic City, New Jersey, Bill Dickey was drafted, although he was 37 years old and had sinus trouble. Two days later, Joe Gordon was drafted. "The Yankees have lost a ballclub," wrote Dan Daniel. "The race is as open as it ever has been, or ever will be."

Daniel was not exaggerating. The Yankees had lost every starter from their 1942 championship team, and the war was challenging their depth as well. The armed forces had taken four Yankee catchers—Dickey, Aaron Robinson, Ken Sears and Ken Silvestri. Rolfe, the regular third baseman, had retired; the service had taken his stand-ins, Hank Majeski and Bill Johnson. With John Sturm and Buddy Hassett gone, the Yankees were working on their third first baseman of the war, Nick Etten. Five Yankee outfielders were in service—DiMaggio, Henrich, Keller, Selkirk, and Weatherly. Among the starting pitchers, Red Ruffing and Marius Russo were in service, and Spud Chandler had been classified 1-A.

The team's ace relief pitcher, Johnny Murphy, had a war-plant job and might have pitched part-time, but Yankee President Ed Barrow was offended by the notion. "A man is either a major league player, or a war worker or bricklayer," Barrow said. "I think that using part-timers would demean big league ball. It would give us a semi-pro tone. The New York club wants none of it in any circumstances." With so many players gone, Yankee Stadium was to echo that season to the names of Bud Metheny, Mike Garbark, Oscar Grimes, and Monk Dubiel.

From Washington's runners-up of 1943, the service took first baseman Mickey Vernon, second baseman Gerry Priddy and catcher Jake Early. Cecil Travis and Buddy Lewis were by then Army veterans. Cleveland finished third in 1943, but then lost pitcher Chubby Dean, catcher Gene Desautels, and outfielders Gene Woodling and Hank Edwards. Pitchers Bob Feller and Tom Ferrick, catcher Jim Hegan, infielders Bob Lemon and Eddie Robinson and outfielders Soup Campbell and Buster Mills already were in service.

The Chicago White Sox, fourth in 1943, lost shortstop Luke Appling, the 1943 American League batting champion, second baseman Don Kolloway, and pitcher Eddie Smith. White Sox players remaining in service included pitching star Ted Lyons, infielders Bob Kennedy and Dario Lodigiani and outfielder Taft Wright.

Detroit's young outfield star, Dick Wakefield, joined the Navy Air Corps after leading the league in hits and doubles as a rookie in

1943. Also taken from the Tigers after the 1943 season were second baseman Jimmy Bloodworth and three starting pitchers—Virgil Trucks, Tommy Bridges, and Hal White. Detroit front-line players already in service included pitchers Al Benton, Fred Hutchinson, and Les Mueller, catcher Birdie Tebbetts, infielders Charlie Gehringer and Billy Hitchcock, and outfielders Hank Greenberg, Barney McCosky, Hoot Evers, and Pat Mullin. Like the Yankees, Detroit had a better team in service than on the field. To shore up their pitching, the Tigers tried Emery Hresko, too young for the draft at 17, and Ralph Siewert, too tall at 6 feet, 11 inches. Neither made it.

The Boston Red Sox, already laid low by the inductions of Williams, Pesky, and Dom DiMaggio, were not spared following their seventh-place finish of 1943. Joe Dobson, a starting pitcher, and Mace Brown, a veteran reliever, were inducted. Previously taken from Poston's pitching staff were Mickey Harris, Earl Johnson, and Charley Wagner.

The Philadelphia Athletics lost their best infielder, Pete Suder, and a good young outfielder, Elmer Valo. Most of Connie Mack's prewar team, poor as it was, had been inducted in previous years. Having traded knuckleballer Roger Wolff to Washington for Buck Newsom, Mack arranged to dramatize his acquisition by ceremonially signing Newsom during the winter banquet of the Philadelphia Baseball Writers Association. Mack brought the contract and a glowing smile, but Newsom failed to appear.

The Cardinals, unlike the Yankees, were lucky in war. From their 1942 championship team, five of the eight regulars and two of the best pitchers were still on hand in 1944. So were Ray Sanders, who had played well at first base in 1943; Harry Brecheen and George Munger, good rookie pitchers in 1943; and Danny Litwhiler, the outfielder acquired from the Phillies during the 1943 season.

Johnny Hopp was moved to center field. He was flanked by Litwhiler and Musial, Harry Walker having entered service. Kurowski, the third baseman, was 4-F; he suffered from osteomyelitis as a child, and had had a piece of bone removed from his right arm. Catcher Walker Cooper and shortstop Marty Marion had infirmities that moved them down the draft list because they could serve only in a limited capacity. Marion recalled his injury:

When I was nine years old we were playing cowboys and Indians down in the woods. I jumped off about a twenty-foot bank and hit wrong and broke my leg. My bone was sticking out, and the kids I was playing with ran off and left me. When my Daddy got home, he asked the kids, "Where's Martin?" And they said, "The last time we saw him he was laying down in the gully." So Daddy came down through the woods and found me. I had been laying there a couple of hours. I remember him picking me up and taking me to the hospital. It was Grady Hospital, a charity hospital in Atlanta, where we lived.

They set it, and I guess I was in the hospital about two and a half months. Then they X-rayed my leg and found out it was about an inch and a half shorter than the other leg. So they put me on the operating table, and for two hours and a half, they cut my leg. So my right leg is wired together, and I have forty-eight stitches up the thing. I walked on crutches for about a year. Although the broken part of my leg never bothered me playing ball, the knee was injured, too. All through my high school days, when I'd play ball, all of a sudden my knee would slip out, you know? I'd lay down on the ground, they'd jerk it back in, and I'd get up and play again. The docs said, "Marty, it will get stronger as you grow older." And it did. I didn't have any trouble with my knee in pro ball until I was, oh, 30 or 31 years old, maybe.

Mort Cooper, the Cardinals' best pitcher, also was 4-F because of an old knee injury. Max Lanier, who won seventeen games in 1943, had not been drafted. Four more good Cardinal pitchers were inducted: Al Brazle, Murry Dickson, Howie Krist and Ernie White. That gave Ted Wilks an opportunity to move up to the major leagues. He was 28.

Stan Musial's deferment illustrated the uneven character of draft calls from one community to another. There was no hint that Musial sought or received special consideration; he was just lucky. Age, number of children conceived before Pearl Harbor, and occupation were weighed by each local draft board in deciding who should be drafted and who should be deferred. Some draft boards had to take virtually every able-bodied man between the ages of 18 and 38; others had more than enough eligible men and had to make choices.

Musial was healthy and 23. He had one son born before Pearl Harbor, and supported his parents as well; Musial's father had contracted black-lung disease while working in the Pennsylvania coal mines. Musial worked during the off season in a war plant. He was deferred until after the 1944 season. Again purely by luck, the draft took many players who were older than Musial and had larger families—for example, Ruffing and Dickey of the Yankees, Luke Appling of the White Sox, and Lonny Frey of the Cincinnati Reds, who was 32 years old and had three sons.

During the winter of 1943-1944, Sam Breadon, the Cardinal owner, ventured some self-pity. "There isn't a club in either league which has lost as many regulars as we have," he said. It was not true, and by March even Breadon had taken heart. "I don't see how anybody can beat us," he said. Forecasting the 1944 pennant races for the *Sporting News*, Dan Daniel had little to speculate about in the National League. "If the Cardinals are able to maintain their current lineup for even half the season, it will be downright murder," he said.

The Dodgers, so strong and proud before the war, were in terrible distress. "All I can say is that we will have a large number of human beings at the training camp," Branch Rickey said in March. The team's only two solid infielders from 1943, second baseman Billy Herman and third baseman Arky Vaughan, were missing in 1944. Herman entered military service, and Vaughan elected to work on his ranch year-round until the war ended. Desperate enough to put aside his thrift, Rickey offered Vaughan a raise, a bonus to cover the additional cost of living in Brooklyn, an apartment, travel expenses for the whole Vaughan family, and three workers at $10 a day to perform the ranch chores. Vaughan declined.

Manager Durocher, 38, puffed himself into a semblance of shape and announced himself as Herman's replacement at second base. Durocher's first fielding chance of the season was a bad throw from rookie shortstop Gene Mauch, 18. The ball broke Durocher's thumb in two places and he returned to the bench.

Dixie Walker, 33, the veteran outfielder, was tried at third base, but his throws were so wild that even Howie (Steeple) Schultz could not reach them. Other infielders who toiled for Durocher that season included Tommy Brown, 16, Eddie Miksis, 17, and Eddie Basinski, 21, who in high school and college had played the violin but not baseball.

Dodger outfielder Gene Hermanski and pitchers Rex Barney and Kirby Higbe also were inducted. Higbe was scheduled to report to Fort Jackson, South Carolina, in late October, but was persuaded to enlist a few weeks early so he could pitch in an Army championship game. The opposing team protested Higbe's appearance on grounds that he had not pitched for Fort Jackson during the season. He was barred from the game but remained in the Army, which did not offer to refund the precious weeks of civilian life that Higbe had given up.

The Cincinnati Reds, second in 1943, lost second baseman Lonny Frey, ace pitcher Johnny (Double No-Hit) Vander Meer, infielder-outfielder Bert Haas and outfield prospect Hank Sauer. The Pirates lost first baseman Elbie Fletcher and outfielder Maurice Van Robays. Hi Bithorn, the Cubs' pitching ace, was inducted; so were catchers Clyde McCullough and Mickey Livingston, and outfielder Harry (Peanuts) Lowrey. The Boston Braves lost shortstop Eddie Joost and first baseman Johnny McCarthy.

The Phillies lost second baseman Danny Murtaugh, third baseman Pinky May, outfield prospect Del Ennis and veteran pitcher and pinch hitter Schoolboy Rowe. The Giants gave up pitcher Ken Trinkle and infielders Dick Bartell, Mickey Witek, and Sid Gordon. Pitcher Johnnie Wittig, who lost fifteen games as the Giants finished last in 1943, and Sal Maglie, a pitching prospect, left baseball for war-industry jobs.

The Browns' relative good fortune was not so evident before the 1944 season began. To retain their deferments, Galehouse and Laabs were tied to war-plant jobs in Akron and Detroit, respectively. Muncrief was expected to stick with his war-plant job in Houston. Potter was in Chicago; having undergone his physical exam, he expected to be drafted.

With only a few players signed, the Browns postponed the beginning of spring training from March 10 to March 20, and the Cardinals from March 15 to March 20. "Players continue to be uncertain about leaving war jobs, being doubtful of the effect on their draft status, and those who are willing to play feel they are in the driver's seat and can dictate their own terms," reported the *Sporting News* in early March.

Mort Cooper of the Cardinals was demanding a raise of $5,500, and Bill DeWitt said the infection had spread to the Browns. "Why, one of our players with nothing but Class AA experience has asked for a salary that we would pay a regular after four or five years in the majors," DeWitt told a *Sporting News* correspondent.

The *Sporting News* reported that club owners often did not know whether an unsigned player was really holding out for more money or was merely waiting to see whether he would be drafted. Many players, including Stephens and McQuinn of the Browns, were on several occasions tentatively reclassified 1-A and scheduled for induction, but again flunked their physical examinations. Tex Shirley, the new Brownie pitcher, was examined and rejected seven times; he had a hernia.

In addition to uncertainty about individual draft classifications, the number of men called for military service fluctuated so much that winter and spring that men had little idea when or whether they would be called. In December of 1943, General Hershey estimated that two million men would be drafted by July. On February 26, 1944, President Roosevelt criticized the Selective Service System for "over leniency" in granting occupational deferments, he said that there was a "grave shortage" of manpower for the armed forces. General Hershey barred occupational deferments for men 26 or younger except in critical cases. As usual, his edict was interpreted by local draft boards according to local conditions. A Wisconsin board deferred twenty-four young men as vital to the cheese industry.

In April of 1944, the military suddenly and temporarily suspended induction of draftees 27 or older, arousing an unexpected protest from some men who had made elaborate preparations after receiving their draft notices and had already bade their families long and emotional farewells. The Navy agreed to take these men so their rituals of departure would not go to waste.

The winter of 1943-1944 was a brighter and more optimistic season for the United States. Times Square was again ablaze with light as the new year began. "The crowds were gayer, greater than they were last New Year's Eve," reported the New York *Times*. "The whole picture seemed to have changed since then, from dark foreboding to the certainty of victory."

In Detroit and elsewhere, business was looking forward to the end of the war. Alfred P. Sloan, Jr., chairman of General Motors Corporation, announced that GM would spend $500 million to reconvert its factories for car production. Sloan predicted a postwar boom in automobile sales, but warned that postwar prosperity depended on constructive government policies in place of the "destructive" ones of the New Deal.

In Washington, Chairman Doughton and other members of the House Ways and Means Committee promised to simplify the federal income tax. Instead, new war taxes were imposed. The admission tax on baseball tickets was raised from 10 percent to 20 percent.

Baseball was looking both forward and backward that winter. In St. Louis, the owners of the Cardinals and Browns told the press that one team or the other should leave town. "St. Louis can no more support two major league clubs than Kansas City could support one," said Sam Breadon of the Cardinals.

In Cleveland, Alva Bradley, owner of the Indians, said in an interview that he would rather close for the duration than sell substandard baseball during wartime. Bradley apparently changed his mind, since the Indians neither suspended operations nor, until the end of the war, improved the quality of their play.

In Brooklyn, Branch Rickey, described by Dan Daniel as the "chief tocsin ringer of the diamond," warned that baseball's place as the nation's preeminent sport was in jeopardy. "Baseball must take heed, or football will become our national sport," Rickey said.

Rickey's warning aroused little comment. Football was then so secondary a sport that the *Sporting News* had not covered it at all until the fall of 1942, believing that sports fans would rather read about off-season baseball gossip than real football competition. When football coverage did begin, the *Sporting News* felt obligated to educate fans about the game, much as a television network in more recent years ran primers on hockey. One *Sporting News* story described line plunges, forward passes, and other plays under this headline: "Basic Football Plays Few, but Variations Add to the Fun."

Baseball had maintained its popularity largely because the minor leagues provided strong and widespread grass roots that other sports could not match. Rickey's concern stemmed at least partly from the wartime deterioration of the minor leagues. The draft had so dried up the supply of players that only nine minor leagues, with a total of sixty-two teams, had operated in 1943, down from a 1940 peak of forty-three leagues with teams in 314 cities. Following the war, Rickey suggested, about seventy-five minor leagues should be placed in operation. He was unaware, of course, of an impending development that would have an even more devastating impact on minor league baseball than a world war, and would greatly enhance the popularity of professional football: television.

Seeking a brighter image, the Philadelphia Phillies conducted a contest that winter to find a new name for the team. The winner was Mrs. John L. Crooks, who with her husband was caretaker of the Odd Fellows Grand Lodge in Philadelphia. She was described by the *Sporting News* as a demure little woman, and the name she bestowed upon the Phils was the Philadelphia Blue Jays. The Phils lost more than their name that winter. The team's owner, William Cox, 34, a wealthy lumberman, was thrown out of baseball by Commissioner Landis for placing bets of twenty-five to one-hundred dollars a game on his own team. There was not the slightest suggestion that Cox might challenge Landis's authority. He meekly sold the team to Robert R. M. Carpenter, Sr., a DuPont heir, who presented the Phillies, or Blue Jays, to his son, Robert, Jr., 28: Here, kid, have fun. Young Carpenter was drafted, becoming the first major league club owner conscripted into military service.

During the winter baseball meetings, Judge Landis and the club owners received a delegation of Negroes headed by Paul Robeson, the famous singer. Robeson argued for the admission of Negro players to organized baseball. Just a few months before, the Negro Giants had defeated a team of major and minor league stars in an exhibition game, 4 to 3, with Satchel Paige striking out fourteen batters.

Told that the American public would not tolerate such a thing, Robeson said that conditions had improved since his days as an All-American football player at Rutgers. "They said America never would stand for my playing Othello with a white cast, but it is the triumph of my life," Robeson said. *Othello* was then running in New York.

Of course, baseball's barrier against blacks was unwritten. "The Negro delegates were told by Landis that there was no baseball rule against the signing of members of their race and there the matter was left, just where it had been," reported the *Sporting News*.

Having spent the 1941 season in the Army, Hank Greenberg of the Tigers empties his foot locker at Fort Custer, Michigan, and prepares to return to civilian life. Discharged on December 5, 1941, Greenberg reenlisted·when Pearl Harbor was bombed two days later. (UPI Photo)

Bob Feller (center) is sworn into the Navy by Lieutenant Commander Gene Tunney (right) as Lieutenant David N. Goldenson, Chicago recruiting officer, looks on. (UPI Photo)

Hugh (Losing Pitcher) Mulcahy of the Phillies, the first major league player drafted for World War II, works out in the spring of 1945 after missing four seasons. Weakened by illness contracted in the South Pacific, Mulcahy was unable to regain his pitching skills. (UPI Photo)

President Roosevelt receives an annual baseball pass for himself, and a handbag and pass for Mrs. Roosevelt, from Ford Frick (center), president of the National League, and Clark Griffith, owner of the Washington Senators. The date is April 10, 1942, the eve of the first wartime season. This annual ritual helped Griffith gain Roosevelt's ear and persuade him to give baseball a "green light" for continued operation during the war. (UPI Photo)

George McQuinn of the Browns slides safely into third base after advancing from first on Mark Christman's single in the second inning of the fourth game of the 1944 World Series. The Cardinal third baseman is Whitey Kurowski. (UPI Photo)

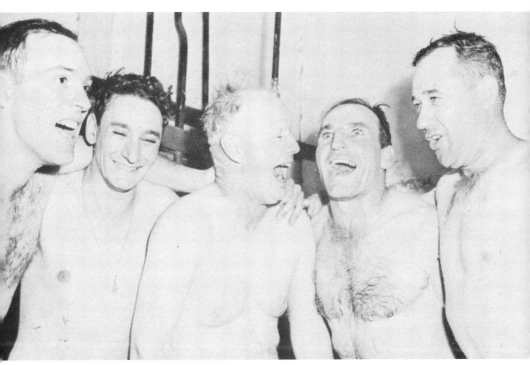

Singing in the shower after winning the 1944 World Series are four Cardinal players who would not have been with the team were it not for the war. Left to right, Danny Litwhiler, acquired from the Phillies; Augie Bergamo, who played in the major leagues only during the wartime seasons of 1944 and 1945; coach Buzzy Wares; Pepper Martin, who retired after the 1940 season but was reactivated in 1944 at the age of 40; and Debs Garms, 36, a former National League batting champion who was called up from the minor leagues during the war. (UPI Photo)

Celebrating the victory that clinched the 1945 pennant, Manager Charlie Grimm of the Cubs playfully messes the hair of his star pitcher, Hank Borowy, who in turn shakes the hand of rookie Andy Pafko, who drove in the winning run. (UPI Photo)

Joe Nuxhall, 15, pitching for his junior high school team in May of 1944, just three weeks before pitching for the Cincinnati Reds. The youngest player ever to appear in a major league game, Nuxhall pitched two thirds of an inning against the Cardinals and yielded five runs. (UPI Photo)

Pete Gray, the Browns' one-armed outfielder, practicing in Yankee Stadium before a May, 1945, game. Note Gray's thin glove, worn on his fingertips so he could quickly discard it and throw the ball. Although popular with fans, Gray was disliked by his teammates, some of whom believe that he cost them the 1945 pennant. (UPI Photo)

CHAPTER 11

That Glorious 1944 Season
Part I: Spring Training and a Fast Getaway

March 19, 1944. One Brownie catcher and four pitchers filed off the train at Cape Girardeau, Missouri. They were welcomed, and outnumbered, by the eight members of The Cape Girardeau Baseball Committee, chaired by Mayor Ray Beckman.

Spring training began the next day, and by then nine Brown players were on hand. There was one outfielder, veteran Frank (Baldy) Demaree, who was not destined to make the club, and no infielders. It was the first day of spring, but temperatures were below freezing. The Browns trained indoors. Their top farm club, the Toledo Mud Hens, trained with them.

Conditions were no better for most other teams. New York suffered one of the coldest first days of spring in years, with four inches of snow. At Bear Mountain, New York, the Brooklyn Dodgers' training camp, six inches of snow left only one visible trace of the baseball diamond, a signboard behind home plate that said, "Durocher Field." At French Lick, Indiana, pitcher Paul Derringer severely wrenched his right ankle when he stepped on a rock in the horse barn where the Chicago Cubs were training.

The war had turned strongly in the Allies' favor. Russian troops were rolling back the Germans and the U.S. was scoring victories in the Pacific. In Algiers, Pierre Pucheau, a former Vichy interior minister who was convicted by the French of collaborating with the Germans, was executed by a firing squad. He refused a blindfold and gave the firing order himself.

In Washington, the Office of War Information said that U.S. war casualties so far included 38,846 killed, 58,964 wounded, 35,521 missing, and 31,730 prisoners of war. In Moscow, the Soviet Union reported that the Germans had suffered thirteen million dead and wounded since invading Russia on June 22, 1941.

In St. Louis, the Federal Alcohol Tax Unit said that many bars were watering whiskey to stretch tight supplies, and the alcoholic content of most St. Louis beers had been reduced. Nine persons convicted of speeding were deprived of their gasoline rationing coupons for a month or more.

In the Gilbert Islands, the Navy discovered that a combat veteran, James Eugene Richardson, was only 14 years old. He was 6 feet tall and had lied about his age when he enlisted. Richardson was discharged and sent home. At Cape Girardeau, the Browns were told that an outfield prospect, Teddy Atkinson, was only 14 years old. He had been brought to training camp by Don Gutteridge, the first infielder to report. Atkinson was not offered a contract.

After a week of indoor practice, the Browns played their first exhibition game, beating Toledo, 5 to 4, on three hits by catcher Frank Mancuso. The infield was intact; McQuinn, Gutteridge, Stephens, and Christman were on hand. Christman had a weekday job making military fire engines at Central Fire Truck Company in St. Louis and was training on weekends only.

To play alongside Demaree in the outfield, Sewell used pitcher Virgil Brown and an outfielder borrowed from Toledo. The other Brownie outfielders were still missing. Mike Chartak and Al Zarilla were hesitant about leaving their war-plant jobs, which provided draft deferments. Chet Laabs had passed his Army physical examination and was awaiting a draft call in Detroit, unaware that a change in draft policy would postpone his induction for more than a year. Milt Byrnes was holding out for a higher salary. Mike Kreevich simply had not been heard from.

But these were passing worries. Members of the team soon trickled into camp, including Kreevich, who said that an ailing leg had been strengthened by his winter job as a milkman. Byrnes and pitcher Jack Kramer, the only holdouts, signed their contracts and reported to Cape Girardeau. Bad weather kept the team indoors most days and put Demaree and Nelson Potter in the hospital with the flu, but Sewell maintained a strict regimen of workouts.

Weather aside, the Browns were blessed with a superb spring training camp. They used the gymnasium at Southeast Missouri State Teachers College; an arena, built for horse shows, that had a dirt floor and thus could be used for infield practice; an outdoor baseball field; and a sandstone quarry, protected from the wind, with a running track.

Batting cages were set up in the arena with nets to stop batted balls. While some other clubs whiled away inclement days waiting for sunshine, the Browns trained hard. Sewell turned up the thermostat in the arena so his players would sweat and get accustomed to the hot summer days ahead.

The results were not immediately apparent. The Browns lost three of their five games with Toledo before winning the final two games for a bare edge against the minor leaguers. Hollingsworth joined Potter on the sick list. Jakucki and Shirley pitched well enough to make the team but were inconsistent.

In an upbeat description of Jakucki, the *Sporting News* reported that the big right-hander "is confident that he will be able to make the grade this time and blames a playboy attitude for his previous failure to get into the big leagues. Now, Jack declares, he is all business and plans to remain."

In truth, Jakucki and other members of the team, while training hard, were getting acquainted with other aspects of Cape Girardeau as well. Jakucki, Shirley, and Kreevich, among others, quickly discovered the two or three bars in town, one of them the back room of a drugstore.

Shirley was sensitive about his premature baldness, and was easily recognized by the cowboy hat that he wore almost always, even indoors. As the summer wore on, Shirley's attempts to hide his bald pate had the effect of accentuating it. When he was forced to remove his hat in hotel dining rooms and other proper establishments, his white pate stood out against his suntanned face like snow on a mountaintop.

Among his teammates, Shirley's skill at keeping his hat on his head was a subject of frequent comment. Bob Bauman, the team's trainer:

Shirley and Jakucki were sitting in a place in Cape Girardeau one night having a few beers. Jakucki was in a booth back of Shirley, minding his own business. Tex thought he was being funny; he took a pitcher of beer and poured it over Jakucki. Jack knocked him right out of there, into the gutter. Shirley rolled over, came up, and still had his cowboy hat on.

George McQuinn:

One night Sewell decided to make the rounds. I think there were only about two bars in the whole little town. There was Mike Kreevich sitting up at the bar. So Luke says, "Mike, you've had enough." Luke drove him back to the hotel, took him up to his room, took the key, and locked Mike in the room. So Luke went on his way, and after half an hour or so he decided to make the rounds again. He walked back in the same bar and there's Mike up on the same stool. Kreevich had left his hotel room via the window and fire escape.

The Cape Girardeau city fathers were thrilled to have a major league team, and treated the Browns kindly. Brownie officials had to commute occasionally between Cape Girardeau and St. Louis. Gasoline rationing was too tight for the 240-mile round trip, but fire departments were allowed all the gasoline they wanted. The baseball officials were invited to fill up their cars at the local fire station.

In return, the city fathers asked one favor. Not unaware of the reputation that athletes had earned for their off-duty recreational activities, these civic leaders wanted Bill DeWitt and Luke Sewell to keep their employees from preying on the innocent lasses of Cape Girardeau. The girls, as it turned out, did not cooperate.

DeWitt:

When we went down there, the guy at the Chamber of Commerce and the mayor and everybody talked to us, and said, "You know, this is a small town, and a very religious town, and there's a lot of gossip." Well, Jesus, there were more gals chasing ballplayers down there than there were in St. Louis [laughs].

On April 2, the St. Louis *Globe-Democrat* headlined the Russian army's drive toward Odessa. General Douglas MacArthur's airplanes destroyed eighty-two Japanese planes on the Caroline islands of Hollandia, Dutch New Guinea, and Truk. In Washington, the War Food Administration said that the U.S. was glutted with eggs, having increased production by 80 percent since the war began. Representative Hagen of Minnesota said that hatchery operators were drowning chicks; it was too expensive to raise them into laying hens with eggs fetching only 20 cents a dozen.

In St. Louis, Mayor Aloys J. Kaufmann proclaimed the week beginning the following Wednesday as Negro Health Week. The *Globe* paraphrased his honor as saying that "ill health in any group contributes to ill health for all other persons in the community." Racism was rarely challenged then, and was certainly not challenged in baseball. At Sportsman's Park in St. Louis, blacks sat in the right-field pavilion, a distant vantage point from which they viewed the game through a screen that stretched from the outfield wall to the roof above.

From Cape Girardeau that April day, *Globe-Democrat* sportswriter Glen L. Wallar, a master of the ancient cliché, wrote darkly about the Browns. "Manager Luke Sewell is getting somewhat worried over what he is going to do for pitchers," wrote Wallar. "Prospects for a competent twirling staff were none too bright when the club arrived at Cape Girardeau on March 19 to start spring training, and after two weeks of work the hustling leader of the Brownies has no reason to show much enthusiasm about his hurlers." Sportswriters always save an angle for another day's story; three days later Wallar wrote that the Browns weren't hitting, either.

Although neither Sewell nor his players were anticipating a Brownie pennant, trainer Bauman recalled a rare balmy day at Cape Girardeau that aroused prophetic springtime dreams:

We happened to be outdoors one day, at one of the parks there. You could see this beautiful lake with ducks and geese and swans swimming around. Nelson Potter, Jack Kramer, and I were all sitting there talking about the schedule, and I said, "Yeah, we wind up playing the Yankees in the last series of the season. Wouldn't it be nice if we came down to the final part of the season and played them for the pennant?" Somebody said, "I'll buy that! I'll take that chance anytime!"

On April 8, the Browns broke camp and traveled to St. Louis for a "City Series" of six exhibition games against the Cardinals. In the first game, Cardinal pitchers Al Jurisich, Bud Byerly, George Munger, and Fred Schmidt walked fourteen Browns; Brownie rookies Tex Shirley, Weldon West, and Sam Zoldak walked twelve Cardinals. Trailing 8 to 2 in the ninth inning, the Browns scored four more runs before succumbing.

The Browns beat Mort Cooper, 5 to 2, in the second game. Christman doubled home three runs in the fourth and was tripled home in turn by Mancuso. In the eighth, Gene Moore homered off Harry Brecheen.

Jakucki held the Cardinals to two runs in the first six innings of the third game. But Zoldak was then pounded, and the Cardinals won, 8 to 6. Taking turns in right field for the Cardinals that day were rookie Augie Bergamo and veterans Debs Garms, 36, and Pepper Martin, 40; Martin had last played in the major leagues in 1940. The weather was dreadful, and paid attendance was only 354.

The Cardinals won the fifth game, 3 to 2, in five innings, with the Brownie runs coming on consecutive home runs by McQuinn and Stephens in the first inning. The sixth game was rained out. The Browns, who usually won the City Series before returning to losing form once the season began, had indicated little promise. They had lost four of the five games, and their rookie catchers had yielded ten stolen bases.

On April 15, Clark Griffith dropped by the White House with season passes for President Roosevelt, who was vacationing in the South. "I know the President is pleased to see baseball continuing," said Stephen T. Early, a Roosevelt aide.

On April 16, General Douglas MacArthur issued a statement in response to reports that the Republican Party might draft him to run for president. "I have not sought the office nor do I seek it," MacArthur said. "... My sole ambition is to assist our country to win this vital struggle by the fulfillment of such duty as has been, or may be, assigned to me."

MacArthur did not say whether that duty might include the presidency. The general had many things on his mind. That same day, he landed in another column of the front page by siding with temperance spokesmen in a flap over fighter pilots. It all started when Major Richard I. Bong shot down his twenty-seventh Japanese airplane, breaking the record of twenty-six set during World War I by Captain Eddie Rickenbacker. Captain Eddie, a gracious man, congratulated Bong and promised him a case of scotch whisky.

That aroused O. J. Christgau of the Iowa Anti-Saloon League. In a wire imploring Rickenbacker to withdraw the offer, Christgau asked the hero to recall his own ordeal at sea after being shot down. "What good would a case of scotch have done you while you were on that life raft?" he asked.

Stepping in firmly, MacArthur said that he did not consider "liquor or spiritous wines as appropriate recognition" for Bong's feats. He noted that the ace had been promoted to major, a sufficient reward.

In Washington, Chester Bowles, administrator of the Office of Price Administration, proclaimed an end to the rationing of lard. At Fort McClellan, Arkansas, Army Chaplain Opie S. Rindahl, a Lutheran minister from Bismarck, North Dakota, announced that he had surveyed the German war prisoners there and discovered that they were not pagans as he had assumed, but Christians. Many of them were Lutherans. Moreover, their favorite songs were "Pistol Packin' Momma" and "Mairzy Doats," current leaders on the Hit Parade.

The sports page that day opened itself to the annual pre-season baseball predictions by presidents Will Harridge of the American League and Ford Frick of the National League. War, peace or famine, these league presidents could be depended upon to predict exciting pennant races, the better to lure fans through the turnstiles. "Every club in our league has a chance at the pennant," wrote Harridge. Atop that paragraph, the *Globe-Democrat*, believing a partial disclaimer was in order, inserted this subhead:

Even the Browns

The St. Louis Browns? Certainly not, in the opinion of most observers. On the same sports page, Jack Hand of the Associated Press named the New York Yankees, Washington Senators, and Chicago White Sox as pre-season favorites. Hand listed the Browns last. The *Globe's* own Martin J. Haley weighed in with a piece picking the hometown Cardinals to win their third straight National League pennant. Haley relegated the Browns to the fourteenth paragraph, skirting the team's deficiencies by saying that the Browns "entertain hopes which, if realized, would carry them into the thick of the American League flag contention for 1944." A St. Louis writer could not preview a baseball season without saying something positive about the Browns, and Haley did. He said it was the team's forty-third straight season in the American League.

Had the Brownies themselves voted, they probably would not have rated their team much higher than the sportswriters did. Luke Sewell:

I thought just like anyone else, that we'd be lucky to get through the year. It was such a makeshift club. Quite a few of the players were marginal, from a major league standpoint.

George McQuinn:

I don't think any of us who had been with the Browns for a number of years ever gave a thought to winning the pennant. Oh, no. We were the Browns and had never done anything like that.

Don Gutteridge:

That was the trouble with the Browns. They had some pretty good ballplayers but they had a defeatist attitude. They didn't think they could do it; they didn't have the confidence. They said, "Oh, what the hell, we're going to lose anyway." And that attitude was eating up the Browns, really, year after year.

To face the Tigers in the season opener at Detroit on April 17, Luke Sewell selected Jack Kramer, career record sixteen and twenty-six. At least he had pitched in the major leagues. Three opening-day pitchers were rookies, including the Giants' Bill Voiselle, who earned the honor by losing twenty-one games for Jersey City in 1943. In Washington, the first ball of the season was thrown out by Vice-President Henry A. Wallace, a wartime fill-in for President Roosevelt.

"The season will provide the biggest opportunity for rookies since Abner Doubleday tossed out the first ball," wrote Jack Hand of the Associated Press.

Kramer outdueled Dizzy Trout in the opener, 2 to 1, shutting out the Tigers until Pinky Higgins homered with two out in the ninth. It was the eighth straight time that the Browns had won their opening game.

The next day, Steve Sundra pitched a three-hitter for a 3 to 1 St. Louis victory. Gene Moore singled home George McQuinn in the first inning, and Gutteridge stole a hit from Eddie Mayo in the third to squelch a Detroit rally. "Don Heffner was on first at the time and very probably would have reached third had the Brownie not corralled the leather," wrote Wallar of the *Globe-Democrat,* corralling another cliché.

In the third and last game of the series, the Browns knocked out Hal Newhouser in the third inning. Jakucki pitched the 8 to 5 victory and Stephens drove in three runs with two singles. Above the Browns' box score, the *Globe* looked ahead to the next day with a WELCOME HOME headline.

The Chicago White Sox were in town for the Brownie home opener, and the festivities included military musical ensembles with both male and female performers. The Coast Guard provided a band with vocalists, and the Navy Spars Drum and Bugle Corps marched and played under the leadership of Ensign Aileen Kirkhart.

Mayor Kaufmann threw out the first ball. He had plenty of room for his windup, only 3,395 fans having come, including a thousand servicemen and children who got in free.

Sewell appeared to be taking a risk by starting Nelson Potter, who had not pitched an inning of exhibition baseball because of illness. But everything was working for the Browns. Mike Kreevich, who in the past three seasons had hit a total of one home run, slammed a three-run homer in the first inning and followed with another home run. Potter:

Sewell started me, and he said, "If you can go four or five innings, fine, good." I kept going, going. He'd say, "How do you feel? I'll get someone in." I said, "No, I feel good." I ended up going all the way.

The Browns won, 5 to 3. The only Chicago runs were scored in the eighth on a home run by Hal Trosky, a power-hitting first baseman whom the White Sox had lured back after two years of retirement; Trosky had left baseball for the peace of his farm because he suffered from migraine headaches.

After four straight victories, sportswriter Wallar's turn-of-the-century tune changed from dirge to hosanna:

Sewell is in high spirits in regards to the work of his team in the four games played. The boys have been fielding in sensational form, hitting timely and playing heads-up baseball to take advantage of the fine pitching the team has been getting. (Breath) The work of the infield has been especially pleasing to the Brownie boss. Gutteridge, Stephens, and Christman have been making sparkling plays to cut down the opponents' hit column while McQuinn has come to the rescue of the three on the occasions they have made poor throws. George has stretched far, wide and handsome to eliminate errors.

On April 24, the *Globe* had more good news. General MacArthur announced that his forces had trapped 140,000 Japanese soldiers, on islands from the Solomons to New Guinea. "Time and combat will be required to accomplish their annihilation, but their ultimate fate is now certain," said the general. "Their situation reverses Bataan." The U.S. and Britain were launching a nonstop air assault against Germany in preparation for invasion of the Continent.

And good Lord, the Browns swept a doubleheader from the White Sox, 5 to 2 and 4 to 3, extending their streak to six games, within one of the American League record for consecutive victories at the start of a season, set by the 1933 Yankees.

Kramer pitched the first game and hit a two-run homer. Caster won the second in relief of Shirley. Trailing in the eighth, the Browns scored the tying and winning runs on a walk, an error, and singles by Moore and Zarilla. The doubleheader drew 7,709 paid fans, a big crowd by Brownie standards. In Chicago, the Cardinals won two from the Cubs; the St. Louis teams had a combined record of 11 and 0.

The Browns had open dates the next two days, and Wallar weighed in with some nostalgic gallows humor. "There was once a time when the Browns welcomed a two-day rest. Their pitchers could rest up from overwork in attempting to retire enemy batsmen. Infielders could recover from the nervous shudders incurred in ducking line drives. Outfielders could rest their weary legs from chasing wallops to the far corners of the ball park." But now the Browns were anxious to play.

During the two-day lull, the vagaries of the Selective Service System again bestowed blessings upon the Browns and boils upon a rival. Pitcher Bob Muncrief was allowed to leave his job at Brown Shipbuilding Company in Houston and join the Browns. The Yankees' best pitcher, Spud Chandler, a twenty-game winner in 1943, was drafted.

Commando Kelly, hero of the Italian campaign and World War II's first winner of the Congressional Medal of Honor, was welcomed home at Pittsburgh County Airport by his widowed mother, eight brothers, and a crowd of several thousand. "Gee, but I'm glad to be here," the hero said. Sewell Avery, the president of Montgomery Ward, defied President Roosevelt's order to bestow full rights on a labor union, and Roosevelt had the Army seize the mail-order house. The photograph of two soldiers carrying Avery from his office building is now considered historic, but the *Globe-Democrat* buried it on page six.

In London, General George S. Patton told an attentive audience that it was the destiny of the British and Americans "to rule the world, and the more we see of each other the better." Estimating his victims at 177,000, Patton said he had been busy "welcoming Germans and Italians into hell," and said he hoped soon to "have a chance to go and kill the Japanese." An eleven-day air assault on

Germany had cost Britain and the U.S. 2,300 airmen. Republican primary voters in Pennsylvania gave Thomas E. Dewey an overwhelming victory.

The Browns tied the record the next day, beating Cleveland 5 to 2 as Sundra outpitched young Allie Reynolds. A triple by Gutteridge and a double by Stephens highlighted a four-run rally in the sixth inning. The game was played in St. Louis, and paid attendance was 960.

Potter pitched the record-breaker the next day, beating the Indians 5 to 1. "It may be stranger than fiction," wrote Wallar in the *Globe-Democrat*, "but it is a fact nevertheless—the St. Louis Browns have deprived the famed New York Yankees of one of their many records."

Kramer stretched the streak to nine the following day, winning his third of the season with a 3 to 1 victory over Cleveland. The Browns were three and a half games ahead of second-place Washington. That was enough. The White Sox ended the streak with a 3 to 2 victory. That same day, Ted Williams finished his pilot training at Pensacola, Florida.

It had all happened too quickly for the St. Louis fans to grasp, as the poor attendance indicated. But the team was as high as a kite.

Sewell:

When you get nine wins behind you, you got a talking point. So I just talked pennant all year long to them, and it probably caught fire a little bit.

McQuinn:

After winning nine in a row to start the season, we began to think we could win the pennant. We realized that DiMaggio and Williams and all the rest of the big stars were off in the service. We were just as good as anybody else.

Gutteridge:

We looked around after we went around the league one time. The other clubs looked bad, and we said, "Hey, we can play as good as they can." There wasn't no Joe DiMaggios. We won the first nine ball games, a record. And the guys said, "Hey, this is fun, let's do it." That changed our whole season.

We were a different attitude.

That Glorious 1944 Season
Part 2: The Race Tightens

The opening streak placed the Browns in an unaccustomed position of prominence in the sporting world, and subjected them to deep and serious analyses. Their strength, the experts concluded, was in superior weakness.

The Browns led the major leagues in 4-F players—men physically unfit for military service. The team started the season with eighteen 4-Fs and thirteen of them made the squad for the long pull: George McQuinn, first base; Don Gutteridge, second base; Vern Stephens, shortstop; Ellis Clary and Floyd Baker, utility infield; Milt Byrnes, outfield; Red Hayworth, catcher; and, among the pitchers, Jack Kramer, Al Hollingsworth, Sig Jakucki, Nels Potter, Tex Shirley, and Sam Zoldak.

Catcher Frank Mancuso was just as exempt from the draft as any 4-F player, although his formal category was 1-C, honorable discharge. As the *Sporting News* said, "Luke Sewell could put a pretty fair 4-F team on the field."

The New York Giants, who finished last in 1943, opened the 1944 season with sixteen 4-F players, tops in the league, and won their first five games. "The Giants now are almost as well fixed with men with creaky backs, twisted knees and other rejection ailments as the Browns," reported the *Sporting News*. The Giants had cornered the market in old 4-F catchers with Gus Mancuso, 38, Ernie Lombardi, 36, and Ray Berres, also 36. Their five best pitchers were all 4-F—Bill Voiselle, Harry Feldman, Ewald Pyle, Rube Fischer, and Ace Adams. Adams was the first of the great workhorse relievers; he had set a record in 1943 by pitching in seventy games.

The Giants' early pace was matched by the Cardinals, who could not match the Browns or Giants in quantity of 4-F players but bested them in quality. The Cardinal 4-Fs included first baseman Ray Sanders, third baseman Whitey Kurowski, second baseman Emil Verban, and pitchers Mort Cooper, Harry Brecheen, and Ted Wilks.

The *Sporting News* noted that 4-F players were more important in evaluating a team's pennant chances than healthier players who might be drafted. Publisher J. G. Taylor Spink said that things had come to a pretty pass "when pennant chances are rated in direct proportion to the number of physically handicapped performers retained by the various clubs."

The superiority of the Brownie 4-F cast had not been noticed as recently as a month before. In March of 1944, sportswriter Tom Swope reported in the *Sporting News* that 157 major league players were exempt from the draft. No team had fewer than four or more than fourteen. (By April, of course, those numbers had changed.) Other players were deferred, most of them because they were fathers, but they could be drafted at any time.

Of the 157 draft-exempt players, ten were 38 or older, and six were citizens of Cuba or some other Latin American nation. The others were 4-F.

Swope did not pick any club as having an edge in its draft-exempt roster, but he did select a 4-F all-star team of Sanders, first base; Gutteridge, second base; Snuffy Stirnweiss, Yankees, shortstop; Kurowski, third base; Jim Russell, Pirates, left field; Augie

(Goo Goo) Galan, Dodgers, center field; Dixie Walker, Dodgers, right field; and, behind the plate, Lombardi; Ray Mueller, Reds; and Ken O'Dea, a Cardinal substitute.

Swope selected nine 4-F pitchers: Cooper and Brecheen; Adams; Rip Sewell and Max Butcher, Pirates; Al Smith, Indians; Dutch Leonard, Senators; Orval Grove, White Sox; and Atley (Swampy) Donald, Yankees.

The Browns' gradual accumulation of misfits had not been without its embarrassments. The previous October, Representative Elston of Ohio, reacting angrily to a newspaper story, asked General Hershey how the Browns could get away with boasting of a 4-F infield. Brownie officials hastened to reply that it was not a boast, merely a statement of fact.

Even while the Browns were tearing off their winning streak, Congress was considering the conscription of 4-F men for military labor or war plant jobs. The *Sporting News* pleaded for mercy. "Would it be against the best interests of this nation to appeal to Washington to let our 4-F players remain in the major leagues, where they could do America the most good, doing the thing they can do best?" the publication said. To the good fortune of baseball in general and the Browns in particular, the legislation did not pass.

Despite the streak and the impressive disabilities of the Brownie players, most baseball writers restrained their praise of the Browns. "Here in the East," sniffed Dan Daniel, "we still adhere to the notion that the American League race will settle down to another battle between the New York and Washington clubs." Daniel called the Browns "the Sewell surprises, the Luke Lallapaloosas."

Daniel appeared to be correct. After winning nine straight, the Browns lost ten of their next fifteen games and slipped to third place, behind the Yankees and Senators. Steve Sundra, one of the Browns' best pitchers, was inducted into the Army on May 9.

The Yanks were not without their own wartime nobodies. They won six in a row behind the pitching of veteran Bill (Goober) Zuber and rookies Monk Dubiel, Emerson Roser, and Joe Page; in later years, Page would distinguish himself as a relief pitcher.

On July 2, Yankee shortstop Oscar Grimes made three errors in one inning, a feat that was matched, also during the war, by Lew Riggs of the Dodgers and Catfish Metkovich of the Red Sox. They fell one short of the four errors committed in a wartime inning by shortstop Lennie Merullo of the Cubs.

The Yankees benched Grimes, who could neither field nor hit, and inserted Mike (Mollie) Milosevich, 29, a rookie who could field. During nine years in the minor leagues, Milosevich had never hit .300 or won an invitation to spring training with the Yankees. He was a coal miner who hadn't finished high school. Playing left field was a more cultured man, Arthur Beauregard (Bud) Metheny, another 29-year-old who had been making a career in the Yankee farm chain. Metheny was 4-F because of an injury suffered while playing football for the College of William and Mary. In the Yankees' sixth straight win, a 4 to 3 decision over Boston, Metheny drove in the winning run with a drive that knocked down Joe Cronin, the 37-year-old Red Sox manager. In desperation, Cronin was playing himself at first base.

Although the Cardinals were leading the National League, the rest of the standings were slightly askew. The Philadelphia Blue Jays won five straight in early May to take second place. The Cubs lost thirteen straight, and Charlie Grimm was brought in from Milwaukee to manage them.

On April 30, before a crowd of 58,063 at the Polo Grounds, the Giants beat the Dodgers 26 to 8 in the opener of a doubleheader. In the Giants' second, Johnny Rucker doubled; the next six batters walked. Like overgrown Little Leaguers, Dodger pitchers Rube Melton, Les Webber, Al Zachary, Fritz Ostermueller, and Tommy Warren walked seventeen batters altogether and yielded eighteen hits.

Mel Ott walked five straight times. Phil Weintraub, 36, a retread who had not played in the major leagues since 1938, drove in eleven runs. Ernie Lombardi drove in seven, and Leo Durocher was thrown out of the game in the sixth inning for venting his anger at the umpires. Giant fans ushered Durocher to the showers with oranges and apples; a vengeful Dodger fan caught Giant left fielder

Joe Medwick in the groin with a pop bottle. Suffering considerable pain, Medwick retired for the afternoon. He already had three hits.

On May 1, Pulitzer Prizes were awarded to Richard Rodgers and Oscar Hammerstein II for *Oklahoma!*; to Ernie Pyle of the Scripps-Howard Newspaper Alliance for war correspondence; and to the New York *Times,* owlish in war as in peace, for a survey of the teaching of American history.

The Paramount Theatre in New York premiered *Going My Way,* a movie starring Bing Crosby and Barry Fitzgerald as kindly priests and now immortalized on the late show. In one scene, Crosby appears in the basement of a church rectory, wearing a Brownie cap and jacket. "Always in the cellar," remarks a character in the movie, which was filmed before the 1944 season. "At any rate," remarked the *Globe-Democrat,* "with the Browns in first place Crosby isn't kidding when he sings 'Swinging on a Star.'"

Other movies playing in New York included *Gaslight,* which starred Charles Boyer and Ingrid Bergman and was paired with live music by Phil Spitalny's All-Girl Orchestra. Around the country movie houses were showing *Andy Hardy's Blonde Trouble* with Mickey Rooney, and *See Here, Private Hargrove.*

In Hollywood, Warner Brothers named Humphrey Bogart to star in *God Is My Co-Pilot.* Judy Garland filed a divorce suit against Sergeant Dave Rose, a composer in civilian life *(Holiday for Strings, Winged Victory).* At a British air base, Major James Stewart was awarded the Distinguished Flying Cross for leading an air raid over Germany. "I guess I'd better send it home," the movie star drawled, fingering his medal. "I'm mighty proud of it."

In Washington, Robert E. Hannegan, chairman of the Democratic National Committee, predicted that President Roosevelt would seek and win reelection to a fourth term. "Despite the malicious whispers to the contrary, I can assure you the president is fit and ready for the fight," Hannegan said.

At a Philadelphia meeting of the American Psychiatric Association, Dr. Harry Freeman of Worcester, Massachusetts, said that suicides in the U.S. had dropped to a new low of twelve per 100,000 people, compared with a high of seventeen per 100,000 in 1932. Freeman attributed the decline to the increase in employment and to the war, which turned aggressive feelings outward against the Germans and Japanese.

In the funny papers, Dick Tracy was pursuing a villain named Flattop aboard a ship. Flattop sneaked away in a rowboat, abandoning his partner, Vitamin. Orphan Annie was staying with a poor but virtuous woman named Mazie, who rented her parlor to pay a debt. The new tenant was an amazing man named Sinsin the Swami, who read minds and confided to Annie that he knew her old ally, Punjab.

Pensive, a 7 to 1 shot with Conn McCreary up, won the Kentucky Derby. The War Production Board selected more than a thousand hospitals to handle limited civilian distribution of a new curative called penicillin. Wrestling with a different kind of drug, the board said that it might soon let distilleries make a little whiskey.

A pitcher named Ralph Branca won his fifth straight for New York University, beating Colgate, 10 to 5. He was 18 years old and soon would join the Dodgers, who already were using another 18-year-old rookie, Calvin Coolidge Julius Caesar Tuskahoma McLish. McLish, called "Cal" or "Buster" by his teammates, was billed as a switch-pitcher who could throw fast balls with either arm. He settled on the right arm once competition began.

Another young Brooklyn pitcher, Hal Gregg, had a no-hitter against the Blue Jays until rookie Ted Cieslak singled in the seventh. With Oklahoma City in 1939, Cieslak got in the way of a pitch from Dizzy Trout and suffered a fractured skull. In charge of an army gymnasium program a few years later, he met head-on with a medicine ball. Severe headaches eventually led to his discharge from the army. Cieslak went unannounced to the Blue Jay training camp at Wilmington, Delaware, in 1944, played well in practice, and was installed at third base. His major league career lasted eighty-five games.

Some older players also were doing well. The Tigers got an unexpected lift from rookie outfielder Chuck Hostetler, 40, who after three weeks of play was batting .444. Hostetler had retired from pro ball after ten years in the minor leagues, but had kept his hand in as a semi-pro player. At one time, so the story went, Hostetler had been so fast that he chased a fox for two miles, finally throwing his coat over the panting animal.

Mel Harder of Cleveland won the 200th game of his career and his third straight of the season. Harder was 34 and was sometimes relieved by a man nine years his elder, Joe Heving, the major leagues' only playing grandfather. Heving had a good sinker ball. Lou Boudreau, the Indian manager and shortstop, was declared 4-F because of arthritis in his left ankle. He had broken it three times. Throughout his career, Boudreau played with the ankle taped almost as stiffly as if it were in a cast. He was a superior shortstop nevertheless.

Feasting on weak wartime hitters, Bucky Walters, 35, of Cincinnati, beat the Boston Braves for his fifth straight win and third shutout. Connie Ryan was the only Boston base runner, reaching first on a broken-bat single. In fifty-eight innings, Walters had yielded five earned runs. Another Cincinnati veteran, Clyde Shoun, 32, did Walters one better, beating the Braves 1 to 0 and allowing no hits. Mike Ryba, 40, was pitching excellent relief ball for the Boston Red Sox.

Toward the end of May, the American League had settled into a tight race among mediocre teams. "Nobody is going to run away with the flag," said Steve O'Neill, the Detroit manager. On May 25, the Browns were in second place, two and a half games behind the Yankees and only three games ahead of the last-place White Sox.

But the Browns were working to alleviate their weaknesses. High in priority were steps to reclaim pitcher Denny Galehouse and outfielder Chet Laabs, who were anchored to war-plant jobs in Akron and Detroit, respectively. Both men were deferred from the draft because of a combination of circumstances. They had defense jobs, were older than 26, were married, and had children conceived before Pearl Harbor. In both cases, the opportunity to play part-time led to full-time playing status before the season was over.

When Steve Sundra was drafted off the mound, DeWitt asked Galehouse to sign on as a Sunday pitcher. Galehouse was expecting the offer, and had been working out as best he could in Akron.

Galehouse:

DeWitt said, "Well, why don't you try it? Since it's only once a week, we'll pay you half a salary." I had been making only $9,000 or $10,000; the Browns weren't making any money and it was our misfortune to be members of a team that wasn't drawing.

I was an employee of Goodyear Aircraft, working with Selective Service, trying to get draft deferments for the employees. It was my job to determine who was essential and who was not. It was a tough position to be in. We worked six days a week, sometimes as much as sixty-five or seventy hours. I worked out at the noon hour with guys who might want to play catch, and with local baseball teams—the high school and the local amateur teams. I did some running. But it wasn't like regular training, where you're bearing down.

On Saturday, I'd get an overnight train to wherever the Browns were playing. You knew the schedule way ahead and made the reservations way ahead, so most of the time I'd get an upper berth. I'd get there at 7:30 or 8 o'clock in the morning. I'd have breakfast and go to the ball park; there wasn't anyplace else to go. We always had Sunday doubleheaders. I'd pitch the first game and then I'd leave and take the train and go back home.

It was a little tiring because I was on the go all the time. At first I pitched pretty good. I wasn't winning, but I kept the opposition low; we didn't score many runs. From a pitching standpoint, the hitters were a little bit easier to pitch to than prior to World War II. But then the fielders weren't quite as good, either, so it would kind of balance.

Then I started getting out of shape. I was way behind in conditioning, and I could see that it was either one thing or the other—quit baseball altogether, or play full time. So I took a trip to Sarasota, Florida, where I had lived during the registration period for the draft. I went to see the chairman of the draft board, and I said, "Now, I am considering quitting the war job, because it looks like we've got a chance to win the pennant. How long would I have before I'm taken into service?"

He said, "You probably wouldn't take your physical before the end of the season." So I took that chance. I quit the job, and finished the season up, and I wasn't taken until April, and all I missed was the 1945 season. No, he wasn't doing me a favor. He was just saying that there were enough men ahead of me to fill the quota for the next few months.

Although a pitcher could be useful once a week, an outfielder could not. A defense job had to be found for Laabs in St. Louis. This, too, DeWitt handled. Laabs:

Bill got me a job in his father-in-law's plant in St. Louis. They made pipes—ten, twelve, fourteen inches in diameter. Our job was to inspect them. I found out later that these pipes were sent down to Tennessee for the atom bomb project.

I got to St. Louis about the first of June. I worked days. Whenever the club was at home, I could play at night and on Saturdays and Sundays.

About the first week in August, I was able to quit the job and play full time.

Ever since their fast start had given rise to dreams of the pennant, the Browns' management had been working on the problem of discipline. Bob Bauman, the trainer:

That was the roughest, toughest club I've ever been with. They were just a rough group; wild. Kreevich, Laabs, Stephens, Caster—you can go down the line. And Jakucki!

Not long after spring training, Luke Sewell came up to me. He said, "We've got a pretty good ballclub and I think we've got a chance to win the pennant. But you know the character of our ballclub. I'm going to have these guys checked on the road, and I'd love to have you do it." I said, "Let me think about it."

I went home that night and thought. I had checked college boys [Bauman was a trainer at St. Louis University during the winter]. But I had never checked pros. The next day I said, "Yeah, I'll check them, Luke. On one condition. You have a meeting, let me talk to the boys."

So I did talk to the players. I said, "Your manager and I have talked. He thinks we have a good chance for the pennant, and I think we've got a good chance for the pennant. But a lot of you have a tendency to go off the deep end. Your manager has asked me to check you on the road, and I've accepted. I'm going to check you every night at 12 o'clock and I want you to be in your rooms. That's all I ask. I don't want any trouble about it. If you've got anything to say about it, say it now, because I don't want any trouble later on."

You could have heard a pin drop. I never had any trouble. Oh, I found Shirley, you know, with a hat on in bed, or someone stiff underneath the bed.

During a ball game you couldn't ask for a better bunch. They worked. Off the field it was something else. In Boston, we had inside rooms facing a courtyard. On a warm night, no air conditioning, people would have their windows open. The players would be hollering at each other across that court. Some of them would have firecrackers. Pretty soon you'd hear a whistle; it would sound like a bomb coming down. Then they'd throw a firecracker down in the courtyard. Bam! People would get scared—it was

World War II, you know. Everything in that hotel would light up right now. The switchboard downstairs would be alive. About that time, another whistle, another firecracker.

Mike Kreevich, the center fielder with a weakness for drink, was such a valuable player, and was so well respected and well liked, that the Browns descended on him like a swarm of social workers. Bill DeWitt:

We called Mike's brother up in Illinois, and we said, "What can we do with him?" He said, "You people can't handle him, but he has great respect for the Catholic Church. If you can get a priest down there who'll take him in tow, you can get him straightened out." So we got a priest in St. Louis to kind of look after him. The priest would come see him, and he'd go see the priest. It kept him sober for quite a while, I'll tell you that.

Don Gutteridge:

Yep, they got a priest, and they got me. They said, "Will you room with him?" I said I would, so I roomed with Mike. I don't drink and they thought I would help him. I'd say, "Mike, let's go to a show or something." Instead of going to a bar. Another thing I did, I'd always make sure there were candy bars laying on the dresser, because if he had sweets he wouldn't be as liable to want alcohol. I was a do-gooder, I guess.

That wasn't all. Luke Sewell told me, "Now, when some fellows come and say, 'We want to talk to Mike,' you get out of the room." It was the AA men. They tried to get him in Alcoholics Anonymous.

During another part of the season, Gutteridge roomed with Vern Stephens, the Brownie slugger. Stephens had a baby face and an insatiable appetite for feminine companionship. After being rousted from the room a number of times so that Stephens could entertain a guest in privacy, Gutteridge told Bill DeWitt that his batting average would be twenty points higher if Stephens would let him sleep. Gutteridge:

Stephens? Oh, he was quite a ladies' man. Quite. I roomed with him for a while; roomed with his suitcase mostly. How he did it—go out like he did and then play as well as he did—I don't know. He was a superman. He was every bit of that.

Mark Christman, the third baseman, recalled an experiment at reform that was conducted by Charley DeWitt, Bill's brother and the team's traveling secretary. Christman:

Stephens could hit the ball. He could swing. He hit twenty-five home runs in that big ball park at Sportsman's Park, a long way for a right-handed hitter. He used to hit balls on out in right field, too, on that pavilion roof. He was that strong. And I still think he had as good range at shortstop as Marty Marion. Not as good hands, but he covered as much ground, and he had an arm like a shotgun.

Charley DeWitt called him in the office one day, and he said, "Vern, for criminy's sakes, we've got a chance to win this pennant. Now why don't you take care of yourself, and quit running around at night, and get in bed and get your rest? Because you can help us, you're the best hitter on the ballclub. With your help we can win this thing and make some money out of it."

So Vern says, "All right." And for three weeks he quit drinking and going out, and never got a base hit. So Charley DeWitt called him in and said, "Go out and stay out!" I really think those guys who did that sort of thing did it to loosen up.

The American League race remained tight. On May 19, the Browns, Yankees, and Senators each were first, second, and third at various times of the afternoon and night, as the outcome of their games came in one by one. On May 21, the Yankees swept the Browns, 4 to 3 and 8 to 1, before 59,161 fans. It was the largest crowd ever to see the Browns play at Yankee Stadium. The next morning's editions of the New York *Times* happily prepared the Browns for burial. "It is questionable if they ever will be the same after what happened to them yesterday," the newspaper said.

On May 24, Laabs made his first appearance of the season. He walked twice as the Browns beat the Red Sox, 7 to 3, for Kramer's sixth victory of the season. Muncrief won the next day, indicating that he was back in shape although he had missed spring training. Potter lost a heartbreaker, and then Jakucki pitched his best game to date, holding the Red Sox to four hits in a 4 to 2 win.

Muncrief, who had a career record of no wins and six losses against the Yankees, beat them 11 to 3 on May 29 as McQuinn and Moore homered. The next day the Browns swept the Senators 6 to 4 and 4 to 2, while Detroit swept the Yankees. On May 31, Jakucki stranded thirteen runners and beat Washington 4 to 3. Detroit again beat the Yanks, this time on a grand slam pinch home run by Al Unser, a bullpen catcher whose son, Del, later played outfield for several major league teams.

In Los Angeles, Count Haugwitz-Reventlow sued his former wife, Barbara Hutton, by then the wife of Cary Grant. The suit sought control of the education and rearing of their son, Lance, 9, who, according to the Count, had been subjected to "coarse and vulgar language" from Miss Hutton and others.

In Detroit, James Hoffa, international representative of the Teamsters Union, announced that striking bakery drivers would resume bread deliveries. In Washington, J. Edgar Hoover observed his twentieth anniversary as director of the Federal Bureau of Investigation.

In a poll of female war workers conducted by the Post-War Planning Committee of the American Legion Auxiliary, nearly 48 percent said that they intended to keep on working after the war. Just over 50 percent said that they planned to quit work and return to their homes. In Washington, Labor Secretary Frances Perkins proposed a postwar economic program designed in part to reduce the role of women in the work force. Her proposals included a bar on shifts of more than eight hours for women and on the use of women on graveyard shifts. She also called for "retiring women who are merely pin-money workers and came into the labor market only because of the war need, in order to make opportunity for girls who must work regularly."

In New York, Professor Albert Einstein urged intellectuals to organize and "fight for the establishment of a supranational political force as a protection against fresh wars of aggression." Einstein said that the organization also should protect the economic position of intellectuals and "secure their influence in the political field."

On June 3 at the Associated Press bureau in London, Joan Ellis, 22, a teletype operator, was working on a machine that she thought had been disconnected. For fun, she punched out this message:

"FLASH EISENHOWER'S HEADQUARTERS ANNOUNCE ALLIED LANDINGS IN FRANCE"

At 4:39 P.M. Eastern War Time, the message was transmitted to the AP headquarters in New York, which instantly relayed it throughout the U.S. and Latin America. Less than two minutes later, the AP caught its error and transmitted:

"BUST THAT FLASH"

But in the meantime the radio networks had broken into broadcasts to announce the bogus invasion. At the Polo Grounds, a game between the Giants and the Pirates was interrupted. The invasion message was read over the loudspeaker; the players and 9,000 fans stood for a minute of silent prayer.

On June 6, the great invasion really began as U.S., British, and Canadian troops landed at Normandy. On the same day, Rome was captured, the first of three Axis capitals to fall.

One of the first U.S. soldiers to enter Rome was Sergeant John A. Vita, 27, a cartoon animator from Port Chester, New York, whose parents had been born in Italy. Vita quickly went to Mussolini's palace and climbed to the balcony overlooking Piazza Venezia. To a crowd of several hundred nonplussed Italians below, Vita shouted "Death to Mussolini" in his best Italian. The Italians applauded, although it was not clear whether they understood him.

The only two major league games scheduled on D-Day were postponed, as was a boxing match in Philadelphia between Sammy Angott and Ike Williams. The Yankees returned home on D-Day from a Western trip in which they had lost eight of thirteen games.

The Browns were back in first place, a game and a half ahead of the Yankees. Detroit had won seven straight and was third, two and a half games behind the Browns. The Senators were last, having lost ten of their last fifteen games.

Thurman (Joe E.) Tucker of the White Sox, whose nickname resulted from his physical resemblance to comedian Joe E. Brown, was leading the American League in batting with .400. Next were Boston's Indian Bob Johnson, 37, at .340; Detroit's Paul Richards, 35, at .339; Hostetler, 40, also of Detroit, at .337; and Cleveland's Oris Hockett, 34, at .336.

McQuinn was batting .310 and was the only Brownie at .285 or better. The team was being carried by its pitching, its defensive infield, and, perhaps most important, its grit. "It doesn't seem reasonable for a team with a batting average of only .237 to continue to set the pace when other clubs are pounding the leather with considerable more force," wrote Wallar in the *Globe-Democrat*.

It was not a reasonable year. The Browns' inferiority in leather pounding remained considerable, but the team stayed on top. McQuinn slumped, but Stephens began hitting. Kramer tailed off, but Muncrief and Jakucki got hot.

On June 17, Jakucki shut out Detroit, 5 to 0, although the Tigers had seven hits to the Browns' six. Christman hit a three-run homer. A week later, Jakucki shut out the Tigers again. The next day the Browns won with unaccustomed ease, downing Detroit 7 to 1 for Muncrief's sixth straight victory. Stephens hit two doubles and two singles; Milt Byrnes had three hits. "Yes," wrote Wallar, "it was quite a day with the willow for the Sportsman's Park lads, who for the most part of the season have been far down in the swatfest column."

The Browns were playing only a bit better than .500 baseball, but no other team was doing better. The Yankees, Tigers, Red Sox, and White Sox waxed hot and cold; the Browns plodded along, never losing more than three games in a row.

The White Sox stormed into second place in late June but fell back. The Yankees fell to fifth, then won six in a row, including the first two in a series at home against the Browns. Milt Byrnes muffed an easy fly to put the Yankees up in the first game. In a battle of wartime pitchers, Jakucki lost the second contest, 1 to 0, to Monk Dubiel, who got his nickname years before when issued a uniform so small that his teammates likened it to the tight little costumes worn by organ-grinders' monkeys.

In the New York *Times*, Louis Effrat wrote of the Browns with disdain. "Even for these subnormal times the Brownies looked like anything but a first-place club," he said. But in the last game of the series, the Browns clung to first place as Hollingsworth won his fifth straight game, 3 to 0, with the help of five double plays.

On July 4, Hal Newhouser won his twelfth of the season for Detroit. Two days later, Tex Hughson of the Red Sox became the first American League pitcher to win thirteen. Muncrief won his eighth the same day in Philadelphia as Stephens homered off Woody Wheaton, an outfielder making his first and last major league start as a pitcher.

At the All-Star break, the Browns had won forty-five and lost thirty-four. Boston was second, two and a half games behind, and New York was third, trailing by three and a half games. Philadelphia, in last place, was only nine games out of first.

Seventh-place Detroit gained hope in mid-summer when Dick Wakefield was unexpectedly discharged by the Navy. The young slugger had completed his pre-flight training with considerably better than a passing grade, but the Navy did not need as many pilots as it had anticipated; cadets in the bottom half of their class suddenly became civilians. Wakefield had to register for the draft, but in the meantime joined the Tigers. On July 13 he returned to the Detroit lineup and singled twice as the Tigers beat the White Sox for Dizzy Trout's eleventh victory of the season.

Detroit had two of the league's best pitchers in Trout and Newhouser, but the team's other pitchers were so weak that the two aces often relieved each other. Veteran outfielder Doc Cramer, 39, benched because of a batting slump, caught Manager Steve O'Neill's eye and was asked to pitch. "Cramer is fast and has a good curve," O'Neill said. Cramer demurred and was returned to the outfield.

The Yankees also strengthened themselves, buying outfielder Herschel Martin, 34, from Milwaukee of the American Association, and regaining the services of veteran shortstop Frank Crosetti, 33, who had been working at a California shipyard. "The Yankees can win," Daniel wrote when Martin joined the team. "The Browns are not their superiors. Team against team, there is no comparison." The vision of Crosetti was, to Daniel, the final nail in the Browns' coffin. "Give us Frankie again at short," he wrote, "and you can have your Browns and all the rest."

The Cardinals were coasting. The loss of three straight to the Blue Jays in early June merely reduced their record to forty-five and eighteen and their lead over second-place Pittsburgh to nine and a half games.

McQuinn and Stephens batted third and fourth for the American League All-Star team. Each got a hit, and Muncrief pitched an inning and one-third without yielding a run. But the National League won, 7 to 1, behind the pitching of the Blue Jays' Ken Raffensberger and the Pirates' Rip Sewell. Phil Cavaretta of the Cubs tripled and singled; another Cub, Bill (Swish) Nicholson, keyed a four-run rally with a pinch-hit double.

Seventeen members of the 1942 All-Star teams and thirteen from the 1943 All-Star teams were in military service. George Munger of the Cardinals, with a record of 10 and 2, was picked for the 1944 National League team but was inducted into the Army the morning of the All-Star game, just as Howard Pollet had been the year before. Munger pitched that night for Jefferson Barracks and beat the Lambert Field Navy Wings, 2 to 1, in a battle of service teams from the St. Louis area.

That Glorious 1944 Season
Part 3: Recalling the Season

A game in St. Louis on July 20, 1944. Nelson Potter was pitching for the Browns; Cal Hubbard was umpiring behind the plate. Hubbard:

A lot of umpires didn't know what in hell a spitball was, but it's a fast pitch and it's got a quick, sharp break down. Once in a while some old guy would slip one in and they'd squeal about it. You couldn't prove it was a spitter, but I told Mr. Harridge, I said, "Christ, you don't have to prove it. If the umpire says it's a spitball it's a spitball." Umpire says it's a strike it's a strike, don't make a damn where the ball was. If he says it's a spitball that's it. You don't have to prove it.

Nelson (Potter) was one of the ones they all accused of throwing spitters. I don't know whether he did or not. He was a kind of sidearm pitcher and the ball broke down a little bit. But [licking motion] he'd do that; go to his mouth, see, and that was against the rules.

This night they were playing the Yankees in St. Louis, and Hank Borowy was pitching for the Yankees. Every once in a while Borowy would do that [licking motion]. He was just kind of wetting his fingers. He wasn't throwing spitters. But Luke Sewell came out and he said to me, "Make Borowy keep his fingers out of his mouth." Course I knew that was going to kick up a storm because they were going to holler like hell about Potter, too.

So I went out to Hank when the inning started. I said, "Hank, Sewell's complaining about you putting your fingers in your mouth. Let's not do it any more." He said, "O.K., my God, I didn't even know I was doing it." He was just as happy. Art Fletcher was coaching third base for the Yankees and he came by me and he said, "What's Sewell squealing about?" I said, "About Borowy putting his fingers in his mouth." And Fletcher said, "Holy cow! Well, make Potter keep his out of his mouth, too." I said, "All right."

So the inning was over, and Potter went out to the mound. I went out and I said, "Nellie"—they called him Nellie—I said, "Nellie, they're complaining about you putting your fingers in your mouth. Sewell complained about Borowy, so we're not going to have any more of that today. Let's don't do it."

He did it again, so I went out to him again, and here comes Sewell running out there. I said, "Now, Luke, I've already told him twice. You're the one that started it, complaining about Borowy putting his fingers in his mouth. Potter does it all the time. I've already told him twice. You tell him now that if he does it any more, we're going to run him the hell out." I said, "Now, Luke, he's your baby. He's your responsibility."

So Luke talked to him. I don't know what in the hell he told him, but when we got ready to play Potter just did this [an obvious and exaggerated licking motion]. He just did it on purpose, see.

I said, "Come on, you're through." I never did say he was throwing spitters. I just said he was violating the pitching rules. I had to put Sewell out, too. I knew he was going to raise hell. But he started it all, and he was a louse anyway, that Sewell; he was always bitching about something.

When I threw Potter out the Yankees had two men on base, and the pitcher they put in got them out without scoring. Dizzy Dean was the broadcaster. So Diz said, "Looks like 'ol Hub changed pitchers just at the right time."

I made out a report to the league, and they suspended Nellie for ten days. He had a wife and I think he wanted a vacation anyway. They said his wife gave birth to a child nine months later. I gave him the chance to be home.

Potter:
I always had a habit of moistening my fingers and then going to the resin bag to get a good grip on the ball. Hank Borowy was pitching for New York this night and he did the same thing. It was a cool, dry night. If you couldn't get a little moisture on your fingers it was hard to get a good grip on the ball.

So we kept moistening our fingers. For some reason, Luke Sewell hollered at Hubbard about Borowy going to his mouth. He should never have done it, but he did. So Hubbard said, "Well, O.K., we'll have no more of that. And that goes for your pitcher, too!"

So Cal kept telling me I couldn't go to my mouth. Well, I started to blow on my hand. I'd make a fist and blow on it. He said, "You can't do that." I said, "Cal, I'm blowing in my hand." He said, "I know what you're doing. You're wetting your fingers."

Which I was, but he couldn't prove it. So he kept warning me to stop it, and I knew that I either had to get a little moisture some way or I was going to have trouble. So I kept doing it and he just run me out of the ball game. Did I ever throw a spitter? No, no. And Cal Hubbard never accused me of throwing a spitball.

I was very surprised when they suspended me. I said to Sewell, "Heck, I might as well go home a few days." And I did; came home, went fishing a couple days. I kind of stretched it out a little bit, and then I got a wire from him. "You better get back here." It cost me about two starts.

Did my wife have a child nine months later? Yeah, this is true. [laughs] They used to kid me about it, but the rest of that story is not true. We did not name the baby Cal Hubbard Potter.

No other pitcher before or since has been ordered out of a game for violating the spitball rule. Potter's ejection prompted an angry outburst from the crowd of 13,093. It was the fifth inning. The Yanks were leading, 2 to 1. Nick Etten was on third and Rollie Hemsley on first with none out. Don Savage had a count of two strikes. Denny Galehouse relieved. He threw Savage a third strike, fanned Milosevich, and got Borowy on a roller to second.

With two out in the Brownie seventh, Hayworth reached first on a throwing error by Milosevich. Stephens walked. Chartak, batting for Gutteridge, homered to the pavilion roof in right. Byrnes walked on four pitches, and McQuinn hit the next pitch onto the pavilion roof.

"Jim Turner went to the hill for the Yanks," wrote Wallar in the *Globe-Democrat*, "and got Laabs on a pop to Milosevich but who cared about what Chet did, for Mike and George had already delivered the knockout punches." The score was 7 to 3.

Luke Sewell:

The only club that looked like it might get out and go that year was the

Yankees. The Yankees should have won the pennant. They had the personnel. A better team? Oh, yes. Their personnel, practically all of them had come through their farm system, and they knew about them.

But you see, McCarthy had a system of baseball. He just turned those big bats loose and let 'em go. Joe's theory was that if he could intimidate you early in the season he didn't have to worry too much. But those big bats weren't there. They were in the Army. He was still playing that same kind of baseball, as if he had DiMaggio, Keller, Henrich, Dickey. Any number of games, if he had dropped some sacrifices in and things of that kind he would have won them from you.

We had improved, and a lot of the other clubs hadn't. Except for the Yankees, it looked like there weren't any better clubs. You see, your wartime baseball was pretty comparable with baseball today, this day and age right now. Back before the war, you had some Double-A [minor league] ballclubs that would be in these pennant races right today. You take the old Newark ballclub, the old Kansas City ballclub, the old Baltimore club and the old Rochester club; those clubs would be winning pennants in the major leagues today. Oh, yes, no question about it.

We had that mediocre ballplayer who is not of major league caliber. Everybody had 'em. We had a bunch of misfits. But some of them surprised us. Jakucki was one; he won thirteen games for us off of the sandlots. Red Hayworth turned into an extremely intelligent catcher. You could teach him things and he could grasp them.

Kreevich was a great little fellow, a great center fielder, and he had a hell of a year for us. Gene Moore hit well for us, when it counted, and he was good in the outfield. I don't think he had a cartilage in either knee. When he'd fall down I'd rest him awhile [laughs]. The only thing we ever did with Laabs was cut his backswing down. He started getting around on those balls and he could whomp 'em. When we were up against pitchers he didn't think he could hit he'd be sick. He'd be up on the trainer's table. When it was a pitcher he could whomp, Chet would be running up and down on the sidelines and bouncing around. I'd use him in the places where he could hit. Zarilla hit well sometimes, although he was better after the war. Byrnes was just a fill-in player.

We had to keep that infield going; we had to keep McQuinn, Gutteridge, Stephens, and Christman going. Vern Stephens, Christ, he could knock the ball from here to the Cuyahoga River out there. McQuinn was a great fielder and a real good hitter, an ideal man for a ballclub. But his back would hurt him; he had to wear a steel brace.

Potter and Galehouse pitched real good for us. Kramer, maybe an astrologist could figure out when his moon was in its crescent. Muncrief had good stuff, but Bob was a fellow that wasn't consistent. You'd put him out there one day and he'd look like a million dollars, and you'd put him out next time against the same ballclub and they'd rack him up. Then late in the season he got a chipped elbow.

Jakucki's fast ball was a natural sinker. I don't know if you remember the old pitcher the Yankees used to have, Wilcy Moore? Well, he was about Jakucki's size, had about the same delivery, and his fast ball sunk the same way. Jakucki was a good fielder, and a better-than-average hitter as a pitcher. If he had just settled down and taken care of himself he could have pitched another five or six years as a relief pitcher in the major leagues.

We were grateful to have anybody who could stand up on the mound [laughs]. Hollingsworth couldn't throw much; he had a bad arm. He'd come through the Cardinal farm system, and when they let someone go you could bet something was wrong with him.

Caster was the only relief pitcher we had who could throw it over the plate. Didn't make any difference if it was 12 o'clock at night and no lights, he'd throw it over the plate. Not too much on the ball, but he could get it over, and the relief problem is walking them in.

July and August are awful months on a ballclub. The players lose interest. They've been at it since spring training. In September, they start thinking about next year's contract and they perk themselves up. Here they come!

But July and August are the two roughest months on a manager. Even though I kept talking pennant, it was hard to keep that idea in front of them. I just kept after them, kept talking to them, gave them little pep talks, switched them around, tried to rest them a little bit, sympathize with them.

Shirley Povich, the Washington *Post* sportswriter:

Toward the end of the season, Luke Sewell was doing more manipulating and more maneuvering with players than anybody I ever saw. He'd platoon, and start this lineup one day and another lineup the next day. Finally I says, "What the hell is going on here, Luke? You change these lineups every day! You must smell these guys on the bench getting hot."

And he says, "No, Shirley, I smell those bums out there on the field getting cold."

George McQuinn:

It seemed to be destiny that we were going to win the pennant. We got the breaks. Everything was going our way. Take those two catchers; so many things happened to them it was unbelievable. They dropped more pop fouls! Every time somebody would pop the ball up with men on base and Red or Mancuso would run after the pop foul, they'd drop it. Nine times out of ten in baseball, the guy gets a base hit after that. But it didn't happen that year; we'd get the guy out.

Hayworth loved to catch Kramer because Jack could throw a ball right through a knothole. Kramer had the most perfect control of almost any pitcher I ever saw. Potter had one of the greatest screwballs in history. I'd say the second best; Carl Hubbell had the best.

Red Hayworth:

Catching in the minor leagues, I never thought anything about a pop fly. Went all over the ball park to catch 'em. But old catchers like Sewell and Hofmann and Taylor told me, "Listen, a double-decker stadium is different. The wind currents are different. Sometimes instead of coming to you it'll come down like a knuckle ball."

So I said, "Well, there's nothing to it." So I was catching Potter at Chicago and a pop foul went up. Routine. I went back, throwed off my mask, and the ball fell about five feet from me. But you soon figured those things out.

Things fell in place that year. Take Al Zarilla, a streak hitter. We were playing the Yankees and they had us beat by one run in the latter part of a game in St. Louis. There's two men out and Gene Moore on first. Zarilla hit a line drive to right field and Bud Metheny caught it. McGowan was umpiring at first, and he jumped up and down. Said, "I had time called." Gene Moore was tying his shoe and they didn't notice it; the pitcher made the pitch. When McGowan calls anything it's called; he was a great umpire. So the pitcher has to pitch again, and Zarilla hits the ball on the roof. Things like that.

Mark Christman:

On a pop fly, poor Frank Mancuso couldn't lean back to see the ball, because his back was in such bad shape. He was all right going forward, but as soon as he got under it he was done.

But the guys were loosy-goosey that season. They were kidding and laughing and joking. There wasn't a guy on the ballclub that didn't like the next guy. We had a meeting every day, and Sewell kept telling us that we had the potential, we had the ballclub, to win the pennant. You're darned right it helped. It kept us going all the time.

We had a better ballclub than the Yankees; we had better pitching. Now, Detroit was in seventh place with about half of the season over, and they got Dick Wakefield back out of service. He started hitting, and it was amazing the number of runs he drove in, and he drove 'em right into first place. They had two kids pitching, Newhouser and Trout. They had nobody else. Newhouser won the Most Valuable Player Award. He won twenty-nine games and Trout won twenty-seven. I think Trout should have won it, because Trout saved half of Newhouser's ball games.

Players who wouldn't have made it without the war? Maybe me. I played after the war, but I only had a good record during the war. I always felt that I was a mediocre ballplayer, and I had to hustle. I wasn't a good hitter. I never had good wrists, and I sprayed the ball all around. I'd hit like seven or eight home runs a year, and I had to work at hitting all the time. You take the good hitters, all they do is concentrate on what the pitcher's throwing and swing the bat. Me, I had to concentrate on keeping my elbows away from my body, the bat away from my head, make certain I got the bat out front to hit the ball better. All those things you're concentrating on, and then you've got to make sure the pitch is a strike. Like I say, I had to work at it.

On our ballclub that year, we just took turns driving in the winning run. If we needed a run, the guy who was up there got the run. It was a pressure ballclub. We were getting two or three runs a ball game and our pitching staff was holding them to one run. We had a pitching staff that was a good one, and on defense we had kids that really had good hands. If you booted a ball you booted the ball game away. I was hitting .300 until about the last six weeks of the season, but I lost twenty pounds that year. I was down to about 155 pounds, and the last five or six weeks of the season I couldn't pick up a bat, I was so tired.

Denny Galehouse:

The Yankees, having lost so many players to the service, were a lesser team. The Browns, realizing the situation, I think were putting more effort into the game. We were giving 100 percent where in the past it wasn't worth it to go beyond 90 or 95 percent. You think, "We've got a chance. Let's go!"

You make some breaks by that extra effort. But still, some balls have to hop for you. That almost has to happen for a team to be a winner. You have a man on third base when you need the tying run, and have a ground ball hop over an infielder's shoulder. Situations like that happened.

Wartime players? This one outfielder with the Browns, who I won't name, cost me three games in '44. The first time, the guy comes charging for the ball; it's over his head, three bases. The ball game is over. Maybe a month later, that's in his mind. He stays back and waits for it, and the ball carries to right in front of his feet. He plays a short hop and it gets by him. The next time it's the reverse again, he charges and the ball's over his head. He just wasn't a good outfielder.

We were leading the league a majority of the time and by a fair amount, and we kind of relaxed, figuring we had it won. I could see the attitude change on the last Eastern trip. Gosh, that's when we got in trouble. We started losing. When we'd win they'd win. Then we'd lose and they'd win. First thing you know, we've lost our lead.

On August 10 in New York, the Browns won their tenth straight as Galehouse shut out the Yankees, 3 to 0. By August 15, the Browns were five and a half games ahead of Boston. Detroit trailed by eight games and New York by eight and a half. "Harridge Loop Prepares to Hail New Champion," proclaimed a headline in the *Sporting News.*

But the race turned. The Tigers beat the Browns three out of four in Detroit, and, a few days later, again in St. Louis. In the latter series, Trout won the opener, 4 to 3. Trapped in a rundown between third and home, Rudy York scored the tying run in the eighth when Mancuso's peg hit him in the back. Pinky Higgins drove home the winning run in the ninth. Two days later, the Browns pulled off a triple play, Christman to Gutteridge to McQuinn, but lost anyway as York and Wakefield homered; Newhouser won his twenty-second game.

After leading the league since June 1, the Browns slipped out of first place on September 4. New York, playing like the Yankees of old, moved on top by sweeping the Athletics, 10 to 0 and 14 to 0, behind Mel Queen and Monk Dubiel. The American League suddenly had its tightest pennant race since 1908. The Yankees were first; the Red Sox were fourth, only three games behind. The Browns and Tigers were in between.

Detroit and New York were considered the most likely winners. The Browns seemed to be playing their way out of the race, and the Red Sox lost out to Selective Service. Within a two-week period in late August and early September, three Red Sox players were drafted—pitcher Tex Hughson, catcher Hal Wagner, and second baseman Bobby Doerr. Boston's competitors could not have chosen the new soldiers any more deftly. Hughson was leading the league in winning percentage with eighteen and five, .783; Wagner and Doerr were the league's top two hitters at .330 and .325, respectively.

In an attempt to cushion the loss of Hughson, Tom Yawkey, the Red Sox owner, bought Rex Cecil and Clem Dreisewerd, both of whom were pitching well in the Pacific Coast League. Dreisewerd startled his teammates with his choice of bullpen catchers. She was his wife, and Dreisewerd, a superstitious man, wanted no one else to warm him up. But neither rookie could replace Hughson. Like an airplane without wings, the Red Sox plummeted out of contention.

A scheduling quirk gave the whole league four straight days off, and the Browns returned to St. Louis for the final seventeen games of the season. Now, with every player needed, the Army threatened to reach into the Brownie outfield.

Bill DeWitt:

Zarilla got drafted, and he was supposed to report about three weeks before the season was over. I talked to his draft board, and they gave me nothing. So I went to talk to a guy down at Jefferson Barracks. I said, "Here's our right fielder. Is there any way I can bring the guy down and get him inducted and then get him a leave until after the baseball season is over?"

He said, "Well, let me talk to the general." They let him play the season out and play the Series. The day after the Series was over, he went down to Jefferson Barracks and into the Army.

The Browns also suffered an entirely unwarranted slur on their integrity. On Friday night, September 15, sportscaster Bill Stern told his network radio audience that a "national baseball scandal" involving the Browns would appear in print the next day.

The story, it turned out, was printed in *Collyer's Eye and Baseball World* (no relation to *Collier's* Magazine), a Chicago publication devoted mostly to horse racing. The Brownie slump, so the story hinted, had resulted from an order by unnamed "major league leaders" who wanted a team with a larger home ball park to play in the World Series.

By the time Stern repudiated his own story four days later, the Browns had taken three of four games from the White Sox. Gutteridge, who had one home run for the season, hit two during the series. Kreevich had eight hits; McQuinn and Christman, who had been slumping, regained their batting eyes.

In the first game, Galehouse stopped the White Sox, 5 to 1. A bumble by manager Jimmie Dykes killed a Chicago rally in the first inning. With two out, Eddie Carnett singled home Wally Moses. Hal Trosky advanced to third and Carnett to second on the throw home. Guy Curtwright stepped up to bat, and Sewell emerged from the dugout waving the lineup that Dykes had turned in before the game. It listed Curtwright following Trosky in the batting order. Carnett was declared out, the run was nullified, and the inning was over.

The next day, Kramer pitched a one-hitter against the White Sox while the Athletics beat the Yankees. St. Louis was back on top; Detroit and New York were tied for second, a half-game back. On September 17, the Tigers swept the Indians and took first place as the Browns and White Sox split a doubleheader and the Yankees lost twice.

Washington came to town and exploded for six runs in the eleventh to break up a duel between Galehouse and Roger Wolff, who hit Stephens with a pitch in the home half of the eleventh. Sewell picked up a bat but did not advance on Wolff. The Browns and Senators had been on the verge of blows all season, and two nights later a fight erupted. The combatants were Tom Turner, a reserve catcher whom the Browns had acquired from the White Sox, and Roberto Ortiz, a Washington outfielder.

Observing the fight with obvious relish were sportswriters Shirley Povich and Red Smith. Smith's account appeared in the *Sporting News* just after the event occurred. Povich described it in an interview thirty-four years later.

Smith:

During Washington's batting practice on the night of September 21, Turner sat on the bench and sought to calm his nerves by playing a word game. This consisted of digging interesting words with a Biblical flavor out of his vocabulary and flinging them at the Senators.

Ortiz, Cuban student of Pan-American diplomacy, walked to the mouth of the Browns' dugout and spoke briefly for the defense, and apparently remembering Luke Sewell's use of a bat, brandished one of George Case's Louisville Slugger models by way of emphasizing his point. Turner suggested that if Roberto would discard the shillelagh, they could do the rest of their talking with their hands.

Roberto dropped the bludgeon. Thomas stepped onto the field of honor. "Goodie!" said their playmates. "Let's you and him fight." They formed a ring around the combatants.

Turner fought from a weaving crouch. Ortiz used the Corbett standup stance, showing a roundhouse right and nice footwork. Once when Turner crouched low in the Arturo Godoy style, Roberto tried a field goal from placement. The kick was partially blocked and the crowd booed.

Up rushed a citizen in civvies trying to foment peace. Fearful lest the fun be spoiled, the Browns' Ellis Clary reached out, grabbed a handful of shirt-front and cocked his right fist. With simple dignity, Ellis offered to bash in the snoot of any officious buttinski. Then he blushed and stammered, recognizing his handful as Umpire Weafer in mufti.

By this time, the pugilists had punched themselves breathless and Ortiz went off to have his thumb treated. Unnoticed in the confusion was the fact that Clary had set a new American League record by speaking before punching. It was the first time in his career this forthright character ever did that.

Povich:

Tom Turner was a popoff. And Tom Turner didn't like Cubans. And Tom Turner started picking on Mike Guerra, a little Washington catcher. Whereupon: "If you want to fight Guerra, you fight me." This was big Ortiz, Roberto Ortiz. He shoved Guerra out of the way.

It was the first time I've ever seen two ballplayers square off and nobody interrupted it. Both teams came over to watch, and the ballplayers were all in a circle. The Browns didn't like Turner; they were hoping he would get the hell kicked out of him.

And this is exactly what happened. Roberto really didn't fight fair. He fought a Cuban fight, and he kicked Turner in the groin. The fight was over, and I think the Browns were just as pleased as the Senators.

The Browns walloped the Senators 9 to 4 that night for Potter's seventeenth win. Ortiz sat out with a broken thumb. The Yankees beat the Tigers, 5 to 2, in ten innings. Having taken two of three from Washington, the Browns swept three straight from Philadelphia, although registering only sixteen hits in the three games. In the final game of the series, the Browns were trailing 2 to 0 with two out in the ninth and two men on base.

Mark Christman:

That game at home against the A's? I remember it very well. It was the funniest thing you ever saw. We're losing by two runs and we had two men on base. Sewell put Tex Shirley in to run for McQuinn at first base.

I got a base hit, between the outfielders in left center. Tex could run, and he wound up coming around third base. And he stumbled. He started to fall, and came down the line just barely keeping his balance, and when he got about ten feet away from home plate he fell. He crawled the rest of the way home, and they threw the ball away and I wound up at third base.

Now get this. There were two outs at the time, and Baker hit a fly ball to center field, and Bobby Estalella dropped it. I scored the winning run.

(Red Smith, the eminent sports columnist of the New York *Times*, was then covering the Athletics for the Philadelphia *Record*. He says that Estalella was in tears following the game.)

The Tigers were just as hot. Playing at home, they won two of three from the Yankees and four straight from the Red Sox. On September 25, the Browns pulled into a tie for first place, beating the Red Sox 3 to 0 behind Potter while Russ Christopher of the Athletics stopped Detroit, 2 to 1. Superb St. Louis pitching continued the next night as Jakucki beat the Red Sox, 1 to 0. Trout, meanwhile, shut out the Athletics, 6 to 0. The Browns and Tigers were tied with five games to go.

Newhouser shut out the Athletics the next day. The Browns and Red Sox were scheduled to play an afternoon game, too, but it was raining in St. Louis. Because of wartime travel restrictions, a postponed game would not be replayed. If the Browns played and won, they would remain tied with Detroit. If they played and lost, they would be one game back. If the game was postponed, they would be a half-game back. St. Louis and Detroit would have four games remaining to play.

Luke Sewell:

It rained all day. We wait and wait and wait until about 4 o'clock in the afternoon. The train to Chicago is at 6 o'clock, and the Red Sox were supposed to be on that train. There was no pullman that night to Chicago, and the Red Sox were out of the race then.

I wanted to play it like nobody's business. So I got hold of Joe Cronin [the Red Sox manager]. Cronin said, "Well, we have to get league permission." So we called Harridge. He said, "If Boston agrees to it, you can play it tonight."

So Cronin said, "Yeah, we'll stay over. We'll probably beat you." It's still raining. He pitched Pinky Woods, big huge fellow. I thought he was doing us a favor. But he beat us, 4 to 1. In the mud. It rained all through the ball game.

When the game was over, Cronin came by. He said, "I warned you." I said. "Well, I'm satisfied. What difference does it make whether I lose the pennant by half a game or a game?"

In a way, Cronin may have been repaying Sewell a favor dating back to 1933 when Cronin, at 26, was in his first year as a manager, and turned for help to his veteran catcher, Sewell, who was six years his elder. The team was the Washington Senators, and they won the pennant.

Sewell:

It was 19 and 33, and Joe Cronin came to me in the spring of the year and he said, "Luke, I don't know anything about pitching. I want you to help me with the pitching." I said, "In what respect?" He said, "Well, tell me when you think a man begins to weaken, and when we should change pitchers."

So all year long, and during the World Series, when I picked up dirt and threw it toward first base, Joe started a man warming up. When I picked up the dirt and threw it towards Cronin at shortstop, he took the pitcher out. Nobody on the club knew about it except Cronin and myself.

But Cronin's generosity had not helped the Browns after all. In the mud, late at night, before fewer than 3,000 fans, the Browns' pennant hopes appeared to have been all but snuffed out. Trailing Detroit by one game, the Browns had to face the Yankees in the last four games of the season while the Tigers hosted Washington.

The Yanks were strong and motivated. They had beaten the Browns ten of eighteen games that season. Only three games out of first place, they still had a slim chance for the pennant. The Senators were last and had won only three of their eighteen games with the Tigers. After the fight in St. Louis, they seemed unlikely to exert themselves unduly in the Browns' behalf.

Even should the Browns overcome these odds and gain a game on the Tigers, thus ending the season in a tie, the advantage would still lie with Detroit. A one-game play-off would be held, and a coin flip for the home-field advantage was won by the Tigers.

Christman:

We thought we had a chance, although it wasn't much of one after we got beat by the Red Sox. The thing that bothered us more than anything else before the series with the Yankees was that we had already flipped, and if we tied at the end of the season we were going to have to play the ball game in Detroit, and Newhouser was going to pitch it. That killed us, because he beat us every time we were in Detroit.

While the Browns worried, the Russian army pushed into Transylvania; the U.S. Army crossed the Rhine into Germany and broke the Siegfried Line. A dispatch from Stockholm, Sweden, reported that Hitler would escape the Allies in a special submarine loaded with gold and able to travel 20,000 miles without refueling.

Within President Roosevelt's cabinet, Treasury Secretary Henry Morgenthau was espousing a postwar policy of destroying Germany as an industrial nation and settling its people on small farms. Morgenthau believed that Russia would need its manpower at home and would be glad to let the U.S., Britain, and France handle postwar occupation chores.

Cordell Hull, the Secretary of State, and Henry Stimson, the Secretary of War, disagreed with Morgenthau. But his assumptions about Russia were shared by many. As wartime allies, both the Russians and Chinese were held in high esteem by most Americans. Not long before, Vice-President Henry Wallace had visited China. Wallace, too, considered himself able to predict the postwar behavior of other nations. He said that Russia and China would be so friendly that their border would be like the one between the U.S. and Canada.

In Quebec, President Roosevelt and Prime Minister Churchill

met to plan military strategy against Japan. In New York, the newspaper trade publication, *Editor and Publisher,* reported that Thomas E. Dewey, the Republican candidate for president, was supported editorially by 617 daily newspapers with a total circulation of 21,439,768. President Roosevelt was supported by 220 newspapers with a total circulation of 4,676,510.

In Poplar Bluff, Missouri, the entire Butler County draft board resigned when sixty-seven farmers, deferred by the local draft board, were reclassified 1-A by Missouri Selective Service Headquarters, and were drafted. In the funnies, Judge Hedge, a weak man, ordered Annie to leave the poor but virtuous woman with whom she had been living and go to an orphan's home. "He's afraid of Mrs. J. Bleating Hart and her gang of do-gooders," Annie's dismissed guardian said with disgust. Although disappointed, Annie took the judge's order with her usual determination to make the best of a bad thing.

That Glorious 1944 Season
Part 4: The Great Victory
and the Streetcar Series

Although the Browns were behind and faced a tougher opponent, the matchups were straightforward. New York at St. Louis and Washington at Detroit. Single games were rained out Thursday in both cities. So it was doubleheaders Friday, followed by single games Saturday and Sunday. All games to be played in daylight. Gentlemen, retire to your corners and come out fighting.

The Tigers started Ruffus Gentry in the first game, saving Dizzy Trout for the nightcap. Gentry had won eleven games and lost fourteen; he led the league in walks issued. But this day he was sharp. So was Washington's Johnny Niggeling, the old knuckle-baller who formerly had pitched for the Browns.

In the first, Rudy York drove home a run for Detroit with a 440-foot triple. The Senators tied it in the sixth. In the Tiger seventh Wakefield doubled, Jimmy Outlaw singled, Joe Hoover walked, and Gentry and Doc Cramer singled. Three runs scored. Detroit won, 5 to 2, as Gentry scattered nine hits and walked only three.

The Tigers had a leg up, winning a game without using either Trout or Newhouser. But in the nightcap Trout was bombed. Washington's Stan Spence hit a three-run homer in the third.

Trout was lifted after yielding six runs and six hits in four innings. Mickey Haefner, another knuckle ball pitcher, gave up twelve Detroit hits, including three by York, but the Tigers could not put them together. The Senators won, 9 to 2.

In St. Louis, the Yankees started fast. Snuffy Stirnweiss, the lead-off batter, singled. He moved to second on a bunt, to third on an infield out, and scored when Johnny Lindell bounced a single over the head of Jack Kramer, the Brownie pitcher.

Ernie Bonham, pitching for the Yankees, led off the third with a single and Stirnweiss followed with his second straight hit, a double that put two men in scoring position with no outs. Kramer retired Bud Metheny and Hersh Martin. But against Lindell, Kramer's superb control left him and he threw a wild pitch. Bonham ran for home, but catcher Red Hayworth scrambled after the ball and nipped Bonham at the plate.

The exertion may have tired the Yankee pitcher. In the home half of the third, Kramer doubled, Gutteridge beat out a bunt, Kreevich singled, and Laabs singled: two runs. In the eighth, Stephens singled and McQuinn homered. Kramer meantime stifled the Yankees. The Browns won, 4 to 1.

The second game gave the Browns an opportunity to tie the pennant race. But they were batting against Hank Borowy, New York's best pitcher, and he was throwing well. In the first, Gutteridge doubled, advanced to third on a wild pitch, and scored on an infield out. The Browns did not score again, and got only one other hit, a single by Stephens in the seventh.

Nelson Potter was pitching superbly for the Browns. He allowed only six hits, and the Yankees threatened to score only twice. Potter:

There were a couple of men on and two out. Big Lindell was with the Yankees then, and he hit one to left center that was hit good. I turned around, and little old Mike Kreevich was already on his way. He pulled it down just at the last minute. Beautiful catch.

In the ninth, they had the tying run on second and Paul Waner was the pinch hitter. He hit a kind of a little nubber. It looked like it might be a base hit, over Gutteridge's head. And Gutteridge just backpedaled and made a jump at the last minute and it stuck in the web. That ended the ball game.

The Browns won, 1 to 0.

The race was tied. On Saturday, Hal Newhouser struck out seven and won his twenty-ninth game of the year, 7 to 3. Already leading 2 to 0, the Tigers scored three in the sixth. York homered, and Cramer doubled two runs home.

In St. Louis, Brownie hitters kept the pressure on Brownie pitchers. This time Galehouse watched his teammates squander two scoring opportunities. In the first, the Browns loaded the bases with no one out and scored only one run. In the second, they loaded the bases with two outs and failed to score.

In the Yankee second, Lindell rammed a line drive toward the left-field corner; Christman leaped and caught it, the force carrying him backward so far that he almost fell. With Stirnweiss on base in the Yankee fourth, Kreevich made a diving catch of Martin's low line drive. In the Brownie sixth, Gene Moore hit his sixth home run of the year, his fourth against the Yanks. No Yankee reached third base and only two reached second. The score was 2 to 0.

The Yankees had scored only one run in the three games, none in the last twenty-six innings. But for the last game, the Browns were down to Jakucki, the least reliable of their starting pitchers. Jakucki had his own way of preparing for a big game. Bob Bauman, the trainer:

The night before our last game, we were staying at the old Melbourne Hotel. Jakucki was going to work on Sunday, and this meant everything; it meant the World Series. So the boys were watching him about drinking.

So Sig comes in the hotel about 11 o'clock at night carrying a big bag. A bag of whiskey; that's the way he carried it. Taylor was a coach, and he hollered at him, "You're not going to take that to your room!" Jakucki says, "You're not going to take it away from me!" Taylor says, "You're not going to drink that tonight, I'll tell you that." Jakucki says, "I tell you. I won't drink tonight." Taylor says, "I don't believe you." Jakucki says, "I promise you I won't take a drink tonight. But don't try to take the liquor away, or there'll be trouble."

So the next thing I saw of Jakucki was at the ball park the next day. Before the ball game, I'm working on him. I can see he's been drinking. He says, "I kept my promise last night. I told him I wouldn't take a drink last night but I didn't promise I wouldn't take one this morning."

Denny Galehouse:

The night before the game, Jack Kramer got him, and he said, "Hey, now, Sig, this is important. This could mean the pennant to us. Can't you, one night, lay off the stuff and come in shape. Because we really need you."

He was putting it on thick. "We got to have that game tomorrow and you can do it if you stay in halfway decent shape. Will you do it for us, for the rest of the team? We're all pulling for you."

So Sig said, "Well, yeah, O.K." I guess maybe he did, because the next morning Jack said he saw him and said, "By golly, attaboy, Sig!" Sig said, "I got to have a little something before I go out there." So I think he had a couple of snorts before he went to the park, to kind of straighten himself out.

In Detroit, Emil (Dutch) Leonard, the Washington pitcher, was facing pressure of a different kind. Shortly before leaving the Book-Cadillac Hotel for the ball park, Leonard got a telephone call. He recalled it thirty-two years later in an interview with Milt Richman, sports editor of United Press International. Leonard:

I picked up the phone. This man on the other end said, "Hello, Dutch," and he sounded so friendly I assumed it was someone from back home in Southern Illinois, because the war was still going on and a lot of people from back home were coming up to Detroit to work in the factories.

"You're pitching today, aren't you?" this fellow said. I said, "Yeah, I think so," and he said, "Good. You have a chance to make a lot of money." I said, "What do you mean?" and he said, "I'm authorized to offer you better than $20,000 if you don't have a good day."

It didn't dawn on me what he meant. I said, "What are you talking about?" He said again, "If you don't have a good day, you can make yourself better than $20,000." Then it dawned on me. This was some gambling syndicate or something. I said, "Go to hell" and hung up.

I'll tell you the truth, I was scared. I was just a small-town boy and I didn't know what to do. But George Case was my buddy, and on the way out to the ball park I told him about the call. He said, "Dutch, somebody might have heard that conversation. You'd better tell somebody about it, Ossie or someone." [Ossie Bluege was the Washington manager.]

When we got to the ball park I told Clyde Milan, one of our coaches. He went over and told Ossie, then came back with a new ball, handed it to me, and said, "You're still the pitcher."

The game in Detroit started an hour ahead of the one in St. Louis. A crowd of 45,565 was on hand; Leonard, still another knuckle-ball pitcher with the Senators, faced Trout, pitching with only one day of rest. In the Washington fourth, Joe Kuhel singled and Stan Spence, who had homered off Trout in the second game of the series, did it again. The Senators scored a third run in that inning and a fourth run in the eighth.

Leonard stopped the Tigers until the ninth. Two pinch hitters, Chuck Hostetler and Don Ross, singled. Doc Cramer's long fly brought Hostetler home. But Leonard retired Eddie Mayo and Pinky Higgins. The Senators won, 4 to 1. Most of the Detroit fans stayed in their seats to watch the results of the Brownie game posted, inning by inning.

Although a lot better than usual, the Browns' attendance had been disappointing all season. The opening win streak did not awaken much fan interest, and neither did the close pennant race. Going into their final home stand of the season, the Browns were last in the league in attendance. It was as if St. Louis fans could not believe that the Browns had finally put a winning team on the field.

The final four-game series against the Yankees should have played before packed houses. But the Friday doubleheader, played on a cloudy and cool day, drew only 6,172 paid fans. That was the day the Browns tied the race; surely the fans would pour out for the Saturday afternoon game. In fact, the park was less than half filled; paid attendance totaled 12,982.

On the final day, with the pennant at stake, St. Louis awakened. At 7 A.M., fans started lining up on Dodier Street for general admission tickets. An hour before game time, the streets around Sportsman's Park were so jammed with cars and people that Margaret DeWitt, wife of the Brownie general manager, had difficulty getting to the gate. Clifford Kachline, a young *Sporting News* correspondent who is now historian at the National Baseball Library in Cooperstown, stood on a railing, the press of fans on all sides preventing a fall. The attendance was 35,518 paid and 37,815 altogether; 15,000 more were turned away. It was the first time the Brownies had filled Sportsman's Park since Phil Ball expanded the seating capacity in 1925.

As the game began, the Brownie defense began to show strain. With two out in the Yankee first, Herschel Martin tripled. Lindell grounded to short, but Stephens threw the ball over McQuinn's head, Martin scoring. In the second, Christman fumbled a grounder by Stirnweiss, who reached first and promptly tried to steal second. Hayworth threw the ball into center field, Stirnweiss reaching third. Metheny grounded to Christman, who caught Stirnweiss in a rundown. But Martin doubled Metheny home.

Mel Queen stopped the Browns without a hit for three innings. Kreevich singled in the fourth, bringing up Laabs, who was just beginning to hit after a dismal season in which he had registered only three home runs. Laabs caught a fast ball and hit it high into the left field bleachers, tying the score. A few minutes later, the final score in Detroit was posted on the Sportsman's Park scoreboard.

With two out in the fifth, Kreevich again singled. Laabs pounded a curve ball 400 feet into the left-center field bleachers. In the eighth Stephens hit a home run onto the pavilion roof in right.

Jakucki pitched masterfully. In the last six innings, only one Yankee reached third base. In the Yankee ninth, with the Browns leading 5 to 2, Lindell lined deep to Moore in right-center. Etten singled past Gutteridge. Crosetti lined to Kreevich in center. Oscar Grimes popped a foul ball toward the Yankee bullpen on the first-base side. An easy chance for veteran George McQuinn.

Luke Sewell:

The greatest play that I ever saw in baseball? George McQuinn made it on the last day of the season in 19 and 44. There were two out in the ninth inning and Grimes was at bat and he hit a pop fly, about fifty or seventy-five feet high and about ten feet outside of first base. McQuinn caught it and it was the greatest play I ever saw in baseball.

It cinched the pennant for us. We were milling around and everything, and I was shaking hands with the boys, and Don Barnes came out. He owned the ballclub. I looked at him and he was crying, tears just running down his cheeks. I never came as near crying myself, on a baseball field.

When the shock of winning the thing was over, it was a tremendous feeling. You got a little weak in the knees.

It wasn't a runaway. We had a lot of fun out of it.

Even during that final game. Don Gutteridge:

Ellis Clary, our utility man, as funny a man as I've ever seen, was quite an avid football fan. He liked to bet those football cards. On the last day of the season, it was either win or lose the pennant, and he had a radio there, listening to the football game. The Chicago Bears were playing Green Bay, as I remember, and he had some money on it.

And Al Zarilla, he said he was going to be a golfer. This was during the game, and he had a golf club, and he was up in the clubhouse. He was using the big box of sand where everybody spits tobacco juice, and he was hitting like he was in a sandtrap.

That just shows you how loose and cool everybody was.

The Browns won the pennant with eighty-nine wins and sixty-five losses. Their winning percentage of .578 set a new low in American League history, and was indicative of the war's leveling effect; in 1945, the Tigers were to win the pennant with a percentage of only .575.

The 1944 Browns may have been as good, or nearly as good, as the Tigers and Yankees, but they won largely on pluck, getting more runs out of their hits than any other team in the league. The Browns' team batting average of .252 was seventh in the American League, but they finished second to Boston in runs scored.

Stephens hit twenty home runs, second to Etten among American League sluggers, and led the league in runs batted in with 109. Kreevich hit .301, eighth best in the league, and was the Browns' only .300 hitter. Among the pitchers, Potter was nineteen and seven, Kramer was seventeen and thirteen, Muncrief was thirteen and eight, Jakucki was thirteen and nine and Galehouse was nine and ten, winning most of his games during the stretch drive. Caster had six wins, six losses, twelve saves, and an earned run average of 2.44, best on the team.

No Brownie pitcher came close to matching the exploits of Detroit's aces. Trout won twenty-seven, lost fourteen, and led the league in ERA with 2.12. Newhouser was voted the league's most valuable player for his twenty-nine victories. Trout finished second in the voting, Stephens third, and Dick Wakefield, who played in only seventy-eight games, was fourth.

By September 1, a month before the season ended, the Cardinals already had ninety-one wins, more than the Browns were to total for the whole season, and could barely stay awake. No other team in the National League could touch them. Pittsburgh tried, winning nineteen of twenty-one games during an August streak without gaining a single game on St. Louis.

Other teams in both leagues were so desperately short of manpower that they imposed heavy burdens on their capable players. Ray Mueller of Cincinnati and Frankie Hayes of the Philadelphia Athletics each established a record for consecutive games caught in his league. Walker Cooper, the Cardinal catcher, played in only ninety-seven games; Ken O'Dea, the second-stringer, was better than most catchers in the league. Disdainfully flicking crumbs to their hungry rivals, the Cardinals sold pitchers Preacher Roe to Pittsburgh, the second-place team, and Harry Gumbert to Cincinnati, the team in third place.

As a team, Cardinal batters in 1944 led the league in hits, runs, batting average, doubles, and home runs. Musial hit .347, Hopp .336, and Cooper .317. The Cardinal pitching staff led the league in strikeouts, shutouts, and earned run average. The league's three top pitchers in winning percentage were Cardinals: Wilks, seventeen and four, .810; Brecheen, sixteen and five, .762; and Mort Cooper, twenty-two and seven, .759.

Although they dozed through a long losing streak in September, losing fifteen games out of twenty, the Cardinals finished with 105 wins and forty-nine losses for a .682 percentage. The Pirates were second, fourteen and a half games behind.

The Cardinals were not only better than the Browns but also more experienced. Despite the age and vagabond background of many Brownie players, not a single one of them had ever appeared in a World Series.

St. Louis bookies quoted the Cards at one to two, the Browns at eight to five. Reserved seat tickets were snapped up at six for $37.50, and scalped at six for $150. The center-field bleachers, kept empty during most games to provide a dark background for the hitters, were sold out for the Series. Shirt-sleeve weather would mean a background of white shirts, ideal for fast overhand pitchers like Cooper, Lanier, and Galehouse.

Mayor Aloys P. Kaufmann proclaimed the week beginning October 2 as "St. Louis Baseball Week," and a glorious event it was. Lesser activities were shunted aside; a federal grand jury recessed for the week. Most baseball historians live elsewhere, and the 1944 World Series has gone down in print as the St. Louis "Trolley Series." That term benumbs any resident of St. Louis, where the public conveyances were always called streetcars; and the Series, appropriately and alliteratively enough, was called the "Streetcar Series."

(Indeed, so remote are the historians that an otherwise fine reference book, *The Sports Encyclopedia: Baseball,* places the final Brownie series of the season in Yankee Stadium, apparently on the assumption that that is where all historic American League games are played. Not on your Griesedieck Bros. Beer billboard [right field corner, Sportsman's Park] were those games played in New York.)

The first clash between managers Luke Sewell and Billy Southworth was over a place to sleep. With housing short in wartime, the Sewells and Southworths had shared an apartment all season. One closet was for men, with Sewell's clothes at one end and Southworth's at the other. The Browns and Cardinals were never in St. Louis at the same time. As Sewell would be leaving with the Browns, Mrs. Sewell would entrain for the family home in Akron, and into the Lindell Towers apartment would come the Southworths.

However admirable this display of interleague cooperation might have appeared during the season, it would never do for the opposing managers to sit in the same living room after a World Series game, sipping bourbon and chatting politely with their wives. Besides, Sewell wanted to invite his mother, and Mrs. Southworth could hardly be expected to put up with a mother-in-law from the wrong family and, indeed, the wrong league. To the relief of both couples, another resident of the building was out of town in October and graciously let the Southworths use his apartment.

Southworth named Cooper to start the first game. Sewell was coy, privately telling Galehouse that he would start but pledging him to secrecy and telling no one else until shortly before the game.

Both pitchers were strong. In the Cardinal third, Hopp and Sanders singled, and Musial advanced them to scoring position with a sacrifice. Walker Cooper was intentionally passed to load the bases. Galehouse then struck out Kurowski, and got Litwhiler to bounce into a force play.

The Browns were hitless until two were out in the fourth. Then Moore singled to right and McQuinn hit a line drive that barely reached the pavilion roof in right. The Browns got no more hits, but the Cardinals got no runs until the ninth, when Marion doubled, advanced on an infield out, and scored on a fly ball. The Browns won, 2 to 1.

As things turned out, the Series turned on four plays in the second game. It was another pitchers' duel, Potter versus Lanier. The play that still torments Sewell was vintage Brownie stuff, and occurred in the Cardinal third. Emil Verban led off with a single, and Lanier bunted.

Sewell:

We made six misplays on the ball. That's pretty difficult. He popped a little ball down the third-base line. Potter and Christman came over to it. They looked at each other and let the ball drop, and Potter picked it up and he rolled it up his arm. That's two misplays.

He threw it to Gutteridge at first. Little Don was trying to hold his foot on the bag and get the ball, when he should have gotten off and caught the ball. It went down into right field. That's three.

Chet Laabs let it hit that right field wall there, reached over to pick it up and it rolled through his legs. That's four. He picked the ball up and fumbled on his pickup, that's five, and threw it away at second base. That's six misplays on the one ball.

Two errors were charged on the play, both to Potter. While the Browns threw the ball around, Verban raced to third base. Augie Bergamo drove him in with a ground out.

An inning later, another Brownie error helped the Cardinals score their second run. With one out, Sanders walked and Kurowski singled him to second. Marion grounded sharply to Christman, who had a chance for a double play but instead fumbled the ball (or "leather-covered pill," as the *Sporting News* account had it). Verban drove in Sanders with an outfield fly.

With two out in the seventh, the Brownies tied the game. Moore singled, Hayworth doubled off the left field wall, and Mancuso, batting for Potter, singled Hayworth home.

Kreevich opened the Brownie eighth with a double. Blix Donnelly relieved for the Cardinals and struck out the side. Muncrief was pitching for the Browns, and the two relievers held until the eleventh. The Browns were the visiting team. McQuinn led off the eleventh, and was the hapless victim of two critical plays.

The screen that stretched from the top of the right field wall to the pavilion roof extended sideways to right center, and then stopped. A ball hit over the wall to the left of the screen was a home run. McQuinn drove one to right center, just a bit too low to reach the roof and just a bit too far to the right to fall into the stands. It bounced off the screen for a double.

Christman bunted perfectly down the third-base line. Donnelly grabbed the ball quickly and threw it to third base. The throw was perfect, hitting Kurowski's glove low. McQuinn was already sliding and slid into the tag; Kurowski would not have had time to move his glove.

Sewell:

Donnelly made a hell of a play on the ball, wheeled around and threw it and the umpire called it [clap] just quick like that. I said, "OH NO!" He said, "I'm right." I said, "You are, but you called it too damned quick."

The Browns did not score. In the Cardinal eleventh, Sanders singled, was sacrificed to second by Kurowski, and was driven home by Ken O'Dea's pinch single. The Cardinals won, 3 to 2.

Sewell:

I had brought my mother up from Alabama. She had never seen a professional game in her life; wasn't very interested in the thing. I said, "Now, you come on up. I want you to see this. You'll probably never see us again in another World Series."

So I got her up to St. Louis, got her a car and a driver, got them two seats right by the exit where they could just walk out, and I got them a special parking place right across the street. And I said, "Now, any time you get tired and you want to get home, you just tell this fellow, and he'll take you home."

So she stayed the first day, nine innings, and went home. Everything was lovely, we had a nice visit. After that second game, I must have stayed up in the clubhouse an hour and a half. Finally I got out and went to the apartment.

She liked a rocking chair, my mother. Well, I had a rocking chair for her and she was rocking away. I went up, put my arm around her shoulder, and I said, "Mom, what did you think of that game today?" They had beat us in eleven innings, you know. "Oh," she said, "I was awfully glad when someone won because I was getting mighty tired."

It just about broke my heart.

The Browns won the third game, 6 to 2, as Kramer struck out ten. The Browns, for once, hit well. With two out in the fourth, they scored three runs on successive singles by Moore, Stephens, McQuinn, Zarilla, and Christman. In the seventh, Gutteridge doubled and eventually scored on a wild pitch, and McQuinn doubled home a second run. Both Cardinal runs were unearned.

The Browns led, two games to one. Had they won the second game as well, they would have been up three to nothing, a lead that might have been insurmountable.

The two-to-one edge was not. In the fourth game, Jakucki was touched for two runs in the first on a home run by Musial, and two more in the third on a single by Musial. The Browns hit Harry Brecheen rather well, totaling nine hits, but could not bunch them and fell afoul of the superior Cardinal defense. In the first, Kreevich singled with one out and Moore lined a ball toward the center field wall. Hopp made a spectacular catch. In the eighth, Moore walked, Stephens singled him to third, and Laabs grounded hard through the box and toward center field. Marion caught the ball and flicked it to Verban to start a double play. It was the kind of play that, during the season, had earned Marion the designation as Most Valuable Player in the National League and Player of the Year in the major leagues. Not bad for a man who hit .267. The Cardinals won, 5 to 1.

In the fifth game, Cooper struck out twelve and Galehouse struck out ten; their total of twenty-two set a World Series record that stood for nineteen years. The Browns did not score. Sanders and Litwhiler homered for the Cardinals, both hitting fly balls that, according to Galehouse, would have been caught had the wind not blown them out of the park. The Cardinals won, 2 to 0, to go ahead, three games to two.

Potter faced Lanier in the sixth game. In the second, Laabs tripled to center and McQuinn, by far the best hitter in the Series, singled him home. In the third, Verban and Lanier singled for the Cardinals, but Potter struck out Litwhiler and Hopp.

With one out in the Cardinal fourth, Walker Cooper walked and Sanders singled him to third. Kurowski grounded to Stephens. A double-play ball, Stephens to Gutteridge to McQuinn. But both runners were called safe; Gutteridge had failed to touch second, and Kurowski had beaten the throw to first. Cooper scored on the play. Verban and Lanier singled, driving in Sanders and Kurowski. The Cardinals won the game, 3 to 1, and the Series, four games to two.

It was a defensive Series. The Cardinals made only one error, setting a record for a six-game Series with a fielding percentage of .996. Partly because of the background of white shirts in center field, ninety-two strikeouts were recorded, a record for a six-game Series that still stood thirty-two years later. As a team, the Browns batted .183; the Cardinals batted .240. McQuinn batted .438 for the Browns. Verban, the Cardinals' weakest hitter and the only man in their lineup whom the Brownie pitchers had not bothered to discuss before the Series, hit .412.

The fan support appeared to be about evenly divided. The *Sporting News* said that the crowds were polite, perhaps because so many fans were ambivalent. In St. Louis, neighborhood boundaries did not determine one's baseball loyalties. It was not like Chicago, where South Siders root for the White Sox and North Siders root for the Cubs, or New York, where, at that time, Brooklyn residents supported the Dodgers and the rest of New York supported the Yanks and Giants.

Even in a championship season, the Browns were not able to

reap the usual financial rewards or gain a proper degree of dignity.
By Brownie standards, home attendance was marvelous. By baseball standards, it was mediocre. Outdrawing the Cardinals for
once, the Browns attracted 508,644 fans to their home games. It
was the Browns' highest attendance since 1924, but ranked fifth in
the American League for 1944.

October 9, 1944, was a harbinger of the Browns' future. The
sixth game of the World Series was played that day and drew
31,63C fans. In Baltimore, a Little World Series game the same
day drew 52,833. Altogether, World Series gate receipts totaled
$906,122, the lowest amount since 1939. The individual players'
shares of $4,626 for the Cardinals and $2,744 for the Browns were
the lowest since 1920. (Jakucki, so his teammates said, spent his
before leaving town.) Even so, the Brown and Cardinal organiza-
tions had to give half of their respective shares to war relief agencies, and the players had to take 10 percent of their meager shares
in War Bonds.

Mark Christman:

By the time Uncle Sam got his share, we wound up with about $2,400
cash. That was terrible; worst I ever saw.

Bill DeWitt:

When we won the pennant that year, Landis ruled that half of the pro-
ceeds that were to come to the clubs were to be given to Army-Navy relief.
I said, "Jesus, here we are losing money, and for once we get a chance to
make some money in the World Series, and we have to give half of it
away."

After the Cardinals won the Series, Don Barnes and I went into Sam
Breadon's office to congratulate him. And he said, "If we'd have lost this
Series to the Browns, I'd have had to leave town. It would have been a dis-
grace to lose to the Browns."

Showing superior manners, Barnes and DeWitt managed to
laugh at Breadon's gross joke. Barnes ventured the opinion that
the pennant would purify the team's history and remove "the curse
of the Browns" in dealing with promising amateur players, who in
the past had often blanched at the prospect of a career with the
Brownies. To grace the Sportsman's Park flagpole, said Barnes,

"I'm going to buy the biggest pennant that the OPA [Office of Price Administration] will allow."

But history could not so easily be forgotten. During the winter, Bob Sieger of the Detroit *News* tabulated the all-time American League standings for the *Sporting News*. The Yankees were first. The Browns were last, 802½ games behind.

The Browns, still laughingstocks in their championship year. Would that feeling be tempered by thirty-two years of hindsight? Marty Marion:

We thought we were going to just walk through them. Who in hell's the Browns, you know. By the time we got in that first game, we found out they were a pretty good ballclub. Yes, sir. We had a hell of a time beating those boys. They were tough. If they'd have beat us that second game we'd have probably been in trouble. We had a good ballclub but it wasn't great. They had quite a bit of pride.

That Streetcar Series. [pause] If the Browns had beat us, that would have been really a disgrace.

CHAPTER 12

Winning for Dear Old Navy

America's best baseball teams during the war may not have been in the major leagues at all, but rather in the Army and Navy. The Navy was particularly adept at stationing its outstanding baseball players at Norfolk, Virginia; Great Lakes, Illinois; and Pearl Harbor, Hawaii, where their skills could be used to improve morale, inspire enlistments, sell War Bonds, and satisfy the ego of sports-minded Naval brass.

Captain Harry Adrian McClure, commander of the Norfolk Naval Operating Base, had a leg up in this kind of competition. Before Pearl Harbor, Gene Tunney, the former heavyweight boxing champion, was commissioned a Naval lieutenant commander and told to organize a physical fitness program for the Navy. Tunney's program was located at Norfolk, and he was empowered to recruit athletes, coaches, and physical education specialists, granting them immediate rank as chief petty officer, the highest rank an enlisted man could achieve in the Navy.

Tunney's recruits were nicknamed "Tunney Fish." After a few months of training, most of them were sent to Naval bases around the country, where they conducted calisthenic and athletic programs. But McClure was anxious to keep his baseball stars, and turned for help to an old Navy friend, Admiral Randall Jacobs, who happened to be chief of Naval personnel.

With Lieutenant Commander Tunney bringing them in and Admiral Jacobs keeping them there, Norfolk quickly became a baseball power. In 1942, playing exhibition games against minor league teams and other service squads, Captain McClure's team won ninety-two games and lost only eight.

Fred Hutchinson was twenty-three and one; Bob Feller was nineteen and three. Vinnie Smith of the Pirates caught and Sam Chapman of the Athletics played in the outfield. The rest of the players were competent minor leaguers.

In 1943, McClure added first baseman Eddie Robinson of the Indians, catcher and outfielder Don Padgett of the Dodgers, and pitchers Walt Masterson of the Senators and Charley Wagner of the Red Sox. With the help of Admiral Jacobs, Dom DiMaggio of the Red Sox was transferred in to play center field. McClure was rich with shortstops; he kept Phil Rizzuto of the Yankees and let the Norfolk Naval Air Station have Pee Wee Reese of the Dodgers.

It was this squad that took on, and defeated, the Senators at Griffith Stadium in the big War Bond game promoted by Shirley Povich of the Washington *Post* in 1943. McClure always sat in the dugout with his players, but was a brusque Naval type who would not permit unauthorized intrusions.

Povich:

Bing Crosby was going to sing, and was in the dugout talking to some of the players. McClure chased him off. He said, "Get Crosby out of here."

His ignorance of baseball was tremendous. I was down there one time, had written a story about the base. He must have liked it, because he called me in. He'd hold court every morning, with thirty or forty people waiting. When I arrived they ushered me right in.

There was the captain sitting there, and he said, "I'm glad to see you, Mr. Povich, and I want to thank you for coming. I called you because I have a question to ask you. Did you ever hear of a pitcher named John Vander Meer, and do you think he would help this team?" Of course, Vander Meer had pitched back-to-back no-hitters a few years before. That was how ignorant the man was.

McClure was solicitous of his help but never forgot the perquisites of his own rank. When Dom DiMaggio fell in center field, apparently injured, McClure rushed out to help him—in a chauffeured jeep. Late for a game one day, he told an aide that the game could begin but the Norfolk players should withhold their scoring until he arrived. They did so, although unintentionally.

As a recruiter, McClure met his match in Mickey Cochrane, the great Athletics and Tigers catcher of the 1930s, who was given a Navy commission to coach the baseball team at Great Lakes. Cochrane's team was sixty-three and fourteen in 1942, and fifty-two and ten in 1943. In 1944, Great Lakes won thirty-three games in a row and finished the season with forty-eight victories and two losses. Its final game of the season was a 17 to 4 drubbing of the Cleveland Indians.

Playing for Great Lakes at one time or another during the war were first basemen Johnny Mize of the Giants and Johnny McCarthy of the Braves; second basemen Billy Herman of the Dodgers and Johnny Lucadello of the Browns; shortstops Alban Glossop of the Dodgers and Eddie Pellagrini, who later played for the Red Sox; third basemen Merrill May of the Phillies, Ken Keltner of the Indians, and Pinky Higgins of the Tigers; catchers Walker Cooper of the Cardinals, Clyde McCullough of the Cubs, and George (Skeets) Dickey of the White Sox, younger brother of Bill Dickey; outfielders Barney McCosky of the Tigers, Joe Grace and Red McQuillen of the Browns, Whitey Platt of the Cubs, and Gene Woodling of the Indians; and pitchers Bob Feller and Tom Ferrick of the Indians, Virgil Trucks of the Tigers, Bob Klinger of the Pirates, Johnny (Bear Tracks) Schmitz and Vern Olsen of the Cubs, Johnny Rigney of the White Sox, Denny Galehouse of the Browns, and Clyde Shoun of the Reds. Schoolboy Rowe of the Phillies both pitched and played the outfield for Great Lakes in 1944. Johnny Groth, then 18 years old and just out of high school, made his mark in the Great Lakes outfield and was signed by the Tigers, for whom he later starred. (Grace, Feller, and several others played at various times during the war for both Norfolk and Great Lakes.)

Gene Woodling entered the Navy at the age of 21, after being called up from the minor leagues in time to play eight games of the 1943 season for Cleveland. After the war, he was traded to the Yankees, where he played on Casey Stengel's championship teams of the early 1950s. He says that the Great Lakes squad may have been as good as the Yankees. Woodling:

I was drafted into the Navy in the fall of '43 and sent to Great Lakes. I was just going through regular basic training, and word had gotten out that I was a professional ballplayer. So they called me over to mainside.

A fellow named Tony Hinkle, who was quite a basketball coach at Butler, was the athletic director at Great Lakes. He asked me if I would like to stay the next year in ship's company, as they called it, and play for Great Lakes. Well, would I like to! Yeah! I like to jump through the ceiling. And that was not realizing the type of ballclub we were going to have. My Lord, all the great ones were there.

Well, we hardly lost a ball game. We played all the major league clubs; all sixteen of them. We beat them all. Never lost. That was in '44.

Roy Hartsfield was with the team, the guy who's managing the new Toronto franchise. Roy and I were just the kids. Gee whiz, young guys like Roy and myself getting a chance to play with these guys! Billy Herman had better baseball sense than any guy I've ever been around. My Lord, I learned a lot. It helped my career.

Bob Feller touched all bases, going from Norfolk to a combat assignment and finally to Great Lakes. Feller:

I went right down to Norfolk after enlisting, and went through the whole routine, basic training and all. I knew I was going into Tunney's physical fitness program, but I didn't know anything about playing ball. Sam Chapman was in my class. Then I pushed a platoon that Sam Snead was in.

When the spring came, we were playing ball. I pitched War Bond games in Newark, Washington, Baltimore, Boston, and so forth. Sold a hell of a lot of Bonds, put on exhibitions. Sam Snead occasionally put on golfing exhibitions at home plate before the game. He'd drive balls down the runway at the air base.

But I told them I wanted to get out of the Tunney program and get into combat; wanted to do something besides standing around handing out balls and bats and making ball fields out of coral reefs. I went to gunnery school at Newport, Rhode Island, but then they got to hassling about my services. Cochrane wanted me at Great Lakes. At the Emmerton Hotel in Baltimore, Tunney and McClure got into a hell of an argument, and Mc-

Clure won. McClure was a great sports fan. He liked the athletes, liked to be around them, would do anything in the world for them.

So I went back to Norfolk, to the gunnery school there. And I went on the U.S.S. *Alabama* that fall. We left the states in December of '42 and came back in April of '45. I had a forty millimeter anti-aircraft crew. I could walk out on that ship now and show you my battle station. It was right out in broad daylight.

We spent the first six or eight months in the North Atlantic. I was playing softball in Iceland in the spring; 2 o'clock in the morning and the sun was still up. I used to go and help a woman stack her peat moss. All the rest of the guys would go to a bar. I'd walk out in the country a few miles, alone, help her stack her peat moss, drive her two cows in, milk 'em, and drink about a quart of milk before I went back to the ship. Only fresh milk I got.

We came back in the later part of the summer, went right through the Panama Canal and over to the South Pacific. We hung around the Fiji Islands for awhile, and then when we got the fleet assembled, and enough men and equipment to start a successful attack, we hit Kwajalein and the Gilberts and the Marshalls and then across to Truk.

We were doing shore bombardments and anti-aircraft protection for about twenty carriers. One day our fleet shot down 400-and-some Jap planes; the Marianas turkey shoot they called it, just the day after the landings at Saipan. Did I get any of them? I don't know. You can't tell; everybody's shooting and the planes are falling all around the place. So who the hell knows who hit them?

Scary? Yes, particularly at night. You're zig-zagging at high speed, and the plane comes in low. You've got all your other ships out there, and it was nothing unusual to have the ships in the periphery get raked by bullets from our own guns, and a lot of guys get killed.

One time we were called to our battle stations. I ran out on the port side aft, where my battle station was, and this other fellow ran out up above. We hit a big swell, going at high speed, and the water picked him up, and I saw him go by. I was on the phones to the sky control, and I told them. By God! As luck would have it, some kid on a destroyer was looking for him, saw him wave. He threw a life raft at him and the son of a bitch, he grabbed it.

I was the only guy who saw him. It was dusk; in five more minutes it would have been all over. He came back, and I get a letter from him every Christmas.

I worked like a son of a bitch while I was in the Navy aboard ship. I was keeping myself in great shape. I had about three lockers tied up with my athletic equipment. I had my rowing machine, my punching bag in the boiler room where it was hotter than hell. And I did my chin-ups and push-ups, and skipping a rope, and roadwork on the beaches, and running around the ship on my jogging track. Had guys aboard ship lined up waiting to take turns catching for me. Even when you're standing around the guns doing nothing, you can do pushups, deep knee bends, deep breathing exercises, high kicking exercises, stretching exercises. There's all these things you can hang from to keep your muscles in shape.

We got back in the spring of '45, landed at Bremerton, and I went to Great Lakes shortly thereafter. I played badminton there with Paul Brown, who coached the football team, took sauna baths, got massaged, and loosened up.

I took Cochrane's old job at the Lakes, and oh, hell, I had a good ballclub. We played all the air bases, because I liked to fly.

I was pitching great. Beat the Cubs; that's the year they won the pennant. But most of the time I coached third base. I had young guys who wanted to pitch, and we had Denny Galehouse. We had Clyde Shoun, too. He was a little bit of a screwball. He gave me some lip, and I threw him off the ballclub. I sent him out to OGU [outgoing unit] and they sent him to the South Pacific. No bullshit, either; tomorrow, pack your sea bag. Zoom!

Even at Norfolk and Great Lakes, the tenure of athletes usually was limited to one year. Some were then dispatched to normal duty assignments, or to conduct athletic programs. Others were dispatched to another Navy baseball team. In late 1944, the action shifted to Hawaii and the South Pacific, where Admiral Chester W. Nimitz, commander-in-chief of the Pacific Fleet, took a personal interest in the baseball program.

Barney McCosky, the star outfielder for Detroit:

I enlisted, wanted to be a pilot. I went somewhere in Ohio to pre-flight school and, hell, I was 25 at the time, and when I got in that school there were kids 19 and 20, just out of college. I couldn't keep up with those guys. I said, "What the hell am I doing here?"

So I called Great Lakes; Mickey Cochrane was a commander there. I said, "Mickey, get me out of this end of it. Get me over there; I'll be a sailor." About a week later I was in Great Lakes. I played ball for him that summer; that was in '43. Tom Ferrick was there, Johnny Mize, Skeeter Dickey, Schmitz of the Cubs, we had a real good ballclub.

Then we were sent to Bainbridge, Maryland. That's where we were sent through Gene Tunney's physical fitness program. From there we went to Treasure Island outside San Francisco. We had a Navy team there, and we played for maybe two or three weeks. Nimitz (in Hawaii) said, "Get those ballplayers out here!" But the captain in San Francisco didn't want to let us go, and kept putting our names at the bottom of the list.

Finally one night all our names were called over the loudspeaker. The next day we were aboard the U.S.S. *Birmingham* and we were on our way to Hawaii. Did the Navy purposely put its best ballplayers on Hawaii? Oh, yeah. That's for sure.

But they didn't put us all on one team. They scattered us out where each team had maybe three or four big league ballplayers. We filled in with minor leaguers and amateurs. I managed Aiea Barracks.

In our barracks we had Bobby Riggs, the tennis player, and Buddy Blattner of the Giants. They would put on great Ping-Pong matches, and the sailors would bet like hell. That Riggs. My God! I had him in my platoon, and I had to put him at the back of the line. He couldn't walk a straight line. In tennis you've got to move sideways, so he duck-walked. Same with Willie ᴾep, the boxer. I had him in my outfit at Bainbridge, and he couldn't march. I put him in front as a platoon leader, but he couldn't walk a straight line, so I had to put him in the middle of the line.

In our baseball league in Hawaii, we also had Aiea Hospital, Kaneohe Bay airbase, and the Pearl Harbor submarine base. We recruited, and had tryouts, and picked the best ballplayers.

We were the chief specialists in the recreation end of it. We had to give exercises, umpire ball games, set up basketball tournaments, be instructors, all this stuff. Everybody played hard, and we really enjoyed playing out there. We had the best equipment. I had Johnny Lucadello and Eddie Pellagrini. Johnny Mize was with the air base.

Hugh Casey was with the air base, and I could hit him like I owned him. This one game, the first time up I hit a home run off him. This was a big game; we were going right down to the championship. The next time up, I bent down to get some dirt in my hand, with my back turned to the pitcher, and bang! He threw the ball while I was bending over and got me right in the middle of the back.

So I walked right out to the mound, and said, "Did you mean that?" He said, "Yeah." With that, I hauled off and whacked him right on the mouth. We had a fight right on the mound. That night, somebody said, "You're going to be shipped out for fighting." Sure enough, that night right after dinner, here comes the page on the loudspeaker. "Chief Specialist McCosky report to headquarters."

I walked in there and saluted our captain. He said, "Relax. You know why I called you in here?" I said, "Yeah, I believe I do. That incident on the field?" He said, "Yeah. Well, if you hadn't gone out after him your ass would have been shipped out of here." So he shook my hand and I walked out.

While the Navy was concentrating its baseball firepower at a few bases, the Army was dispersing its players more widely. Outfielder Terry Moore of the Cardinals and pitcher Mickey Harris of the Red Sox played on opposing teams in the Panama Canal Zone. Moore was given a furlough to attend the 1943 World Series; thirty-three other Canal Zone soldiers wrote to *Yank*, the Army newspaper, complaining that many GI's had been there longer than Moore without receiving so much as a three-day pass. Not that Moore was above Canal Zone activities; he managed the campaign of one Penny Flack, a candidate for War Bond Carnival Queen.

Enos Slaughter and Howard Pollet, Cardinal teammates before the war, played on the same Army Air Force team in Texas. Like most of the big leaguers in service, they put in a full day of work, too, supervising calisthenics and recreation for thousands of servicemen.

Indeed, spokesmen for all the military services repeatedly stated that baseball players received no special treatment, a claim that could not be demonstrated by the case of Private First Class Phil Masi of the Bronx, New York. Stationed at Fort Dix, New Jersey, Masi went twenty-two days without kitchen police duty. He wondered why until a sergeant brought him the paraphernalia of a baseball catcher, whereupon Pfc. Masi confessed that he was not the Boston Braves' catcher of the same name. The next day, Masi was on KP.

By the summer of 1944, the Army, like the Navy, had collected quite a few baseball players in Hawaii. The soldier athletes included Joe DiMaggio and Joe Gordon of the Yankees, Walt Judnich of the Browns, Dario Lodigiani of the White Sox, Mike Mc-Cormick of the Reds, Gerry Priddy of the Senators, and Johnny Beazley of the Cardinals. Anxious to strengthen its baseball brigade, the Army began tapping others. One was Red Ruffing, who did not want to go to Hawaii and worked out a compromise; his orders allowed him to return to stateside duty after he had given Hawaii a try. Ruffing:

I had to fly to San Francisco first, to catch a plane. I got there in the evening. So I talked to the sarge up there; I says, "How long will I be around?" He says, "About a week, but report in to me every morning, see if your name's called." I go in the next morning and my name's called. He comes over to me, he says, "That can't be. Jesus Christ, that fast? They must really want you over there. I got to see those orders."

He comes back, he says, "You know they threw a general off to get you on that plane?" So I was gone that night. Got in there the next morning. And they met me, Joe Gordon and all those, Walt Judnich, DiMaggio. We played a few games over there, played the Navy.

Exercising his option, Ruffing soon returned to his former assignment at Long Beach. But the Army nonetheless agreed to play the Navy in a Hawaii World Series. Admiral Nimitz threw out the first ball and his forces took it from there. The series proved to be one of the Army's most humiliating defeats since Corregidor. The Navy won six straight games. The series was extended to eleven games so servicemen at outlying Hawaiian bases could be entertained. The final tally was eight wins for the Navy, two for the Army, and one tie.

That aroused Army brass in Washington, including Colonel Larry MacPhail, the former general manager of the Dodgers. Enos Slaughter of the Cardinals was then stationed at the Army Air Force Cadet Center in San Antonio, Texas. Slaughter:

Well, the Navy was beating the hell out of the Army in Honolulu. Larry MacPhail was working with the government then in Washington, and he got every major league player in the whole United States who was in the Army Air Corps. In seven days' time I had my orders, and I was at a base in Utah. There were forty-eight of us. We had Birdie Tebbetts catching, Billy Hitchcock, Joe Marty, Howard Pollet, Buster Mills, Ferris Fain, Sid Hudson, Taft Wright, Stan Rojek, Lew Riggs, Max West, Tex Hughson. We stayed there and got shots, and they were supposed to fly us to Honolulu. Instead they took the football players and flew them over there and we went by boat.

When we got over there, it was too late; all the Navy was gone and the Marines were gone.

The Army assault force had indeed been outmaneuvered. It was early 1945, and twenty-eight Navy baseball stars had been dispatched from Hawaii to entertain the American troops who by then had seized most of the Pacific islands from the Japanese. The Navy had added even more outstanding players to its Pacific baseball fleet. One team was captained by Mace Brown, the Red Sox relief pitcher and the only officer among the touring athletes. Brown:

Somebody got the bright idea of all these ballplayers taking a six-weeks tour of all the islands in the Pacific. We had two teams, most of them ex-big leaguers.

Who were they? First off, some non-ballplayers. We had George Abrams and Freddie Apostoli, two prizefighters you probably know of. Apostoli was a champion middleweight and Abrams was the number one middleweight challenger. They put on boxing exhibitions.

Then we had Bobby Riggs, the tennis player, and Buddy Blattner, who played shortstop for the Giants. Buddy was a real great Ping-Pong player; he and somebody won the world doubles championship when he was a kid. He was also a real good tennis player, and Riggs was real good at Ping-Pong. So they'd put on exhibitions in tennis and table tennis.

Here are some of the ballplayers. We had Mickey Vernon and Johnny Mize, Pee Wee Reese, Elbie Fletcher, Barney McCosky, Joe Grace, Virgil Trucks, Johnny Rigney, Tom Ferrick, Johnny Vander Meer, Bob Klinger, Merrill May, Hall White, Vinnie Smith. And Del Ennis; he was just a kid then, hadn't been in the big leagues.

I guess we did have good teams!

The first island we went to, Johnston Island, wasn't big enough to have a game. Then we went to Kwajalein, and Eniwetok, Peleliu, Tinian, Saipan, Guam, Roi-Namur, and Ulithi. They didn't even have a field on a lot of these islands until we got there to play, and then they just took a bulldozer and scraped 'em off. There wasn't any grass; it was all coral rock and dirt. We played up in Saipan, and there must have been 15,000 boys there—a whole division and then some. They were everywhere, all around the field. That night they left for the invasion of Okinawa.

Were we contributing to the war effort? I sure feel so. My goodness sakes, you take 15,000 boys who are going on an invasion tomorrow. If you can entertain them a little today, I'd have to think that's worthwhile.

Barney McCosky:

Nimitz says, "Now, you guys have been here long enough. We're going to play on all the islands." So out we went from Hawaii, and we played on

Ulithi, Guam, Saipan, Tinian, all these islands. The fields? Every time you hit a ball it was in the ocean. After the tour, they split us up and sent us to various islands to run the recreation programs. I went to Saipan.

The islands were secure, but there were still some Japs in the caves. They knew the island was secure but they didn't want to give up. They had our Navy clothes on; our dungarees, everything. Stolen them? Oh, yes. They had guts; they had nerve. They were watching our ball games! They were coming out of the hills.

While the game was going on, the MP's were up there in the hills, what they called the bleacher seats, and they were plucking the Japs out of there as fast as they could walk around. They would pluck one, two, three, four, five, out of the stands while the game was going on. The Japs like baseball, you know. They thought the island was secure and nobody would bother them. Over in Saipan, we watched four or five every day come into our chow line and eat, with our uniforms on. We knew who they were but we didn't bother them. They'd be right in line with us. They weren't bothering anyone.

Having missed connections with the Navy, the Army baseball stars went on their own island-hopping tour. Enos Slaughter:

See, the Japanese really like baseball. On Saipan, there were plenty of 'em back in those holes and caves. They'd come out and see us play ball, they'd sneak around and watch the ball game.

We built our own ball diamonds, put up our own tents. On white coral; took bulldozers and built 'em. We had a nice ball park over there. We set bomb crates up for stands. Shoot, we got five or ten thousand every ball game. That was in July of '45. We had two Army teams on Tinian. Then we went over to Guam; somebody over there built ball diamonds. Then they built ball diamonds for us on Iwo Jima.

We had some real battles. Major league quality? Oh, heck, yes. I slid and played just as hard over there as I played here. Everybody played to win.

Of course, not all the major leaguers in service played baseball, and not all the baseball played in military service was by professional players. Major Clark Gable played first base for a bomber group team in England. In 1944, Army and Navy teams played a "little world series" in North Africa. Right field sloped into the Mediterranean, and Italian war prisoners were lined up on the beach to retrieve balls that otherwise would be lost at sea.

After the surrender of Germany, the Army built a baseball field in the Nazi stadium at Nuremberg, where Hitler had been honored with military parades. Al Kermisch, a retired Army colonel who once played semi-pro baseball, recalls playing first base for Dachau, the Army having built a baseball field at the infamous concentration camp. At Heidelberg, Lieutenant Warren E. Spahn, who had last pitched for Hartford and hoped for promotion to the Boston Braves, honed his skills against inferior competition, allowing only one run, unearned, in four games, and striking out seventy-three.

Many professional baseball players served in combat assignments. Two players who had made brief appearances in the major leagues were killed in action. Elmer Gedeon, an outfielder who played five games for the Senators in 1939, was killed in France on April 15, 1944. Harry O'Neill, who caught one game for the Athletics, also in 1939, was killed on Iwo Jima on March 6, 1945.

Minor league players killed in action included Hank Nowak, a pitcher for Houston and New Orleans; Billy Hebert, an infielder with Oakland and other teams; Marshall Sneed, who played for Topeka; and Art Keller, who caught for Toledo. Gene Stack, a pitcher who was about to be promoted to the White Sox when drafted, died suddenly after pitching an Army baseball game on June 26, 1942. Gordon Houston, an outfielder with Texarkana, Texas, died when his airplane crashed during a training flight early in 1942.

Billy Southworth, Jr., son of the Cardinal manager, won a Distinguished Flying Cross and an Air Medal for piloting his Flying Fortress on twenty-five bombing missions in Europe. Unhurt in combat, he died February 15, 1945, when the bomber he was piloting overshot LaGuardia Field while attempting an emergency landing, and crashed into Flushing Bay.

Lou Brissie, a minor league pitcher before the war, was badly wounded by shell fragments on December 7, 1944, while fighting in Italy. Both feet were broken, his left ankle was smashed, his left leg was broken between the knee and ankle, and both hands and shoulders were wounded. Brissie nevertheless developed into a star pitcher for the Athletics after the war, and became a symbol of courage for handicapped veterans.

Cecil Travis of Washington, an outstanding hitter before the war, suffered frozen feet in the Battle of the Bulge and could no longer play well. John Grodzicki, a bright Cardinal pitching prospect before the war, suffered a wound that impaired the use of his right leg. He could no longer pitch effectively. Frank (Creepy) Crespi, a young Cardinal infielder, broke his leg in an Army game, broke it again in the hospital during a playful wheelchair race, and did not recover fully enough to return to the major leagues.

Others survived combat assignments and successfully resumed their baseball careers. Buddy Lewis of the Senators was awarded the Distinguished Flying Cross for his service in India and Burma. Harry Walker, a Cardinal outfielder, was wounded in Europe, where he earned a Bronze Star. Earl (Lefty) Johnson, a Red Sox pitcher, also was awarded the Bronze Star for bravery in European action.

Phil Marchildon, the Athletics pitcher, was a tail gunner; his bomber was shot down while laying mines off the coast of Denmark. Of seven crewmen, Marchildon was one of two survivors. He spent a year in a Nazi prisoner-of-war camp and lost thirty pounds.

Marchildon returned in June of 1945. He was too weak to pitch, but Connie Mack coaxed him into one appearance. The Athletics were drawing about 3,000 fans per game, and Mack knew that his returned hero would help roll in dollars at the box office. Mack staged a "Marchildon Night." About 35,000 fans turned out. Marchildon pitched three innings and was awarded a $1,000 War Bond for his heroism. Mack kept the rest of the night's profits. In 1946, Marchildon regained his skills.

CHAPTER 13

The Halt, the Lame,
and the One-Armed Outfielder

A succession of shadowy figures flitted in and out of baseball during the war. The most memorable wartime players were three men and a boy who made the major leagues despite severe handicaps. Bert Shepard, a pitcher, was missing a leg. Joe Nuxhall, a pitcher, was too young. Pete Gray, an outfielder, was missing an arm. Dick Sipek, an outfielder, was deaf.

Unlike Gray, Nuxhall and Sipek, Shepard probably would not have played in the major leagues had it not been for his injury. With the Bisbee, Arizona, Bees of the Arizona-Texas League in 1941, his record was an unimpressive three and five.

An Army Air Corps pilot and lieutenant, Shepard was shot down on May 21, 1944, while strafing a German truck convoy. He woke up ten days later in a German hospital for prisoners of war, and found that his leg had been amputated between the knee and ankle.

Another prisoner made him an artificial leg, and Shepard was running within a month. He returned home in an exchange of wounded prisoners, and was sent to Walter Reed, the Army hospital in Washington, D.C.

To improve the morale of other wounded men, the War Department sent Shepard, 25, to the 1945 spring training camps of the Yankees and Senators. About 100 convalescing war veterans watched him work out with the Yankees at Atlantic City. On March 13, Shepard appeared at the Senators' camp at the University of Maryland, and asked Manager Ossie Bluege for a trial. Bluege agreed, and was not aware of Shepard's artificial leg until he saw him dressing. Shepard pitched competently, and in batting practice hit two sharp line drives.

The Senators pitched Shepard in a spring exhibition game against the Norfolk Naval Training Station team. The game attracted 8,000 fans. Shepard walked the first batter. The second man bunted; Shepard ran in, fielded the ball, and threw the batter out. The next man grounded to first baseman Joe Kuhel. He handled the play unassisted, but Shepard ran over to cover the bag in case a throw was needed. The next batter flied out.

Shepard was signed as a coach. His pitching was not considered up to major league caliber, although he made one relief appearance in 1945, yielding only three hits and one run in five innings. On July 10, 1945, he beat the Dodgers in an exhibition game played to benefit war charities.

Joe Nuxhall was not the only teen-ager to play major league baseball during the war, but he was the youngest. On June 10, 1944, before 5,469 fans at Crosley Field in Cincinnati, Manager Bill McKechnie of the Reds sent in left-hander Nuxhall to pitch against the Cardinals. At 15, Nuxhall was, and is, the youngest player ever to appear in a major league game. Nuxhall:

I was just a big kid, that's all. When I was in grade school we had a city basketball league with the other elementary schools, and our principal made me stay on the defensive half of the floor, simply because I was so much bigger than the other kids. Otherwise there was no competition, you see. When I think about it now I get a little perturbed at him. After all, when you get out on the basketball court you do want to make a point or two.

When I was 12 years old, in junior high school, I was maybe 6 feet tall, 160 pounds. I played in an amateur baseball league in Hamilton, Ohio, with my dad. He was a sports nut. He would have been 32 or 33 years old at that time. I was 12, and we were playing with guys 18 and 19 and in their

20s. He was a pitcher and first baseman, and I pitched and played first base.

We were in the same league, but I was on a different team. They called it the Sunday League. We had about ten teams, and it was all guys who were 4-F or back from the Army. The Reds had reports on my dad, and three scouts came up one Sunday—Bill McCrory, Pat Patterson, and Eddie Reitz. They were coming to check him out as a pitcher.

At the complex where we played, all the diamonds were in one big area. Our team was playing on Diamond One, which was right by the offices. These scouts drove up, and they wanted to know where my dad was pitching. His name was Orville, and they called him "Ox"; that was his nickname. So the playground director told them he was on Diamond Three, way up in a corner by the tennis courts.

Our game had already started, and I'm out on the mound pitching. I'm 14 years old at that time. As the story goes, they saw me pitching, and they asked, "Who is the young kid out there?" They told them that I was Orville's son. They said, "Well, hell, we want to check the kid out."

Which they did, and they talked to my dad later on. They wanted me to sign an Ogden, Utah, contract. I was about 6 feet 2 and weighed 180 pounds. I told them I didn't want to sign then, because our basketball team at Wilson Junior High School was very good, and we had a chance at winning the conference for the third straight year. So I didn't sign, and we won it.

Then after the basketball season, why, we signed a contract. I got $500 to sign and $175 a month. When I signed I was about 190, 195 pounds and 6 foot 3, and I could throw hard. A fast ball was all I had at that time. They wanted to sign my dad too; they wanted to give him $150 a month or something like that. He just couldn't see it. Pretty difficult to raise a family of seven on $150 a month.

There was a lot of publicity about me signing a Cincinnati contract, the youngest ever to sign a contract. I expected to be somewhere in the Reds' minor league system. But I was part of the Reds' roster until school let out in June. I would just come down on weekends and for night games. Frank McCormick lived not far from me, and I always rode the bus down to the ball park with him. Until I signed the contract, I had seen maybe four major league games.

I only made one road trip with the team. We stayed at the Coronado Hotel in St. Louis. One of the players had breakfast with me and told me they had the best apple pie a la mode in the country, so I had a piece.

This game I was in happened on a Saturday. I'm sitting there, and the

Cardinals are just killing us; it's thirteen to nothing. Finally Mr. McKechnie told me to go warm up. Really, he yelled twice. The first time he said "Joe," I didn't pay any attention, figuring he was talking to somebody else. The second time it was a little louder, and I went down and warmed up.

I was surprised. Jeez God, scared to death. Who warmed me up? Al Lakeman. He would yell, "Follow through!" and this, that, or the other thing, trying to help me, but I was throwing the ball over his head and all over the damned place.

Then I got in the game. I started the ninth inning. I'm nervous, quite nervous, and I walked a guy, but I got a couple of guys out; got the third guy on a three-and-two popup. That's when I started realizing exactly what the hell was going on. Here I am, two weeks prior to this I'm pitching against a junior high school. Now I'm pitching against the potential World Champions. Seemed like there were 40,000 people there.

Then all hell broke loose. I don't recall the sequence or the hitters but I know it was bad. I walked five, gave up two hits and I think a wild pitch. I was just scared to death. Finally, McKechnie just walked out and said, "Well, son, I think you've had enough." I kind of tended to agree with him. I just took my glove and left.

But, you know, I've often thought about that darned thing. Because of the conditions—you know, the war—had I retired the side in order, would I have been given another chance? Been kept around? I really don't know, but I've often thought about it.

(The Cardinal ninth: George Fallon was retired on a nice play by shortstop Eddie Miller. Mort Cooper walked, and advanced to second on a wild pitch. Augie Bergamo popped out. Debs Garms walked. Musial singled, Cooper scoring. Ray Sanders, Walker Cooper, and Danny Litwhiler walked, two runs scoring. Emil Verban singled, two runs scoring. Jake Eisenhardt relieved Nuxhall. Fallon walked, filling the bases. Mort Cooper fouled to McCormick. Five runs, two hits, no errors, three men left on base.)

After learning to pitch in the minor leagues, Nuxhall returned to the Reds in 1952. He pitched sixteen seasons in the major leagues, winning 135 games and losing 117. When interviewed during the summer of 1976, Nuxhall was the play-by-play broadcaster for the Reds. To keep in shape, he also pitched batting practice for his old team.

Pete Gray was born Peter J. Wyshner in Nanticoke, Pennsylvania, a scruffy coal-mining town near Wilkes-Barre. At the age of 6, he hopped a farmer's provision wagon, fell off, and caught his right arm in the spokes. The arm was mangled, and had to be amputated above the elbow.

Pete's father was a coal miner, and the family was considered prosperous by local standards. Neighbors called their house "the white house," and coveted invitations there. Wyshner was a Lithuanian name. Ethnic names were not in vogue during the 1930s and 1940s, so the Wyshners changed their name to Gray.

Despite his handicap, Gray was determined to play professional baseball. Although originally right-handed, he learned to bat from the left side. He had a superb batting eye and was a fast runner. Gray mixed line drives with well executed bunts, some down the third-base line, others dragged past the pitcher.

Gray's handicap hindered him more in the field than at bat. For a man with two arms, switching the ball from the glove hand to the throwing hand takes a fraction of a second. Any extension of that time would allow runners to take an extra base. With only one arm, Gray had to catch the ball with a glove on and throw it with the glove off.

He managed this cleverly and deftly. Removing almost all the padding from his glove, Gray wore it on his fingertips with his little finger out. He would catch the ball, stick his glove under the stump of his right arm, draw the ball clear with his left hand, and throw it to the infield.

Gray excelled at local semi-pro ball, but professional teams would not grant a tryout to a player with only one arm. He played semi-pro for Three Rivers, Quebec. Emboldened by his success and determined to earn his way into organized baseball, Gray traveled to Brooklyn in hopes of playing for the Brooklyn Bushwicks, an outstanding semi-pro team whose players often were scouted by major league clubs.

It was 1940, and Gray was 23 years old. Max Rosner, the promoter-manager of the Bushwicks, scoffed at Gray when he requested a tryout. Gray handed Rosner a ten dollar bill. "Take this, and keep it if I don't make good," he said. Rosner was impressed; besides, he knew that a one-armed player would attract fans.

Gray made the Bushwicks, and played two seasons for them. In 1942, Three Rivers, Gray's old semi-pro club, was admitted to organized baseball as a member of the Canadian-American League. Gray was offered a contract, and jumped at the chance. He missed much of the season with injuries, but batted .381.

Toronto of the Class AA International League summoned Gray for a spring tryout in 1943, but cut him. Gray was ill, and felt that he was not given a fair chance. Another account had it that he angered Manager Burleigh Grimes. He returned home in disappointment, but received a telegram asking him to report to the Memphis Chicks of the Class A Southern Association.

Not even taking time to pack his clothes, Gray joined the Chicks. He played regularly in 1943, batted .299, and began to receive nationwide publicity. In 1944, Gray blossomed into a star with Memphis. He batted .333, stole sixty-three bases to tie a Southern Association record, led the league's outfielders in fielding percentage, and was voted the most valuable player in the league. During two seasons with Memphis, he struck out only fifteen times.

Philadelphia sportswriters voted Gray the "most courageous athlete of 1944." The War Department made movies of his play and showed them to wounded servicemen in hospitals.

The Browns bought Gray for $20,000. At Cape Girardeau in 1945, Gray stung the ball; he was one of the team's best hitters. The Browns were defending American League champions and were expected to contend for the 1945 pennant; they insisted that they had purchased Gray because of his playing skills, not his ability to draw fans.

"Gray is just another player to me," Luke Sewell said in a *Sporting News* interview during spring training. "He has to stand on what he has."

That suited Gray, who loved baseball but was so introverted that he appeared sullen and unfriendly to his new teammates, who had won the 1944 pennant partly because of their friendly cohesion. Al Hollingsworth, the veteran pitcher, roomed with Gray and kept reassuring him that he had been promoted to the major leagues on merit, not as a freak.

Of course, that was only partly true. Gray had earned a major league trial, but the Browns, hungry for attendance, bought him partly as a gate attraction. Gray attracted large crowds, and Sewell was urged to play him more than the manager would have liked.

Sewell:

Did I want him? Well, I did and I didn't. If he could cut the mustard, it would be a hell of a thing. But I had my doubts. Larry Gilbert was down in the Southern Association at Nashville, and I called Larry about him. Larry said, "Well, if he can bunt and drag up there like he did down here, he'll be all right."

When I got him, I knew he couldn't make it. He didn't belong in the major leagues, and he knew he was being exploited. Just a quiet fellow, and he had an inferiority complex. They were trying to get a gate attraction in St. Louis. A lot of people got mad because I didn't keep playing him.

But when he got up here, those infielders just came right in on him, and he couldn't get on with those bunts and drags. He had no power. Pete just couldn't play major league ball.

Gray had his heroic moments. He won a game in Detroit with a line drive past third that drove in two runs. Pitchers tried to blow fast balls past him but were unable to. Bob Feller, who barnstormed with Gray following the 1945 season, said that even he could not get a fast ball past Gray. Gray swung a thirty-five-ounce bat, heavier than that used by most hitters, and started his swing early to compensate for his handicap. American League pitchers soon found that Gray was a sucker for a change-up.

For the Browns in 1945, Gray played sixty-one games in the outfield and was sent up to pinch-hit a dozen times. He batted .218 with six doubles and two triples. He stole five bases. Many of his teammates disliked him personally and resented his presence in the lineup. Although admiring him for overcoming his handicap, they believed that the Browns lost a half-dozen to a dozen games that season because runners often were able to take an extra base while Gray fielded a ball. At least one Brownie player challenged Gray to a fight, offering to tie his own right arm behind his back.

Mark Christman:

Pete did great with what he had. But he cost us the pennant in 1945. We finished third, only six games out. There were an awful lot of ground balls hit to center field. When the kids who hit those balls were pretty good runners, they could keep on going and wind up at second base. I know that cost us eight or ten ball games. Because that took away the double play, or somebody would single and the runner would score, whereas if he had been on first it would take two hits to get him to score.

It caused Mike Kreevich to quit. Kreevich the year before hit over .300 as our center fielder, and in '45 he wasn't playing much. Pete Gray was playing center field most of the time. Mike said, "Gee, if I'm not playing well enough so that a one-armed man can take my job, I quit." And he did. They waived him to Washington.

The fans still remember Pete Gray, though, because he was incredible. At the end of the season in '45, Charley DeWitt got a movie commitment to do the story of his life. Pete refused to act or do anything in the movie, so Charley said, "All right, I'll get a commitment from the company so all they'll do is take a camera along and take pictures of you barnstorming, and put all that in a movie." But he refused it. I remember Charley DeWitt sitting down on the bench, trying to get him to do anything, just anything.

Bill DeWitt:

Charley was Pete's business manager, and he booked some games in California, barnstorming after the season. They had never seen him on the Coast. They wanted to make a movie about him, about the one-armed ballplayer. They were gonna pay him 15,000 bucks for a few days' work.

Gray was baldheaded. So the guy said, "The first thing you have to do is get a hairpiece." And Gray said, "I won't do it. No dice." The guy said, "Bing Crosby wears a hairpiece when he's on the stage and doing commercials and movies. Why can't you?" And Gray said, "Forget the whole thing."

The barnstorming tour featured Gray on one team and Jess Alexander, a Negro outfielder with only one arm, on the other.

When visited in the fall of 1976, Gray was sharing his boyhood home with a brother, Whitey, who still showed the effects of repeated blows to the head during a brief career as a boxer. Pete cared for his brother and cooked meals for them.

They lived in squalor. The "white house" of their boyhood was sooty gray. Located in northeastern Pennsylvania, it was heated only by an old-fashioned stove. Bertha Vedor, a cousin, said that she cleaned it for the brothers perhaps once a year. Dust lay thickly on the floors and furniture.

Aside from his years in professional baseball, Gray never held a job. A heavy drinker for most of his adult life, Gray was on the wagon by 1976. He nevertheless spent much of his time at Mrs. Vedor's neighborhood tavern, watching television and chatting with friends. He played pool and golf frequently, showing the same ability with one hand that he demonstrated in baseball.

Pete Gray on his year with the Browns:

I hit the ball good, but I didn't have a good batting average. I hit line drives. They just always seemed to go at somebody. It was just one of those years.

I knew I couldn't stay up too long. I didn't have the power. It seemed I hit a lot of line drives that they'd catch ten or fifteen feet from the fence. Just not quite far enough.

I was mostly a loner. I'd just come to the ball park. One time we came into Washington, and they called me up and asked me to come over to Walter Reed Hospital. They sent a limousine down to pick me up, and a motorcycle escort. I talked to the fellows, and some of them came to the ball game.

I've been retired since the day I was born. Baseball; that's all I ever did. That movie? They're still talking about it. I just didn't care for it. You say I'm a famous man? [He shakes his head and waves his hand in disgust and disbelief.] I'm satisfied with what I've got.

In 1946, the Browns farmed Gray to Toledo. He did not play in 1947. In 1948, he played for a Brownie farm team in Elmira, New York. That fall, Bill DeWitt was approached by the general manager of the Dallas club of the Texas League, who was ambitiously trying to improve his team.

DeWitt:

He said, "Do you have any players to sell? I'll buy the best players available; money's no object." I said, "Let me think. I've got a player at Elmira that I'll sell you, and the price is $2,500. There's only one thing wrong with him." He said, "What's that?" I said, "He's only got one arm." He said, "I'll take him!"

Gray played for Dallas in 1949, at the age of 32. It was his last year in organized baseball.

Dick Sipek grew up in Chicago. At the age of 5, he fell down a flight of stairs and suffered a blow on the head that rendered him extremely hard of hearing. Unable to keep up in public school, he was sent at the age of 9 to the Illinois School for the Deaf at Jacksonville.

Sipek's house-father there was Luther (Dummy) Taylor, who pitched nine seasons for the New York Giants during the first decade of the twentieth century, winning twenty-seven games in 1904. Taylor was one of only two deaf men who had played major league baseball; the other was William (Dummy) Hoy, an outfielder who played fourteen seasons for various clubs, ending in 1902.

At ISD, as the school was called, Sipek became an excellent student and an outstanding athlete. He was an all-state back in football, starred in basketball and, under Taylor's tutelage, became a skillful outfielder and a powerful left-handed hitter.

Having started his schooling at ISD a few years late, Sipek was just finishing high school in 1943, at the age of 20. Taylor recommended him to several major league clubs; none expressed interest until the Cincinnati Reds invited Sipek to join the Birmingham, Alabama, Barons, a Cincinnati farm club in the Southern Association.

Interviewed for this book during the summer of 1976 at his neat home in Quincy, Illinois, Sipek spoke well, but used gestures and facial expressions to convey much of the story. A gracious host and a jolly man, he recalled his baseball career with the joy and wonder of a man who had been allowed to live in a fairy tale. His lovely wife and their daughter, Nancy, a comely college student, were equally gracious and cheerful.

The train ride from Jacksonville to Birmingham was Sipek's first trip alone. He was excited and frightened. He vividly remembered the hotel clerk who gave him directions to the ball park, the streetcar ride, and the secretary in the Barons' office who showed him to the clubhouse.

The Barons farmed Sipek to Erwin, Tennessee, a Class D team. He hit .455 during the first month of the season, and was recalled by Birmingham. He doubled as a pinch hitter in his first game with the Barons, and was installed in right field.

Playing in the same league with Pete Gray, Sipek batted .336 in 1943 and .319 in 1944. The Birmingham fans loved his hustle, his cheerful attitude and his willingness to sign countless autographs for admiring children. Both seasons, he was voted the team's most popular player.

Johnny Riddle, the Birmingham manager, said that Sipek was remarkably attentive, using his eyes to compensate for his poor hearing. Wherever he played, Sipek trained the center fielder and the second and first basemen to let him decide who was to catch a batted ball. If Sipek called for it, they had to get out of the way, because he could not hear their calls. If he did not call for it, it was theirs to catch.

Sipek was touched by the friendliness of teammates. After a night game in Memphis in 1944, he was walking with some other Birmingham players when some sailors began making fun of him. Sipek had been walking a bit ahead of his friends and did not hear the taunts; by the time he turned around, his teammates were pummeling the sailors for their bad manners.

Sipek was promoted to the Reds in 1945. Unlike Gray, he was not considered a gate attraction, and little was made of him. Sipek played thirty-one games in the outfield and was used frequently as a pinch hitter. He hit .244, with six doubles, two triples, and no home runs. Sipek:

Oh, I had a lot of fun. All the players were nice, really nice. They talked loud [gestures to indicate friendly teasing]. I am hard of hearing, but they drop something right behind me, I can hear. They say, "Go to the Army, go to the Army!" I say, "Noooo."

Bucky Walters and some of the other pitchers came to me during batting practice. They asked me, "How can you hear when the ball's hit?" I say, "Oh, I can hear it. When they hit the ball good, I can hear it." [He indicates that his teammates decided to test this claim.]

I turned my back and looked straight at the fence. [He gestures to show a man batting.] "Did he hit it?" I say, "No." Next time, "Did he hit it?" I say, "Yeah."

My hometown is Chicago. Bill McKechnie always let me play in Chicago. The Cubs had good pitchers. Claude Passeau, I hit two out of five. Hank Wyse, two out of four. Hank Borowy, one out of four. Paul Derringer, one out of four.

The players—Bucky Walters, Frank McCormick—were my friends.

Did they learn the sign language? Yes. Kermit Wahl, my roommate, he learned it very fast, the alphabet and everything. [With many gestures and a few words, Sipek described being called out on a close play. He gave the umpire the sign language for a vulgar word. The umpire did not understand, and was nonplussed when Sipek's teammates burst into laughter.]

My biggest thrill? In Birmingham, my second year, my parents came down on vacation. My mother was in a box seat. When I came up to bat, I got a base hit. [He gestures, indicating elation.] My parents are here! I get four for five. My father and mother were so proud.

In '46, they sent me down to Syracuse. Bill McKechnie said, "So long, Dick." I don't know what I said. But after leaving, I thought I should have said, "I'll be back."

Sipek did not return to the major leagues, but played several more years of minor league baseball, and again was voted by fans as the most popular player on the team. He is proud of having played in the major leagues despite his handicap, and feels a natural kinship with Taylor, his mentor, and Hoy, the other deaf major leaguer. After a game during the 1945 season, Sipek found Hoy, then 83, waiting to meet him.

In his middle age, Sipek turned to golf. He recalled a golf game during a convention for the deaf. Sipek saw a man in a nearby foursome pointing him out, and, with sign language, saying, "He was the last deaf player in professional baseball."

Sipek:

After we got back to the clubhouse, I went up to him. I said, "I don't want to be the last deaf player in professional baseball. I want somebody else to come up."

The war afforded many players the opportunity to draw at least a breath of major league air. Some had been waiting years for that privilege. After pitching a total of ten innings for Brooklyn in 1922 and 1923, Paul Schreiber flunked out of the major leagues. In 1937, he became the Yankees' batting practice pitcher. In September of 1945, Schreiber, at the age of 42, was told to warm up and relieve against the Tigers. He pitched three and one-third innings without yielding a hit or a run. Given another chance in the same series, he was reached for four hits and two runs in one inning. That was it; Schreiber returned to his batting practice chores.

Catcher Bill Steinecke was not so lucky. A minor leaguer since

1925, he batted four times for the Pirates in 1931, went hitless, was returned to the minors and stayed there. During the 1944 season, Rollie Hemsley, a reformed alcoholic who had been catching for the Yankees, was drafted. Steinecke, 37, suddenly found himself elevated from Portsmouth, Virginia, to Yankee Stadium. But Mike Garbark, another wartime catcher, won the job and needed no rest. Poor Steinecke never got into a game.

A few elders acquired new skills. After completing a major league career of twelve years as an outfielder, Ben Chapman, 35, was managing Richmond in the Piedmont League. Playing the outfield, Chapman was batting .348. That was no surprise, but his pitching record of thirteen and six was. The Dodgers brought him up late in the 1944 season, and started him on the mound against Boston. Chapman beat the Braves, 9 to 4, driving in three runs himself with a single and a double. Chapman won five and lost three for Brooklyn that season, and hit .368. In 1945, playing for the Dodgers and then the Phillies, Chapman pitched, pinch hit, and played the outfield and third base. He batted .260 and was three and three on the mound.

Also managing in the Piedmont League was Jimmy Foxx, the great slugger of the 1930s, who had been dropped by the Cubs in 1944. He, too, found his club short of talent. Foxx put himself in to pinch-hit one day and batted into a triple play. So he tried pitching, flashed a screwball and a changeup, and beat Newport News, 3 to 1.

The Phillies bought Foxx, 37, for the 1945 season. In May, he led off second base and was tagged out, victim of the hidden ball trick. But Foxx hit pretty well, and in July the Phils decided to let him pitch; it was the only position he had not played in the major leagues. Stan Baumgartner, a Philadelphia sportswriter of the hope-springs-eternal school, wrote about Foxx as if he were a promising youngster. "He still has a good arm, knows how to pitch and may develop," Baumgartner wrote. Foxx pitched in nine games, won one, lost none, and turned in a sparkling earned run average of 1.59. He also hit the last seven of his 534 career home runs that season.

Many old horses were reharnessed for the war. Pepper Martin,

40, "The Wild Horse of the Osage," hit a home run in his first appearance at the Polo Grounds since 1940. He played in forty
games for the Cardinals in 1944, batted .279, and then returned to
the minors as a manager. Babe Herman, out of the major leagues
since 1937, came back to the Dodgers in 1945. Flashing his old
form, he singled, tripped over first base, fell, and doffed his cap to
the applause. Herman was 42, but hit .265 as a pinch-hitter and,
like Martin, managed one last home run.

Paul (Big Poison) Waner went from the Braves to the Dodgers
to the Yankees during the war. In 1944, at the age of 41, he led the
majors in pinch hits with thirteen. His brother, Lloyd (Little Poison) Waner, three years younger, pinch-hit for the Phillies,
Dodgers and Pirates. Al Simmons' last hurrah was with the Athletics in 1944. He was 42, and batted .500—three for six.

Buck (Leaky) Fausett seized the nettle nine years too late. In
1935, Fausett was playing for Galveston, a Texas League team pa-
ternal enough to find him an off-season job in the winter. The Athletics bought Fausett. Connie Mack offered him a salary lower than
the total of his baseball and off-season earnings in Galveston.
Times were hard and Fausett was cautious. He asked Mack to de-
mote him back to Galveston, and the old gentleman obliged.

In 1943, Fausett, still in the minor leagues, hit .362 as the playing manager for Little Rock, and was given another shot at the major leagues, this time by the Cincinnati Reds. He reported in 1944
at the age of 36. It was too late. Tried at third base, Fausett batted
.097. Tried as a pitcher, he yielded thirteen hits in two relief appearances. He was cut.

Despite the shortage of competent performers, several talented
players who appeared for spring tryouts failed to make the grade in
1945. For those times, they had the worst handicap of all: They
were black.

On April 7, the Dodgers reluctantly granted a tryout to pitcher
Terris McDuffie and first baseman Dave (Showboat) Thomas.
Branch Rickey expressed indignation, predicted that the players'
appearance without invitation would set back the Negro cause, and

said that McDuffie and Thomas did not measure up to major league standards. On April 16 at Fenway Park in Boston, Red Sox Manager Joe Cronin and his coaches watched a tryout by infielder Jackie Robinson, outfielder Sam Jethroe, and one Marvin Williams. None was offered a contract.

Some elders were content to remain in the minors. In 1944, the Trenton, New Jersey, Packers of the Inter-State League signed pitcher Hal Kelleher, who had quit baseball in 1940 after four undistinguished seasons with the Phillies. Kelleher had turned to police work, and liked it. He won twelve games for Trenton and was told that he could return to the major leagues. "I don't want to go back to the big leagues," Kelleher said. "My future is in the Philadelphia police department."

James (Ripper) Collins, the old Gashouse Gang slugger who tied Mel Ott for the National League home run championship in 1934, was the playing manager for Albany in the Eastern League ten years later. He was 40, and batted .396, the best average in the minor or major leagues. Charlie Root, 44, the former Cub star, was manager of the Hollywood Stars of the Pacific Coast League in 1943, and was pitching once a week. By the end of July, he had won ten games.

Some minor league teams were forced to much greater extremes than that. In 1943, the York, Pennsylvania, White Roses of the Inter-State League employed two pitchers whose ages totaled 100. The elder of the two was Tom (Lefty) George, 57, a beer salesman who pitched only when the team was at home. George won four straight games. He had pitched for the Browns in 1911 and for the Boston Braves as late as 1918, and had two grandsons in the Army.

Younger players were not overlooked. Joe Garagiola was catching capably for Columbus at 17. He was two years older than a Los Angeles Angels' catcher, Billy (The Angel Kid) Sarni. Both Garagiola and Sarni caught for the Cardinals after the war.

The Knoxville Smokies signed Cy Roberts, 32, who worked the night shift at the local water plant and had never played professional baseball. Roberts hit safely eleven of his first eighteen times at bat. His manager said that he probably would play even better if he slept at night; Roberts was working a boiler from 10 P.M. until 6 A.M.

Durham, North Carolina, of the Piedmont League played a local fireman named Wilkie at second base, and pitched a felon named Patterson. "When Patterson said he had played at Atlanta, I thought he meant Atlanta in the Southern Association," recalled E. J. (Buzzy) Bavasi, the San Diego Padres general manager who was running the Durham club during the war. "It turned out he was just out of the pen at Atlanta."

CHAPTER 14

1945: Neither Team Can Win

With U.S. troops fighting in both Europe and the South Pacific, military manpower demands accelerated during the winter of 1944 and 1945. Few men older than 26 had been drafted during the 1944 baseball season, but in December that moratorium ended.

James F. Byrnes, director of War Mobilization and Reconstruction, instituted draconian measures. He ordered all horse and dog racing tracks to close by January 3, 1945, and at the same time told General Hershey to re-examine all professional athletes who were classified 4-F or had received medical discharges.

"It is difficult for the public to understand, and certainly it is difficult for me to understand, how these men can be physically unfit for military service and yet be able to compete with the greatest athletes of the nation in games demanding physical fitness," Byrnes said. If unfit for combat, he said, 4-F athletes could perform less demanding military chores or be put to work in war factories.

The result was a draft policy that quite openly discriminated against professional athletes. There were then about 260 4-F players in the major leagues. Even those with serious infirmities, like

George McQuinn with his bad back, were threatened with induction.

The first victim was Ron Northey, outfielder for the Phillies. On January 2, 1945, Northey was classified 4-F because of a punctured eardrum, a heart ailment, and high blood pressure. On January 15 he was ordered to report for induction.

At a Louisville induction center, Hugh Poland, 33, catcher for the Boston Braves, was among forty-five men reporting for physical examinations. "Are there any professional athletes in the crowd?" asked a supervisor. Poland raised his hand, and was placed at the front of the line. Rejected because of a bone deformity in one foot, Poland was told to dress and go home. Before he could leave, an officer rushed in. "It was all a mistake," the officer said. "You're a P.A. You'll have to have an X-ray of that leg."

P.A. meant professional athlete. After undergoing the X-ray, Poland was questioned by a colonel. Poland explained that he played with the foot taped up. "You can play ball with it taped up!" said the colonel. "O.K., you're in." Poland had tried to join the Navy a year before, but had been rejected as physically unfit.

There had been public mutterings throughout the war, but now, for the first time, 4-F athletes became objects of widespread suspicion. Byrnes's statement hinted that something was wrong, although no one presented evidence that athletes had been treated preferentially by the draft system.

J. Edgar Hoover of the FBI rushed to the defense of 4-F baseball players. "If any ballplayers, or other athletes, were attempting to dodge service, it would be our job to look into such cases," he said. "But our records show there are few, if any, such cases among the thousands of ballplayers, and they are entitled to a clean bill of health."

Other public servants were more testy. "They closed down the Kentucky Derby and they ought to close down baseball also," said Representative Andrew May of Kentucky. Senator William A. (Wild Bill) Langer of North Dakota introduced legislation under which 10 percent of the players on every major league team would have to be men who had lost "one or more" arms, legs, or hands.

Neither May's suggestion nor Langer's bill received serious consideration.

Baseball's most outspoken defender within the government was Senator Albert B. (Happy) Chandler of Kentucky, who was anxious to be selected as the next commissioner of baseball. Judge Landis had died on November 25, 1944, at the age of 78. Chandler said that 4-F players were more useful playing baseball than "fiddling around at something else," like war work.

As for himself, Chandler said in response to a question, he would love to be commissioner but could not desert the U.S. government in wartime. "That would make me a slacker," he said. "My term expires in 1949." On April 24, 1945, Chandler was offered the commissionership. He accepted.

While Chandler tilted in the limelight, an obscure freshman congressman named C. Melvin Price quietly went to work on the problem. Price represented East St. Louis, Illinois, just across the Mississippi River from St. Louis, and had once covered the Browns and Cardinals for the East St. Louis *Journal.* He worked during the 1930s for the congressman from his home district, campaigned unsuccessfully for Congress himself in 1942, and joined the Army in 1943.

In April, 1944, Private Price was drafted by the Democrats back home as their candidate for Congress. Army regulations forbade campaigning, but Price was elected anyway. He was discharged from the Army, congressmen being exempt from service, and was appointed to the House Military Affairs Committee, chaired by none other than that champion of horse racing and scourge of baseball, Andrew May of Kentucky. Thirty-two years later, the committee's name had been changed to the House Armed Services Committee, and Price, 71, serving his sixteenth term in Congress, had moved up the seniority ladder to the chairmanship.

Price:

The ballclubs were being raided of playing talent. I was close to the De-Witts, and they called several times. Did they ask me to help out? Yes, because the McQuinn case was so obvious that they thought it was a real injustice.

One part of the official government line was that they wanted the sports to continue to provide relaxation and so forth. But what was actually happening was that if you were an athlete, you were automatically qualified for military service. It pretty much endangered the future of baseball. You were getting to the point where it could have been closed before the end of the war.

I wasn't trying to keep any able-bodied guys out of the service. They shouldn't treat them any differently from anybody else. But if they had a disability that would normally disqualify them, they should be disqualified.

Bryce Harlow was then the administrative aide to the secretary of war, and he was my main contact. He was helpful. On my side? Yeah, all the way. Happy Chandler used to call here all the time and find out how things were moving. He was helping. [Harlow later became an aide to Presidents Eisenhower, Nixon, and Ford, and a lobbyist for Procter & Gamble.]

In May of 1945, the War Department suspended the discriminatory regulation, citing the arguments presented by Price. A realist, Price himself notes that his protest had not made much headway before the surrender of Germany on May 8, 1945, eased the manpower shortage.

Players who were inducted under the policy, and missed the 1945 season as a result, included Northey of the Phillies, outfielder Danny Litwhiler and catcher Walker Cooper of the Cardinals, and outfielder Stan Spence of the Senators. Players who were spared a term in service as a result of the change instigated by Representative Price included outfielder Wally Moses of the White Sox, pitcher Allie Reynolds and outfielder Paul O'Dea of the Indians, and pitchers Dutch Leonard and Mickey Haefner of the Senators.

In addition to Cooper and Litwhiler, the Cardinals lost Musial and pitcher Fred Schmidt to service; Max Lanier was inducted shortly after the 1945 season began. Dick Wakefield was summoned back into the Navy, and the Tigers lost third baseman Pinky Higgins as well. Denny Galehouse and Al Zarilla were taken from the Browns. Thanks to the war, the Cardinals appeared to be vulnerable in the National League; the American League looked utterly devoid of a standout team.

On March 8, 1945, troops of the U.S. First Army crossed the

Rhine south of Cologne in a surprise maneuver that promised to shorten the war. The Russian army was within twenty-five miles of Berlin. On Iwo Jima, U.S. Marines of the Third and Fifth Divisions continued to advance. On Wall Street, the optimistic war news revived fears of peacetime economic difficulties; stocks tumbled one to four dollars a share, with the ticker running four minutes behind.

On April 12, President Roosevelt died at Warm Springs, Georgia. Major and minor league baseball parks were closed April 14 in tribute to the man who had thrown out the first ball of the season eight times. On April 19, Joe Cronin, 39, caught his spikes while running the bases at Yankee Stadium and broke his right leg.

Once again, the New York Giants started fast in the National League. They won twenty-one of their first twenty-six games as Mel Ott, Phil Weintraub, and Ernie Lombardi hit seven home runs apiece. The Giants ranged in height from George Hausmann, a second baseman who stood 5 feet 5 inches, to Johnny Gee, a pitcher who was 6 feet 9. The Dodgers won six straight and were second. Rookie Leroy Pfund, a religious man who would not pitch on Sundays, beat the Pirates, 4 to 1; rookie left-handers Vic Lombardi and Tom Seats beat the Cardinals.

In May, the Reds won eleven of twelve games. With Nuxhall, now 16, farmed out, the Cincinnati pitching staff ranged in age from Herm Wehmeier, 18, to Hod Lisenbee, 46, who in 1927 had won eighteen games for the Washington Senators. On May 16, Mort Cooper walked out on the Cardinals to dramatize his demand for a higher salary. He was traded to the Braves for Red Barrett. The Braves soon discovered that Cooper had a sore arm. Barrett won his first three starts for the Cardinals and went on to lead the league in victories with twenty-one.

The White Sox were winning in the American League, and Manager Jimmie Dykes happily increased his cigar consumption to twenty a day. The Sox were led by Tony Cuccinello, 37, a veteran who had retired from playing after the 1940 season only to be called back for the war. Cuccinello hit consistently and on one occasion embarrassed Lou Boudreau, the Cleveland playing manager, with the hidden ball trick. The Yankees and Tigers were vying with the White Sox for first place.

Germany surrendered on May 8, and the government announced that about two million servicemen would be discharged within a year. Trains were crowded with soldiers, sailors, and Marines, many of them wounded. The All-Star Game was canceled to lighten demands on the trains, and the World Series was considered a likely casualty. Under a program adopted by the major and minor leagues, players returning from service had to be kept at least thirty days of spring training, or fifteen days if the season was under way.

Red Ruffing returned to the Yankees twenty-five pounds heavier after a service tour spent in the U.S. and Hawaii. Bob Feller came back in superb condition, having exercised regularly aboard the U.S.S. Alabama between encounters with Japanese aircraft. He and Ruffing had similar difficulties getting out of service, and used similar tactics.

Ruffing:

I was 41 years old, and they were letting men out. But they were going to send me over to Italy, across the ocean, entertaining the troops. So I decided to contact my congressman, Jerry Voorhis. I told him I'd like to have an interview with the secretary of war.

Which I did. I had an interview with him. I told him my age, that I had a family and responsibilities. I asked if there was any chance of me getting out of the service. He says, "Well, there is something coming through. They're going to leave a lot of people out. We'll see what we can do. Where are you going from here?" I says, "I'm going down to Fort Lee, Virginia. I'm supposed to go overseas."

Well, we go down there. I'm with Buddy Baer, the fighter, and a kid by the name of Simone, a ping-pong champion. Captain says, "You guys ready to leave for Italy?" I was mad by this time. I says, "Sooner the better." So he says, "Report tomorrow morning about eight o'clock."

The next morning, the captain says, "Ruffing, I have to see you privately. Step in the room." I says, "OK." He says, "Something terrible happened down in Washington. I've got to let you out of the Army right quick. You have to go to New York and get your papers."

We go to New York. The moment we hit the door, some colonel in the back room says, "Sergeant Rufffinggg, come back here!" I says, "Yes, sir." He says, "We can't send you over to Italy." I says, "That's what I hear." He says, "Your orders don't call for it."

I says, "Well, what about Buddy Baer?" He says, "What about him?" I says, "He's got the same damn orders. Take a look, see?" He says, "What do you mean? Where is he?" I says, "He's out there."

He called him in. He says, "Let me see your orders." And he's stunned. He says, "God damn." He cussed, you know. "Well," he says, "you're going home, boy."

Ruffing rejoined the Yankees. He was fat, 41 years old, had missed two and a half seasons, and still had nothing but a fast ball. He pitched eight complete games in eleven starts, winning seven and losing three while posting an earned run average of 2.89.

Points toward discharge were awarded servicemen on the basis of time spent in service, particularly in combat. Feller had been in service more than four years, and had spent most of it as an antiaircraft gunner on a battleship that was in the thick of many South Pacific engagements. When his ship returned home, Feller was assigned to the Great Lakes Naval Base north of Chicago. There, he coached the baseball team, pitched, and impatiently awaited discharge. Feller:

You had to have forty-five points to get out. Well, I had enough points so I could have sold forty-five and still gotten out. So I went to the admiral. I told him, "I'm married, my wife's pregnant, I didn't win the war myself but I helped, it's already cost me a half a million bucks, I'm in good shape, and I think the Indians may win the pennant if I can get back there."

He said, "Oh, young man. Take your time and don't worry about getting out. Things don't move very fast in the Navy."

This admiral was a pain in the ass. He couldn't fight. They had taken all his ships away from him. Anyway, another officer gave me an idea of who to call in Washington. I went back and picked up the telephone. I was out the next morning.

Who did I call? The secretary of the Navy. So he sent out a radiogram, "Release Feller and nineteen others tomorrow." Other guys who had enough points to get out; not ballplayers.

I walked up, got my papers at Navy Pier [in Chicago], walked out, they took a few pictures, I jumped on a plane, came back and pitched against Newhouser. Beat him 4 to 2, struck out a dozen. What I liked most was the headline in the Cleveland paper: "This Is What We've Been Waiting For." Which was a nice compliment.

Having been given the biggest sendoff of any baseball player, Feller also was accorded the most lavish welcoming ceremony upon his return. It was a huge civic occasion in Cleveland. A luncheon in his honor was attended by a thousand, including the mayor and governor. Many more were turned away.

When it was announced that Feller would pitch against Detroit the night of August 24, the Indians' switchboard broke down under the avalanche of calls from people seeking tickets.

The crowd numbered 46,477. A committee headed by Tris Speaker and Cy Young, former Indian greats themselves, presented Feller with a jeep for his farm. His teammates gave him a pen and pencil set, and the American Legion presented him with a membership. Feller did beat Newhouser, and went on to win five games against three losses. Unfortunately for the Indians, Boudreau broke his left ankle again two weeks before Feller's return; Cleveland did not contend for the pennant.

Hugh Mulcahy, who had pitched very little while spending more than four years in service, returned to the Phillies underweight from illness suffered in the South Pacific. He never regained his pitching skills. Dick Fowler returned to the Athletics. He lost two games and won one—a no-hitter against the Browns. Charlie Keller returned to the Yankees for the last forty-four games of the season, and hit .301.

The Tigers got a quick boost from Al Benton, a pitcher who was just back from service. He started the 1945 season strongly, yielding only one earned run in his first forty-five innings. Having escaped injury during two years in the Navy, Benton then was hit by a line drive and suffered a broken ankle. Les Mueller, also back with Detroit after two years in service, took Benton's place in the pitching rotation.

Mueller pitched nineteen and two-thirds innings of a game in

Philadelphia that was called after twenty-four innings; the score was 1 to 1. Mueller's tenacity was matched by that of Otto Susneck, the Shibe Park press box attendant, whose daily duties included leaving the press box in the eighth inning and bringing the elevator to dugout level, so Connie Mack could climb aboard after the game and ride up to his office. This day, Susneck left the press box at 4:30 P.M. At 7:48 P.M. he was still loyally holding the elevator for Mack, unable to see what had transpired in the meantime.

The Tigers moved into first place during June. Then came their biggest break of the season. Hank Greenberg was discharged from the Army after serving more than four years. He was 34, and had not played baseball while in service. "Nobody has ever attempted to resume baseball operations after so long a lapse," reported the *Sporting News.*

Greenberg returned to the lineup July 1 before a Detroit crowd of 47,729. He homered against the A's in the eighth inning. Benton relieved Trout that day and yielded no runs, indicating that he had recovered from his fracture.

Buddy Lewis returned to the Senators on July 21, having missed three seasons and part of a fourth. He was given his old Number 2 by Frankie Baxter, the Senators' clubhouse man, who had saved it for him. "I always said I wasn't going to give his number to any of these bushers who joined the club," Baxter explained.

Lewis had played very little baseball in service. Nevertheless, he hit well immediately upon his return, and batted .333 in sixty-nine games. Lewis:

The good pitchers were not in baseball, and with the good pitchers gone my timing came rapidly. The baseball was so inferior that it was almost like playing sandlot ball. I was four years older but still right in my prime, and I had no difficulty hitting.

My first time up, a fellow named Earl Caldwell was pitching for Chicago. He threw the first pitch; it caught about that much of the plate, but the umpire called it a ball. The next one was in about the same place, and he called it a ball.

Caldwell walked off the mound, walked about half the way down to the plate. He said, to the ump, "Boy, what in the hell is going on?" The ump said, "Have you met this fellow up here? This is Lewis, he's coming back to the major leagues. This is his first time at bat." Caldwell said, "God damn, I didn't know you were going to walk him." He motioned the catcher out, threw two more balls and put me on base.

Lewis provided some batting punch for the Senators, who already had pulled into second place by winning eighteen of twenty-four games. The Senators had no power—they hit only twenty-seven home runs that season—but they ran the bases with abandon and had a pitching staff that was the oddest, and most effective, in the major leagues. Four of the five starting pitchers relied primarily on knuckle balls, each in his own way.

Despite its name, a knuckle ball is thrown with fingertips, not knuckles, atop the ball. Johnny Niggeling threw his with one fingertip on top, Dutch Leonard with two, Roger Wolff with three, and Mickey Haefner with four.

Cal Hubbard, the umpire:

That knuckle ball. They outlawed the spitter; Christ, they ought to outlaw that knuckle ball. You don't know where in the hell it's going. You can't hit it, you can't catch it. It's dangerous. Some days, when the atmosphere's heavy and the wind's blowing against it, Jeez Christ, the catchers can't catch half of 'em.

To umpire knuckle ball pitchers, you've got to wait, because if you call it too quick, hell, you're liable to miss it a mile. I remember one day Rick Ferrell was catching for Washington, and Roger Wolff was pitching. He had the best knuckle ball of them all. It cut up more. This pitch, I'll never forget it, when it was right out in front of the plate it looked like it was going to be this far inside [holds hands about a foot apart]. All of a sudden it just went like—that—and went right across home plate.

It was one I called too quick. I called it a ball. Rick Ferrell, the catcher, missed it; it went right by him. He said to me, "Hub, that ball was a strike." I said, "Why in the hell didn't you catch it?" He said, "It fooled me." I said, "Fooled me, too."

I was umpiring in Boston one day, and Wolff was pitching. Joe Cronin put himself in to pinch-hit, and the catcher went out to talk to the pitcher. Joe said, "What shall I do?" I said, "Hit that first pitch. It'll be a little stinkin' curve ball, and then the rest of them will be knucklers." That's what Wolff used to do, see. He'd throw that little old curve to try to make a strike, hoping they wouldn't hit it, and then all the rest of 'em were knucklers.

Old Joe just got ready for that first pitch. He threw that little curve, and Joe hit it right against that fence in Boston for a double. I don't like to tell that, because they'll say the umpire was coaching the batter. But we were just talking.

The Senators also were helped by Joe Cambria, a laundryman turned baseball scout who was the first U.S. baseball operative in Cuba. The Washington roster began bulging with Cubans, and sportswriters, coining a foreign policy slogan, called it "Clark Griffith's Good Neighbor Policy." It could as well have been called Griffith's cheap labor policy; to the unsophisticated Cuban players, the lowest major league salary looked generous. Bobby Estalella, who in 1935 became the first Cuban on Griffith's team, reported with a glove and bat from the Cuban version of Woolworth's.

The Cuban players had another advantage: The U.S. armed forces had a devil of a time trying to draft them. Entering the U.S. on six-month visas as entertainers, the players were allowed ninety days to register for the draft, and two appeals of their classification. That soaked up the baseball season; they then went home for the winter.

Three Cubans made the Washington team in 1945. Gil Torres played shortstop, and brought along an interpreter; some of the Washington players insisted that the man was Torres' valet. Mike Guerra was a reserve catcher, and Jose Zardon was a reserve outfielder. In addition, pitchers Alex Carrasquel and Marino Pieretti were from Venezuela and Italy, respectively. Pieretti stood only 5 feet 7 inches tall but threw a mean fast ball, having gained strength from a winter job killing steers in a San Francisco slaughterhouse. He also played the accordion in a dance band.

All this gave the wartime Senators quite an international flavor, and provided opposing players with objects for taunt and ridicule, foreign athletes not being then in vogue. Latins were stereotyped; the Williamsport, Pennsylvania, Grays of the Eastern League had twelve Cuban players in 1945, and fondly called them the "Rhumba Rascals."

The Browns got off to a slow start in 1945 and could not catch up. Laabs entered military service; Kreevich, Byrnes, Moore, and Pete Gray, the one-armed outfielder, were not hitting. Galehouse was gone; Kramer and Caster were not pitching as well as they had the year before. Jakucki was winning, but in early September Sewell finally lost patience with him.

Bob Bauman, the trainer:

We were leaving Union Station in St. Louis about 8 A.M. I'm standing out there, checking to make sure they all get on the train. Everybody is there but Jakucki. He comes late; he's carrying a bag of liquor in one hand and a suitcase in the other. He couldn't walk straight, he's so drunk.

Sewell says, "You're not getting on the train. Turn around and go back. You're through." Jakucki says, "No, I'm not. I'm going on the train." He drops the suitcase and starts swinging, but he couldn't hurt anybody.

Sewell got on the train, hollered at me to get on, and told the porter, "Don't let him in the car." The porter's standing on the area-way between the two cars. Jakucki climbs up there. He drops his grip and it breaks the porter's toe.

So the train starts. Jakucki's between the two cars. Sewell has the conductor get the police to take him off at Delmar Station [a passenger station in suburban St. Louis]. Shortest road trip in history.

That night about midnight, Charley DeWitt gets a call. Jakucki's in the lobby; wants a room. Know how he got to Chicago? Hopped a freight. They won't give him a room, so he lays down on one of the divans.

Coming down in the morning, it was one of the funniest sights I've ever seen. Here he is peeking around a corner. He's been sleeping down in that lobby all night long. He's got a dirty shirt on; looks like he just got out of jail.

DeWitt told him he was through with the ballclub. That was where his career ended.

In the National League, the Giants swooned, and the Chicago Cubs suddenly roared out of seventh place and into first, winning twenty-six of thirty games in late June and July.

The Cubs were blessed by the impatience of the Yankees and the carelessness of the other American League clubs. The Yankees became disenchanted with Hank Borowy, their veteran pitcher. When Borowy yielded a pinch-hit home run to Zeb Eaton, a Detroit pitcher, on July 15, the Yankees decided to get rid of him.

So the Yankees put Borowy on the waiver list, meaning that any team could claim him for $7,500. The American League team that finished last the previous season got first claim, and so on up. If not claimed within his own league, teams in the other league were then given the same opportunity, in the same rotation.

Since the Yankees could have withdrawn Borowy from the waiver list if he were claimed, no club in the American League bothered to claim him, assuming that the Yankees did not really intend to let a pitcher of Borowy's stature go so cheaply. His name went over to the National League, where the bottom four clubs just as idly ignored it. Next in line were the Cubs, who had just edged into first place but needed another solid pitcher.

Charlie Grimm, the Cub manager:
Here comes the waiver list. Our general manager, Jim Gallagher, is looking it over and he called me up. He says, "Jesus, they're asking waivers on Borowy." I says, "Claim him. Don't fool around. Claim him right now." That was it. We got him just out of the sky. The reason he was having trouble with the Yanks was a blister on his finger. But it healed up for him. He won eleven games for us.

Other teams expressed chagrin when the Cubs got Borowy. Clark Griffith of the Senators said that he would have paid $100,000 for him. But Larry MacPhail, who by then was out of the Army and had purchased a share of the Yankees, knew Griffith better than that. "Griff would not have paid a hundred grand for the pitcher if I had thrown in the Queen Mary," MacPhail said.

Thanks to their manager, the Cubs were a lighthearted team. Grimm was a cheerful man who played the banjo, told jokes, and believed that the best players were happy players. He managed the Cubs from 1932 until the middle of the 1938 season, winning the pennant in 1935 and stepping aside in time for the Cubs to win under Gabby Hartnett in 1938. Grimm was summoned back during the 1944 season, moved the Cubs from last place to fourth, and then built his 1945 team around two veterans of his 1935 Cub champions, first baseman Phil Cavaretta and third baseman Stan Hack.

Grimm:
It was a war year, and the clubs were just feeling around for ballplayers.

We trained at French Lick, and there was a flood. We couldn't get out of the hotel. The water was right up to the front steps.

So we trained in a big solarium there, a ballroom. The pitchers were warming up on one side, we had bunting games on the other. There was a piano there, so I said, "We've got to have a little music around here, boys. Keep you awake." So we had a piano player. My God, we had a grand time.

The White Sox were holed up at some other hotel there. When the water cleared out we played the White Sox one exhibition game, and came back to Chicago to go after the pennant. We all sat there in the clubhouse, and I told 'em, "You old fossils, nobody's going to expect you to run your brains out, but let's play baseball. You know how to play; you've played enough of it." By golly, in the middle of the season they said, "Well, we're going somewhere. Let's keep going." And they did.

Our shortstop, Len Merullo, the day that his first child was born, Len made four or five errors. That's where he got the nickname "Boots." And he named the kid "Boots." Boots Merullo.

Bad Feet Becker? That was Heinz Becker, a first baseman we brought up from Milwaukee to fill in for Cavaretta and to pinch-hit. He had a pair of the worst looking feet you ever saw in your life. Bunions and corns all over 'em. You could just see those feet breathe. He'd go to a foot doctor every day before he came to play ball.

One day a ball went by him he should have caught. He came into the bench after the side was retired. I said, "Heinzapoodle"—I called him Heinzapoodle—"You should have come up with that ball, Heinzapoodle." He said, "You know, skip, my feet are just killing me." I said, "Take 'em off and finish the game!" That was about the fourth inning. He played out there the rest of the game in his stocking feet and played great ball, made great plays.

On August 6, the first atomic bomb was dropped on Hiroshima. On August 15, the major leagues held a post-war planning conference. On September 2, Japan surrendered, ending the war.

Both pennant races were tight. The Cardinals won three straight from the Cubs, raising their advantage for the season to ten wins against three losses. But the Cubs were feasting on the second division teams and remained in front.

Besides Borowy, the Cubs' pitching aces were Hank Wyse, Claude Passeau, Paul Derringer, and Ray (Pop) Prim. Derringer had pitched many a good season but was 38 and had thrown his last fast ball; he got by on a curve. Prim had never had much of a season or much of a fast ball; he was 38, had silvery gray hair and got by on a low screwball.

The Cardinal aces were Harry Brecheen, Red Barrett, and Ken (Frozen Shoulder) Burkhardt, who gained his nickname from a stiff pitching delivery. Burkhardt looked like he was putting the shot, not pitching the ball.

On September 14, the Cubs, leading the Cardinals by two games, split a doubleheader with the Phillies. The Cardinals had a doubleheader in St. Louis with the Dodgers, and insisted on playing it as a twi-night affair, although playing so late would require the Brooklyn players to sit up that night on the train to Chicago.

Enraged, the Dodgers won both games, pushing the Cardinals three games behind. The Cardinals crept closer but fell short. On September 25, the Cubs led by one and one-half games with six games to go, the first two of them at home against St. Louis.

In the first game, the Cubs knocked out Brecheen, who had beaten them four times that season. Borowy won his twentieth game of the season, 6 to 5, as rookie Andy Pafko drove in the tying and winning runs with a broken-bat double.

The Cardinals won the next day. But the Cubs then clinched the pennant by sweeping consecutive doubleheaders from Cincinnati and Pittsburgh. In doing so, the Cubs set a record for doubleheader sweeps in a season with twenty, and tied another record by winning twenty-one of their twenty-two season games against the Reds.

Phil Cavaretta won the National League batting championship with .355, and was elected the league's Most Valuable Player. Hack hit .323 and Pafko drove in 110 runs. Wyse won twenty-two games and Borowy had the league's lowest earned run average, 2.14. He won twenty-one games—ten for the Yankees and eleven for the Cubs.

The American League race ended even more dramatically. The Tigers came to Washington in mid-September, leading by only a half-game. Injuries had sidelined Eddie Mayo, Detroit's sparkplug second baseman, and Hank Greenberg; Hal Newhouser was pitching with a bad shoulder. Nevertheless, the Tigers won three of the four games to complete a spectacular Eastern trip. In twelve days on the road, Dizzy Trout started three games and relieved in three others, winning four and losing one.

Detroit then floundered in the West, but the Senators played just as poorly, losing two straight to the Yankees. Washington then beat the Athletics, 2 to 0, on September 22, with Wolff winning his twentieth game.

In the opener of a doubleheader the next day, the Senators led the A's, 3 to 0, in the eighth inning. Mayo Smith of Philadelphia hit a fly ball to Buddy Lewis in short right field. Umpire Eddie Rommel ruled that Lewis dropped the ball. Ossie Bleuge, the Washington manager, was thrown out of the game in the argument that followed; the A's went on to score three unearned runs and tie the game.

Lewis:

We're in the race, and everybody's cheering each other. A short fly ball hit to right field, and I caught it. George Myatt, our second baseman, was running out, hollering at me, "Attaboy, Lewis," and giving me a big hand. Because he'd run out to me, instead of throwing it I took the ball out of my glove and started pitching the ball underhand to him. As I did, the ball hit my trouser leg, and it went on the ground.

The umpire had turned his back on the play when I caught the ball, and when the ball hit the ground there was a roar. He turned around and saw the ball on the ground and called the runner safe.

It has stuck in my mind because it was not an error. I caught the ball. I had possession. It was a great miscarriage of justice.

The game went into extra innings. In the Washington eleventh, the sun emerged from behind a cloud, and Sam Chapman, the Athletics' center fielder, stopped the game while he went for his sunglasses. The Senators did not score.

With two out in the Philadelphia twelfth, Ernie Kish hit a fly ball to center field. George (Bingo) Binks, the Washington center fielder, staggered blindly beneath it; he had not bothered to get his sunglasses. The ball dropped for a double, and George Kell singled Kish home to win the game.

The Senators won the nightcap, but still trailed Detroit and had to wait the Tigers out. Assuming his team would not figure in the pennant race, Clark Griffith had outfoxed himself the winter before by scheduling the Senators to end their season a week before the rest of the league finished. Griffith's motive was pecuniary; he rented Griffith Stadium to the Washington Redskins football team that week.

Detroit went to St. Louis to close its season. Leading Washington by one game, the Tigers had to win one of their final two games to avoid a play-off. For three straight days, rain prevented play. On September 30, a doubleheader was scheduled. Potter started the opener for the Browns against Detroit's Virgil (Fire) Trucks, who was just out of the Navy.

The Browns were in third place and had been playing well. They led, 3 to 2, in the ninth inning. But Detroit loaded the bases with one out and Greenberg pounded a pitch into the left-field bleachers for a home run. The first baseball star to enter military service had closed the last season of wartime baseball on a dramatic note, and the Tigers were champions of the American League.

Newhouser was again voted the Most Valuable Player in the American League, the first player to win the award two years in a row since Jimmy Foxx did so in 1932 and 1933. Newhouser won twenty-five games in 1945 and led the league in strikeouts with 212 and earned run average with 1.81. Trout won eighteen games and Benton won thirteen.

Greenberg hit .311 and drove in sixty runs in seventy-eight games. He was Detroit's only .300 hitter, but it was not a hitters' year. Snuffy Stirnweiss of the Yankees led the league in batting with .309, edging veteran Tony Cuccinello of the White Sox by one point.

The Cubs were favored to win the World Series. Their team batting average of .275 was fifteen points higher than Detroit's and they had four good starting pitchers in Borowy, Passeau, Wyse, and Prim. The Tigers, as usual, were relying primarily on Newhouser and Trout. Benton had not pitched very well since his injury in May; Trucks was too fresh from military service to be depended upon.

But it was a close call. There was nothing auspicious about the traditions or talent of either team. The Cubs had lost seven of the nine World Series in which they had played, and the Tigers had lost five of six. Sportswriters were asked to evaluate the two 1945 champs and predict the winner. Warren Brown, a witty Chicago writer, said neither team could win a World Series.

Substituting quantity for quality, the Cubs suited up thirty-one players for the Series, and the Tigers thirty. Returning servicemen could be used in addition to the normal roster limits of twenty-five men. The Cubs and Tigers had six service veterans apiece.

No National League team had won the first game of a World Series since 1936, but Borowy broke that string with an easy 9 to 0 victory in the first game, played in Detroit. Newhouser was pounded for four runs in the first, two of them tripled home by Bill Nicholson, and was knocked out in the third, when the Cubs added three runs.

Detroit's fielding was less than spectacular. Two pitches got past catcher Paul Richards, and Nicholson's triple was not threatened by outfielder Roy Cullenbine's clumsy attempt to climb the screen and catch the ball. In another attempt to play the outfield like major leaguers are supposed to, Doc Cramer, 40, speared at a line drive by Chicago's Don Johnson. It went past him for a double.

Returning servicemen won the second game for Detroit. Trucks, out of the Navy less than a week, scattered seven hits. With the score tied at 1 to 1 in the fifth, Greenberg hit a three-run homer off Wyse. The score was 4 to 1.

The third game was the last to be played in Detroit, and word got out that no tickets were available for wounded veterans, who had been brought to Detroit from Percy Jones Hospital in Battle Creek, Michigan. An appeal was made, and 716 fans gave up their tickets. The veterans saw Chicago's Claude Passeau turn in one of the best pitching performances in World Series history. Passeau yielded one hit, a clean single by Rudy York, and one walk. The Cubs won, 3 to 0; Stubby Overmire was the losing pitcher.

The Series moved to Chicago, and a press bus broke down on the Outer Drive; writers hitchhiked to Wrigley Field. Movie starlet June Haver visited both dugouts, kissed Charlie Grimm, and left a smudge of lipstick on his cheek. The Cubs started with new uniforms and an old pitcher, Pop Prim. The Tigers started Trout, who had finally recovered from a cold, sore throat, and aching back.

Prim retired the first ten Tigers, but in the fourth Eddie Mayo walked, Cramer and Greenberg singled, and Roy Cullenbine doubled; two runs scored. Derringer relieved Prim in an exchange of 38-year-old pitchers, and the Tigers added two more runs before the side was retired. Detroit scored no more, but the Cubs scored only one run, and that on two Tiger misplays. Trout yielded only five hits. The score was 4 to 1, and the Series was even.

In the fifth game, Borowy was weak and Newhouser was strong, reversing their first-game performances. Two nice catches by Pafko held the score at 1 to 1 until the sixth, when the Tigers scored four runs. Greenberg doubled and scored in that inning, doubled and scored again in the seventh, and doubled and scored once more in the ninth. Newhouser struck out nine. The Tigers won, 8 to 4.

The sixth game was a riot of misbegotten rallies. In the fifth, the Cubs tried to sacrifice a man around the bases and wound up with four runs instead of one; the Tigers kept playing bunts into hits.

Detroit struck back by putting together three hits, a walk, and a Chicago error. But only two runs scored. Detroit's Chuck Hostetler turned in one of the era's most spectacular base-running feats when he tripped over third while trying to score from second on a single by Cramer. Sprawled helplessly on the basepath, the graybeard was tagged out.

In the eighth, the Tigers scored three runs with only one out, pulling within one of the Cubs. Cramer then hit a low line drive and was robbed of a hit by Peanuts Lowrey, another ex-serviceman. That catch saved the game, because Greenberg followed with a home run that tied the score

In the Chicago twelfth with a man on first base, Greenberg charged a drive to left by Stan Hack. The ball bounced over Greenberg's shoulder and the winning run scored.

Although the Cubs won that sixth game of the Series, 8 to 7, the effort exhausted their pitching staff. Passeau stifled the Tigers through five innings. In the sixth, a line drive by Jimmy Outlaw tore the nail off the third finger of Passeau's right hand. Relieving in turn, Wyse and Prim blew leads of 5 to 1 and 7 to 3.

In desperation, Grimm called in Borowy, whom he had planned to save for the seventh game. Borowy held Detroit scoreless for four innings and was the winning pitcher. But his work and Passeau's injury left the Cubs without a good, well-rested pitcher for the seventh game.

After one day off, Grimm gambled and started Borowy in the seventh game. He pitched to three men, all of whom singled. Derringer relieved, and Paul Richards drove in three runs with a double. Five runs scored in the inning, and the Cubs never drew close. They even tried Passeau in the eighth inning, but he yielded two runs. Newhouser struck out ten for a total of twenty-two in the Series, a record. The score was 9 to 3. The Tigers were World Champions.

Postscript

Wartime baseball ended much more abruptly than it began. The armed forces, conscripted year by year during the war, were demobilized rapidly; the public demanded that the boys be brought back home. During the 1945 season, 384 major league players were in military service. Only twenty-two of them remained in service the following summer. Most of the 4,076 minor league players who served also were back.

Spring training camps were glutted with players in 1946 as service veterans competed with wartime fill-ins. Sam Breadon, the Cardinal owner, was portrayed in the *Sporting News* as the old lady in the shoe, with so many players he did not know what to do. But he did know what to do. He sold Walker Cooper to the Giants for $150,000, Johnny Hopp to the Braves for $40,000, and Jimmy Brown, Al Jurisich, and Johnny Wyrostek to various teams for lesser amounts. Breadon was sure that the Cardinals could win anyway.

Shirley Povich of the *Washington Post* wrote apocryphally of a true American League fan who greeted news of Japan's surrender not with thanks for peace but rather with this comment: "That settles it. The Red Sox can't miss the 1946 flag."

Both Breadon and Povich were right, although the Cardinals just squeaked by, tying the Dodgers for the 1946 pennant and beating them in a play-off. The Red Sox won in the American League by twelve games.

As the quality of play returned to prewar standards, dozens of wartime players were brusquely discarded. Many of them were not even invited to spring training in 1946.

Tony Cuccinello, 37, was leading the American League in batting with two weeks of the 1945 season remaining; he was handed his release, effective the last day of the season. The White Sox just as abruptly released LeRoy Schalk, who in 1945 led the team in runs batted in, and farmed out Johnny Dickshot, who was second to Cuccinello among the team's hitters.

The Red Sox released Bob Johnson, 37, who had hit a solid .280 in 1945, and the Cubs released Paul Derringer, 38, who had won sixteen games. The Tigers set a record for disposal of a world championship team. Of their 1945 starters, only Greenberg, New-houser, Trout, and Trucks played regularly in 1946.

Also gone were Gene Moore, Mike Kreevich, Pete Gray, Dick Sipek, Red Hayworth, Sig Jakucki, Joe Hoover, Luke (Hot Potato) Hamlin, Walter (Boom-Boom) Beck, Mike Milosevich, Mike Garbark, Oris Hockett, Chuck Hostetler, Joe Heving, Debs Garms, LeRoy Pfund, Jimmy Foxx, and many others.

Most service veterans regained their baseball skills quickly. In 1946, the batting leaders were Stan Musial and Enos Slaughter of the Cardinals, Ralph Kiner of the Pirates, Mickey Vernon of the Senators, Hank Greenberg of the Tigers, and Ted Williams of the Red Sox. The leading pitchers were Murry Dickson and Howard Pollet of the Cardinals, Johnny Schmitz of the Cubs, and Ewell Blackwell of the Reds; Hal Newhouser of the Tigers, Bob Feller of Cleveland, and Dave (Boo) Ferris and Bob Klinger of the Red Sox. All except Newhouser were military veterans.

The GI Bill required all employers to give veterans first crack at their old jobs, but baseball by and large ignored that provision when convenient. Tony Lupien, a first baseman, returned to the Phillies for the last two weeks of the 1945 season and hit .315. Lupien:

The next thing I know it's March of '46, and one day I got a call from Philadelphia; I've been traded to Hollywood of the Coast League for an infielder named Ken Richardson. So I questioned Herb Pennock [the Phillies' general manager]. I said, "I thought under a thing called the National Defense Act a man had a chance to get his old job back." He said, "That doesn't affect baseball." I said, "Who the hell are you, to operate above the federal government?"

There was no Players Association then. I wrote Happy Chandler, return receipt requested, but he refused to accept the letters. I got a lawyer and filed a case with the Veterans Administration. All of a sudden I got a wire from Hollywood that they would pay me my big league salary if I went out there.

I had kids and no money. My lawyer said, "Look, these people are going to drag you through the courts for the rest of your life. You better go out there and take the money." So I dropped the case and went out there.

Lupien worked his way back to the major leagues in 1948. Had the Phillies kept him in 1946, he would have had five seasons in the major leagues and would have qualified for a pension. Instead, he fell one year short. Ken Richardson, the player the Phils got for Lupien, was cut after six games of the 1946 season.

The Browns finished seventh in 1946 and never again raised their heads. Don Barnes had sold the team during the 1945 season to Richard Muckerman. The Browns for once had some cash on hand, but Muckerman used it to buy and improve Sportsman's Park. That anchored the Browns to St. Louis, and left the team too little cash for a player development program.

The team went broke, and sold star players like Vern Stephens and Jack Kramer to meet the payroll. Muckerman sold the Browns in 1949 to the DeWitt brothers, who peddled the remains in 1951 to Bill Veeck.

The new owner hired a midget and a clown coach to go with his clownish players, but St. Louis fans kept their noses up and Veeck, too, found himself without money.

In 1953, Baltimore interests were anxious to buy the Browns and adopt the team as their own. Legend has it that American League club owners, anxious to get rid of Veeck and his distasteful showmanship, forced him to accept the deal. But according to Bill De-Witt, who was then working for Veeck as Brownie general manager, that is not exactly the way things happened. DeWitt:

We had a league meeting. Calvin Griffith [Clark Griffith's son, and by then the owner of the Senators] didn't want a team in Baltimore, because his team was in Washington. He said, "Look, instead of moving to Baltimore, why don't you move to Los Angeles?" Veeck said, "I don't want to move to Los Angeles."

After they talked the whole thing over, they agreed that Los Angeles was the solution to the whole problem. Harridge said, "All right, we'll give you permission." Veeck could have kept the team and moved it to Los Angeles. But Veeck's stockholders were very unhappy and they wanted to dump the thing to somebody else; they didn't want Veeck to run it.

Veeck sold the Browns to Jerold Hoffberger, a Baltimore brewing executive, who renamed them the Baltimore Orioles. The Browns' last season in St. Louis was 1953. They finished last.

INDEX